Al-Kindi's famous *Forty Chapters* is Volume I of the horary installment of the *Essential Medieval Astrology* series. It contains a solid introduction to astrological principles, and instructions on numerous topics and questions.

Introductions to Traditional Astrology translates two classic introductions to astrology (by Abu Ma'shar and al-Qabisi), with much commentary and advice from other traditional astrologers. It is an essential reference work for traditional students.

Persian Nativities I-III contains five works on natal techniques and predictions by Masha'allah, Abu 'Ali al-Khayyat, 'Umar al-Tabari, Abu Bakr, and Abu Ma'shar. These works represent the natal portion of the *Essential Medieval Astrology* series.

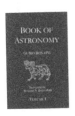

The Book of Astronomy, a huge classic medieval text by Guido Bonatti, is now available in paperback reprints. It is a complete guide to basic principles, horary, elections, mundane, and natal astrology.

Works of Sahl & Masha'allah contains sixteen works by Sahl bin Bishr and Masha'allah, covering all areas of traditional astrology: from basic concepts to horary, elections, natal interpretation, and mundane astrology.

Expand your knowledge of astrology and esoteric thought with the *Logos & Light* audio series: downloadable, college-level lectures and courses on CD at a fraction of the university cost! It is ideal for people with some knowledge of traditional thought but who want to enrich their understanding.

COMING IN 2011

The Book of the Nine Judges is Volume III of the horary installment of the *EMA* series, and will be the primary volume for students. Famous throughout the High Middle Ages and Renaissance, it is a huge compendium of horary advice and judgments from the most important medieval authorities: Masha'allah, 'Umar, Sahl, al-Kindi, Jirjis, Dorotheus, "Aristotle," and others.

COMING IN 2011

The *Logos & Light* audio series continues with complete volumes of lectures on Plato, Aristotle, and the Stoics.

Hermann of Carinthia

The

Search

of the

Heart

Consultation Charts,
Interpreting Thoughts,
& Calculating Victors
in Traditional Astrology

TRANSLATED AND EDITED BY
BENJAMIN N. DYKES, PHD

The Cazimi Press
Minneapolis, Minnesota
2011

Published and printed in the United States of America
by the Cazimi Press
621 5th Avenue SE #25, Minneapolis, MN 55414

Library of Congress Control Number: 2011906231

ISBN-13: 978-1-934586-18-1

ACKNOWLEDGEMENTS

I would like to thank the following friends and colleagues, in alphabetical order: Chris Brennan, Demetra George, Eduardo Gramaglia, Dorian Greenbaum, Deb Houlding, David Juste, and Richard Schacht.

TABLE OF CONTENTS

APPENDICES

Book Abbreviations

BOA	Bonatti, Guido	*The Book of Astronomy*
CA	Lilly, William	*Christian Astrology*
Forty Chapters	Al-Kindī	*The Forty Chapters*
Gr. Intr.	Abū Ma'shar	*Great Introduction to the Knowledge of the Judgments of the Stars*
Introduct.	Sahl bin Bishr	*The Introduction* (in *WSM*)
ITA	Abū Ma'shar, al-Qabisi	*Introductions to Traditional Astrology*
Judges	Various	*The Book of the Nine Judges*
OHT	Māshā'allāh (attributed)	*On Hidden Things* (in *WSM*)
On Quest.	Sahl bin Bishr:	*On Questions* (in *WSM*)
PN	Various	*Persian Nativities* (vols. I-III)
Search	Hermann of Carinthia	*The Search of the Heart*
Skilled	'Ali al-Rijāl	*Book of the Skilled in the Judgments of the Stars*
Thought	Māshā'allāh (attributed)	*On the Interpretation of Thought* (formerly *On the Interpretation of Cognition*), in *WSM*
WSM	Sahl bin Bishr & Māshā'allāh:	*Works of Sahl & Māshā'allāh*

TABLE OF FIGURES

INTRODUCTION

I am happy to present *The Search of the Heart*, the first of three volumes in the horary installment of my *Essential Medieval Astrology* series.[1] Along with al-Kindī's *Forty Chapters* (volume II, 2011) and *The Book of the Nine Judges* (volume III, 2011), it breaks new ground in this important branch of traditional astrology. In 2009-10 I published the natal installments (*Persian Nativities I-III*) as well as an introductory text to the whole series, *Introductions to Traditional Astrology* (*ITA*).

For students learning horary astrology, each of these volumes is helpful in its own way. If you are new to traditional astrology, and horary in particular, you should be familiar with (or have on hand) Books I-V of *ITA*, since that material is used in every branch of traditional astrology.[2] A less complete version of this introductory material may also be found in *Forty Chapters* Chs. 1-4. From there, the student should advance to the books in this series. Following are some of the features of each volume:

- *Search* is the primary source for methods of thought-interpretation and using victors,[3] and has many useful tables for learning the significations of the signs and planets (for example, in describing people and objects). It also contains exotic things such as instructions for finding buried treasure. It gives advice on examining planetary conditions throughout, but does not have much formal, introductory material for the astrology or horary beginner—there is little hand-holding in it.
- *Forty Chapters* is a famous, self-contained book on numerous questions, with much good introductory material. But it does not touch on as many kinds of questions as *Judges*, and not every astrologer agrees with al-Kindī's approach to each topic.
- *Judges* is the most compendious and complete in terms of horary questions (and other matters), but it lacks a detailed primer on horary itself. So, I have supplemented it with more general and helpful material on how to judge a horary chart in its Appendices, drawing on Sahl, Bonatti, and others.

---

[1] See Appendix M for a complete listing as of 2011.
[2] Throughout each book, I make constant reference to definitions and topics in *ITA*, to help the student understand individual concepts and techniques.
[3] See below.

So, each of these has its own value as a course text and for learning how to approach thoughts and questions. *Search* is the best guide to thoughts and victors, as well as some basic ways of approaching a chart. *Forty Chapters* is the best for those wanting a smaller and more manageable introduction to horary and astrological principles. And *Judges* is the best for serious students who know all the basics but want many source texts plus handy guides to horary interpretation.

§1: *The Search of the Heart* and its title

Search is a 12th-Century compilation by Hermann of Carinthia on two little-explored and related areas of handling client inquiries: identifying a client's thoughts (what I call "thought-interpretation"), and the use of victors (or "almutens" or *mubtazzes*).[4]

Both thought-interpretation and victors were important components of what has now come to be called "horary"[5] astrology. This branch[6] of astrology is sometimes called "interrogations" or simply "questions," because it standardly involves a client seeking an answer to a specific concern or question. The client or "querent"[7] poses an explicit question, the astrologer casts a chart,[8] identifies what planets or places in it signify the matter, and then applies various rules to answer the question. Such questions can range from the location of lost pets to the outcomes of wars, which makes it a rather remarkable practice. Some astrologers' reputations (such as that of

---

[4] From the Arabic *al-mubtazz*, "the winner" or "the victor." Victors are planets which play the leading role in signifying something, when there are many possible competing rulers and indicators. Some victors are used to identify the significator of thought, while others act as the primary significators for a certain house or even the whole chart. See below.

[5] Lit., "pertaining to the hour," suggesting questions of the moment or questions posed on the occasion of some matter.

[6] The other three branches are nativities, elections, and mundane astrology. (Astrologers do not normally recognize magical and spiritual astrology as being a standard branch.) Some kinds of charts have ambiguities that make it hard to categorize them neatly, such as "event charts" cast for the time of a past event. On the one hand they seem to be akin to electional charts, but on the other hand astrologers often examine them similarly to horary charts. Still others cast charts for political events and treat them according to mundane significations.

[7] *Quaerens*, lit. "the one seeking/asking."

[8] As we will see below, there was some controversy over *when* to cast the chart.

William Lilly)[9] are built largely upon their horary work, and indeed apart from its versatility one of its chief attractions is that the interpretation process is relatively quick and to the point, compared with the general qualities and lengthy interpretations of nativities and annual predictions. For some astrologers, handling questions is their bread and butter.

Now, many contemporary astrologers cast and interpret "consultation charts" for the time of a consultation (even for natal readings): that is, a chart cast just beforehand in order to get a sense of the client's mood and purpose. If this is done just before a horary consultation, the consultation and horary charts will be extremely similar; and since the horary chart is already supposed to describe the querent's situation accurately, it might seem as though there is little practical difference between interpreting a client's mood or interests, and answering an actual question. For instance, suppose we cast a chart a few minutes before the client arrives, and see that the lord of the Ascendant is in the third house. We might reasonably assume that the client (the lord of the Ascendant) is interested in something pertaining to his siblings (third house), and there will not really be any practical or theoretical difference between identifying this thought beforehand, and pointing out that lord's location once he actually opens his mouth and formally asks the question. In fact, this overlap may even suggest that thought-interpretation is unnecessary, especially since the lord of the Ascendant will already be a primary significator in the chart anyway.

But the older texts did not see things quite this way, and in fact the use of thought-interpretation may originally have predated what we normally think of as horary astrology. The primary difference is that thought-interpretation is focused on identifying a topic that the client has not yet stated, whereas horary questions involve explicit inquiries.[10] There are a wide variety of techniques for identifying the significator of thought, leading to expanded possibilities for types of thoughts, compared with the standard horary significators for the querent.[11] Sometimes the significator of thought alone

---

[9] Lilly (1602-81 AD) was English, and probably the brightest star in the twilight years of traditional astrology. The republication of his classic *Christian Astrology* (on nativities and questions) in the 1980s was one of the primary reasons for the modern revival of traditional astrology.

[10] See for instance *Search* Ch. II.4.1, and Argafalau's material in Appendix I.

[11] In fact, Māshā'allāh even defends the use of such techniques precisely because the Ascendant, its lord, and the Moon (typical significators in horary questions) move and change so slowly that only a few topics could be predicted throughout the working day if we were limited to them. See *Search* Ch. I.10, and the excerpt from *Thought* in Appendix C.

was used both to identify an issue and predict its outcome (such as through its applications and separations).[12] Sometimes the significator of thought was identified *prior to*, and then used *alongside* the usual horary significators in the same chart.[13] Then again, sometimes thought-interpretation seems to have been used specifically as a foil for doubters and skeptics.[14] And sometimes the texts seem to be uninterested in the *outcomes* of the thoughts (unlike in horary), which would be especially true if the purpose of thought-interpretation was to catch skeptics or show off the skill of the astrologer.[15] Below I will explain in a bit more detail what I believe the more important purpose of thought-interpretation really was: identifying a general topic as the basis of further discussion and formulation of an explicit question, and then the selection and analysis of appropriate horary significators. Although my view is hard to prove directly, the texts in this book make it clear that thought-interpretation at least preceded horary questions *procedurally*, and may also have done so *historically*.

And so, thought-interpretation was a distinct approach to handling inquiries, even though in practice it often overlapped with the kinds of horary interpretation we'd expect to follow upon identifying a client's intention or purpose. In order to identify the thought, but also to identify the most important significator of the querent or the topic or even of the whole chart, astrologers often sought victors which would sum up the content of some matter, and act as a proxy for it. In §3 below, I will deal with victors at length.

But what about Hermann's unusual title? The first thing to note is that it is virtually identical to a currently untranslated Arabic work by 'Umar al-Tabarī (d. ca. 815 AD): his *Treatise on the Discovery of Innermost Thoughts*[16] *by the Way of the Stars*.[17] Hermann's *indagatio* ("search") corresponds to 'Umar's "discovery," and refers to the act of tracking something down or searching it

---

[12] Such is the case in Book I of *Search* itself.
[13] See Sahl's *On Quest*. §I.9, in Appendix B.
[14] For example, one might compare what the client *says*, with what the chart indicates is the true nature of the thought. Or, one might respond to a challenge by a skeptic to identify what is in his hand (see Appendices I and J). In the former case, one might still be interested in predicting the outcome of a matter which the client is concealing.
[15] In that case, thought-interpretation would be a stand-alone technique distinct from the answering of specific inquiries.
[16] *Istikhrāj al-ḍamīr*: lit. the "drawing out" or even "solution of," the "conscience, mind, heart, what is innermost."
[17] *Risāla fī istikhrāj al-ḍamīr bi-ṭarīq al-nujūm*. See Sezgin p. 112.

out (as in hunting). His *cor* ("heart") corresponds to 'Umar's "innermost thoughts," and has a range similar to the English and Arabic: the soul and center of thought and emotions, one's sense. We cannot be sure if Hermann had access to this text of 'Umar's, but the uncanny resemblance between the two titles suggests that 'Umar himself may have devoted an entire work to thought-interpretation.

Hermann's notion of a search is important because it allows him to unify three senses of searching found in his book: first, there is the personal sense in which the client is searching for an answer to real problems in life (Book I); second, there is the practical sense of searching for missing objects and hidden treasure (Book II); third, there is the professional and phenomenological sense in which the astrologer is searching for answers.[18] This last sense is not trivial, particularly given how Hermann and his colleagues (Hugo of Santalla and Robert of Ketton) understand the Arabic verb "to signify" or "to indicate." This verb (*dalla*) has the more concrete sense of leading someone to something, of guiding the way—such as when we *indicate* something by *pointing at* it, and so *lead* someone's attention to it. This is precisely the spirit in which Hermann decided to use variants of the Latin *duco* ("to lead") for all types of signification: in his work, a significator becomes a "leader" (*dux*), and its significating activity becomes its "leadership" (*ducatus*). In other words, for the client the chart may indicate a thought or point to a lost watch; but for the astrologer, the *process of interpretation* involves *being led* by the planets to something not directly seen, in being absorbed by and drawn through the intention of one's heart into the heart of something else, into the heart of the client or the heart of the matter.[19] We begin without knowing the client's intention or the objective affairs, but by opening our own hearts and starting out in a spirit of searching and unknowing, we let the chart and the planets lead the way into something else—from the heart, into the heart. To my mind, this is a profound, divinational notion that should command our respect and remind us that in astrology we are ultimately doing something sacred.

---

[18] It is precisely for this kind of reason that I cannot agree with Burnett (2006, p. 99), who suggests that the hidden treasure material in Book II was merely an attempt to compile comparative material on a specific topic. The choice of hidden treasure fits perfectly into the general theme of hiddenness and searching which thematizes the whole book.

[19] Thanks to Chris Brennan for pointing out this English idiom.

§2: Texts distinguishing thoughts and questions

"They even disagree on learning the querent's thought…"[20]

In the previous section, I said that thought-interpretation was distinct from, but sometimes led into or overlapped with, the answering of explicit questions. The texts in this book give overwhelming evidence of this fact, but here are a few of the more striking examples which flesh this out further:

Starting with the oldest-known sources, the *Yavanajātaka* (270 AD)[21] is conspicuous for its use of thought-interpretation. The long section from Chs. 52.7-63 begins with the statement that the positions of various planets in a chart indicate the querent's *thought*, while its *success* depends on such things as the Ascendant (i.e., the default horary significator of the querent). Chapter 53 then begins to discuss "the thought of the querist [sic]," based on "the planet or the sign which is strong." So for example, if the Sun is in the Midheaven, then the client is thinking about authority or starting enterprises (Ch. 54.9); or if the Sun is in a varga of Jupiter, he is thinking about swords, missiles, spells, and so on (Ch. 55.3). But good relationships of benefic planets to the Ascendant will bring about the thought successfully, planets in their enemies' houses indicate bad results, *etc.* (Ch. 54). Other chapters delineate complex combinations of planets, but hardly deal with outcomes at all. Ch. 63 briefly offers a mathematical operation for determining a thought's outcome. Chapters 64-67 offer more advice on outcomes, but without the usual leading formula we see in later horary material, such as "If someone wanted to ask about…": so, it is hard to say whether these chapters describe the outcomes of thoughts, or outcomes of explicit questions, or outcomes of the questions that *devolve from* the thoughts previously identified.

Hephaistio's *Apotelesmatics* (early 5th Century AD) endorses a view elsewhere attributed to the Indians and others,[22] stating that we may foretell the client's thought by looking at the twelfth-part of the Ascendant. Hephaistio then proceeds to list these 144 different possibilities based on the house

---

[20] *Skilled* I.5.2 (see Appendix A).
[21] The Sanskrit *Yavanajātaka* of Sphujidhvaja was a versified version of an earlier Sanskrit prose translation (ca. 150 AD) of an earlier Greek text.
[22] See Hephaistio III.4.20ff (Appendix H below), *Search* I.9.3, and *OHT* §2 (Appendix C). Leopold and ibn Ezra also describe this approach in Appendices G and J.

placement of the sign indicated, its qualities, and its lord. I have translated all of these interpretations in Appendix H.[23]

Sahl's *On Quest*. §1.9 recommends that one use a victor-significator over the chart (which is normally used for thought-interpretation) *alongside* the more usual significators of querent and quaesited (see Appendix B). Hermann does the same thing in *Search* II.4.5.

Appendix A (from al-Rijāl's famous *Book of the Skilled in the Judgments of the Stars*)[24] is filled with material distinguishing significators of thought from the usual significators and victors over the querent, the topic, and the chart. Some of the more striking material is distributed throughout *Skilled* I-III: at the beginning of the material on most houses, al-Rijāl begins by describing what belongs to that house, what its triplicity rulers are, the color attributed to it, and then how to tell whether or not this house is the subject of the question. Take the 2nd house: "And if, in a question, a fiery sign and the thought of the querent were in this house (that is, if the significator of the thought were in it), judge that the question is about assets. But if it were earthen, you should say that it is about entering into a city...". Not only does al-Rijāl identify the thought by the location of its significator, but he even distinguishes the types of thoughts based on the triplicity of the sign itself. I also find it interesting that al-Rijāl's entire book on questions (after running through general significations of the planets) begins with a discussion of finding significators and victors for thoughts, topics, and the whole chart—as though this was a conceptually (and possibly historically) prior practice. Al-Rijāl also highlights the fact that the interpretation of thought is its own area of study, by saying: "They even disagree on learning the querent's thought, and how they can understand it, and what signification they ought to have over him."[25]

A 10th-Century Latin source by a pseudonymous "Argafalau" or Ergaphalau, but undoubtedly based on earlier Arabic material, offers further views on interpreting thoughts and their outcomes, referring to thoughts and topics that are "hidden," "hitherto unshared," "silent," and "not yet asked about." It also includes something a bit more unusual: how to tell what someone holds secretly in his hand. In this case, the identification of objects seems to

---

[23] Hephaistio also offers several other methods of thought-interpretation, including material on their outcomes. See Appendix H.
[24] Abū al-Hasan 'Ali bin Abī al-Rijāl (11th Century AD) is often known as Haly Abenragel.
[25] *Skilled* I.5.2.

be a way of impressing doubters.[26] This *Letter* of Argafalau also deals with more straightforward requests and inquiries, such as whether or not a man's spouse will survive him. I have translated parts of the *Letter* in Appendix I. Abraham ibn Ezra also appropriates this material (but probably from the Arabic source) in his *Particular Treatises*, which I have partly translated in Appendix J.

Hermann himself explicitly distinguishes thoughts and questions, by saying that "every question in astronomy is generally divided into two: for it is either in thought, or in speech."[27] But this does not mean that he distinguishes these two categories in an *absolute* sense, since he then proceeds to point out that planetary configurations (such as transfers of light, *etc.*) and types of answers (such as "when will it happen") are common to both thoughts and spoken questions. Moreover, Hermann groups thought-interpretation and answering questions together, *in contrast* to nativities and their revolutions: "The path of the judgments of the stars is wholly divided into two parts: one is that of the questions of a birth or even of annual [predictions]; the other, that of counsel and the thoughts of men and a concealed thing and the proper quality of persons."

Finally, an intriguing passage in *Skilled* on when to cast the Ascendant, seems to contain the conceptual difference between interpreting thoughts and answering questions in the background.[28] Al-Rijāl cites three views on when to cast the Ascendant: "Valens" says the Ascendant should be taken directly when the querent comes to the astrologer; but "Hermes" says it should be taken at the astrologer's discretion; finally, the "Indians" and others say the querent should decide whether and when to cast the Ascendant, after some discussion with the astrologer. To my mind, "Valens" speaks for the interpretation of thoughts, while "Hermes" and the "Indians" speak for differing views on explicit questions. Al-Rijāl sides with the "Indians," suggesting that since the client has the ability to refuse a consultation, he may also affirm when and what the question is. Two things especially intrigue me about this passage. First, it suggests there was a real practical and conceptual disagreement about what the roles of client and astrologer are, and whether and when a matter even exists—which would not be the case if interpreting thoughts and answering questions were procedurally or concep-

---

[26] See the *Letter* §2 for the hidden object, and §6 for another challenge to the astrologer.
[27] *Search* II.4.1.
[28] *Skilled* I.7, in Appendix A below.

tually identical.[29] Second, for all of his material on how to find significators of thought, and advice on what the client's thought is, al-Rijāl ultimately sides with the more familiar horary practice, without explaining what the *role* of interpreting thoughts then becomes, or what the *relationship between* thoughts and questions really is. I will return to this issue below. Nevertheless we do know that the answering of explicit questions eventually eclipsed (or perhaps, absorbed) the interpretation of thoughts.

As an experiment, let us consider the following two historical charts from Guido Bonatti, and apply the twelfth-part of the Ascendant method from Hephaistio and the Indians.[30] The first chart is a question posed by Bonatti's employer, Count Guido Novello, who was fighting the Italian Luccans at the time.[31] Novello's army was encamped above the Luccans, who were holding certain land with a smaller force. The actual question was "whether there would be a battle between the armies or not," which is normally a seventh-house question. And indeed, Bonatti proceeds immediately to look at the lords of the Ascendant (Novello) and the seventh (the Luccans).

If we look at the table of twelfth-parts in Appendix L, the twelfth-part of the Ascendant corresponds to Capricorn and the second house. According to Hephaistio's list of thoughts, Novello should have been thinking of "warfare or living abroad or encampments," which was precisely the case. If we follow the Indians, we should note that Jupiter is in the second, in his fall: this indicates something of poor quality, namely Novello (the 1st) and his supporters (2nd)—so the thought is at least partly about the quality of the querent himself. Again, following Persian/Arab practice, we see that, of Jupiter's two domiciles, he aspects only Pisces (the 4th), which should relate to territory, which was in fact what Novello was trying to take from the Luccans. What I find especially interesting about this twelfth-part method, is that it reflects Bonatti's own analysis. For the question was "whether" there would be a battle, and so we might expect Bonatti to simply look at the relationships between the lords of the Ascendant and seventh, and say "yes" or "no." But as Bonatti points out, Jupiter in fall in the 2nd "appears to signify the low quality of the querent's side, indeed so that he would not seek

---

[29] Note that if one followed the twelfth-part method of Hephaistio and the Indians mentioned above, it could make a big difference if the chart were cast upon the meeting the client, versus after even a short discussion: on average, the Ascendant will pass through an entire twelfth-part (2.5°) every 10 minutes.

[30] See Appendix H and *Search* Ch. I.9.3.

[31] See *BOA* Tr. 6, questions on the 7th house, Ch. 28.

battle." And so, we might say that the twelfth-part technique helps us not simply to identify the thought, but *what aspect* of the explicit question the analysis should focus on: namely the quality of the querent and his supporters in trying to take the land.

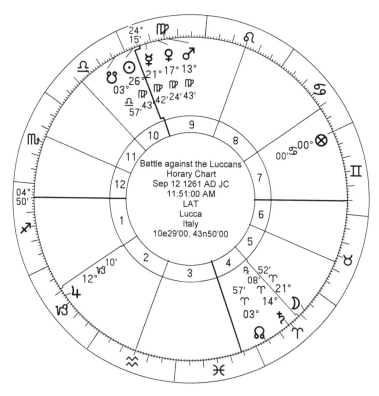

Figure 1: Battle against the Luccans (Bonatti)

The next chart[32] is from the following month, in which Novello was besieging the Luccans and wanted to know if he would occupy their castle. The twelfth-part of the Ascendant corresponds to Sagittarius and the first house itself, so we would expect the thought to concern the general himself (or his side), and not simply the siege and the castle (4th house) which was described in the explicit question. Hephaistio identifies the thought of this twelfth-part as "merchandising in a foreign land," which is not very helpful. But again, Bonatti focuses on the general, saying that the "baseness and

---

32 *Ibid.*, Ch. 29.

sluggishness and tardiness and weakness" was so great that even though they *could* have taken the castle, "they would not apply themselves to those things by which the castle ought to and could be taken," which turned out to be the case. The identification of the thought can therefore be used to focus one's attention in forming a judgment.

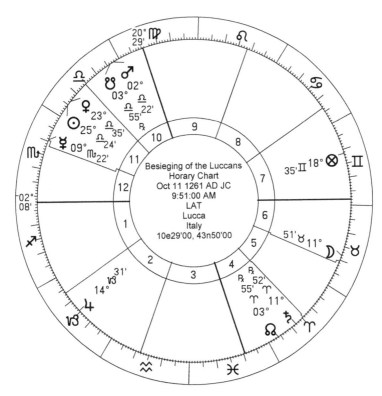

Figure 2: Besieging the Luccans (Bonatti)

§3: Types of victor-significators, and a list

So far, I have spoken in a very general way about thoughts and victors, without being specific about the variety of viewpoints and methods. But before listing the types of victors in *Search* and its Appendices, let me remind the reader of the difference between what we might call a "mere" significator, and a victor. A mere significator is just some planet or place that indicates anything at all: for instance, Venus is a significator of fun and partying, because she signifies those things through her own nature: this is sometimes called a "natural" or "universal" signification. And if in a chart Venus rules the third house or is in it, she signifies siblings because of her rulership of the third or her presence there: this is often called "accidental" signification, because such a signification befalls a planet by location or rulership in a particular chart rather than through its own nature.[33] But a victor is a planet which has superiority over or among *a group* of significators, *all of which* do or potentially do signify that same thing. There are two primary ways to do this:

[1] *A victor among places.* One the one hand we might have a list of general significators for something, and on the other a list of qualifications: we start with the preferred member among the significators, and see if it meets the qualifications. If it does meet them, then it is the victor and we are done; but if not, we discard it and look at the next member to see if it meets the qualifications; and so on. In this way we find the victor *among* a group of candidates. This is used in finding such victors as the natal longevity releaser[34] as well as the querent's significator in certain theories of horary. For longevity, we begin with several places that naturally signify life (the Sun, Moon, Ascendant, and so on), and require the victor to be in certain places in the chart, or in signs of a certain gender, or aspected by one of its lords, and so on. If the chart is diurnal, we start with the Sun and see if he fulfills the criteria: if so, he is the victor; if not, we discard him and look at the next option (the Moon). Turning to Māshā'allāh's theory of horary significators,[35] we assume that lord of the Ascendant is the querent's significator and victor,

---

[33] See a statement to this effect by Hermann in *Search* III.1.1.
[34] Often called the *hīlāj* or *hyleg*, which is Pahlavi for "releaser."
[35] See a similar view of 'Umar's in *Judges* §0.4 (Appendix D below).

provided that it either aspects the rising sign or is applying to a planet which does;[36] if not, we move to the next member on the list (again, the Moon).

[2] *A victor over places*. In other cases, we identify all the significators for something, and assign points or "strengths" to the various rulers *over* those places, sometimes assigning one point per dignity, sometimes different points per type of dignity: the latter is what I call a "weighted" victor because different dignities get different weights or amounts.[37] The planet which has the most points for rulership *over* those places, is the victor. For example, suppose that the Ascendant in a diurnal chart were in the first degree of Scorpio: this is the domicile, bound, and face of Mars, while Venus is the primary triplicity lord. Whether we give equal points to Mars for each dignity, or use a weighted system, Mars gets more points than Venus does, and so is the most authoritative, and therefore is the victor over the Ascendant. In the case of marriage, there are many significators: the Lot of Marriage, Venus, the seventh house, and the lord of the seventh (and even possibly the luminary representing the spouse). In that case, we might create a table in which the various lords over *all* of these places receive points simultaneously, with the victor being the one with the most points overall. I advise students to think of the victor over a single position (such as the Ascendant, above) as a "simple" victor, since it assigns points to the lords over only one place; but the victor over several places at once is a "compound" victor, because its authority is compounded from several places. These are my own terms, and are not found in the traditional literature.

Sometimes traditional astrologers added other criteria, such as giving points for the kind of house the candidates are in, or for their relationship to the Sun. Some inserted house points into the table of dignity points and added everything together indifferently (ibn Ezra, Appendix F), while others cautioned that these categories should not be mixed, and must be considered separately (Hermann, Ch. III.1.1).

To make things clear for the beginner, let us look at the following chart and find two different significators of thought: one according to the Indians

---

[36] Or perhaps the lord is applying to a planet that itself applies to another planet aspecting the Ascendant, so that a chain of planets is involved.

[37] See worked examples in *Search* III.1, and also Appendix F. Note that some of the early thought-interpretation methods give a *different* weight to the bound lord and the primary triplicity lord, than do the versions based on al-Qabīsī (*ITA* I.18, VIII.1.4) and ibn Ezra (Appendix F below). These earlier methods give 3 points to the bound lord and 2 to the primary triplicity lord, whereas later authors often switch these around, giving 3 to the primary triplicity lord and 2 to the bound lord.

(Ch. I.9.3, #1), and a simple weighted victor over the Ascendant according to Māshā'allāh (Ch. I.3.4).[38] Following Hermann,[39] I have used a quadrant-based house system (here, Alchabitius Semi-arcs, used by many medievals).

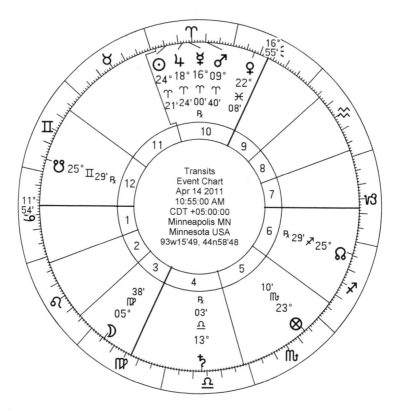

Figure 3: Example chart for two victors

The Indian significator of thought is a victor *among* places. According to Ch. I.9.3, we must find the "stronger" between the bound lord or decan lord[40] of the Ascendant: it, and the planet to which it is being joined, will reveal the thought. The degree of the Ascendant is at 11° 54' Cancer, which is the bound of Venus and the decan of Mercury. Mercury is in an angular sign and received by Mars (and the Sun), but is under the rays, and is

---

[38] I do not claim to know whether the Indians or Māshā'allāh himself really did advocate these methods, but I have no reason to doubt the attributions.

[39] See §8 below.

[40] See Appendix L for tables of Egyptian bounds and "Chaldean" decans or faces.

assembled with and opposed to the malefics. Venus is exalted, direct, and unafflicted, and is in a powerful position next to the Midheaven (of which she is the exalted lord). She is also going to receive the next application of the Moon. So, I would expect the querent's thought to be of a Venusian sort.[41] Since she does not currently apply to any planet, there is no other planet to consider.

Māshā'allāh's significator[42] *over* the Ascendant has two steps: dignities and house rank. First, we must find the simple weighted victor over the degree of the Ascendant by dignities. The lords and their points are as follows: domicile lord (Moon, +5), exalted lord (Jupiter, +4), bound lord (Venus, +3), primary triplicity lord (Venus, +2), decan lord (Mercury, +1). Venus and the Moon are tied with 5 points apiece. The second step is to determine the ranking of their houses, which is especially appropriate in the case of ties, but should probably be examined for the top two planets in any case. Again, let us use Alchabitius houses for the ranking: Venus in the tenth house gets 11 points, while the Moon in the third gets only 5. So, the ranking of houses breaks the tie, and Venus is again the victor.

Using victors like these implies two things: (1) a competition, and (2) a desire to simplify. That is, the impulse is to identify *one* place or planet as a *proxy* for the matter at hand, when there are several competing options. To my own mind, the impulse makes sense in some cases, such as finding the longevity releaser: for the longevity releaser is moved by primary directions, and one doesn't want contrasting primary directions for the same subject-matter. Moreover, the longevity releaser will always be one of the very places which indicated life to begin with. But in other cases it seems to me that the use of victors is a symptom of confusion and uncertainty, and a sign that important lore has been lost. For instance, there are real differences between the Lot of Marriage and the seventh house; but if after calculating a compound weighted victor over all of the marriage-like places, the significator of marriage is a planet with no obvious connection to the seventh, the Lot, the

---

[41] The instructions do not say to take her dignity and house position into account, but it seems appropriate to me.

[42] I note that this victor appears in a chapter on significators of thought, but it could equally be the horary victor over the querent himself. I will treat it as a significator of thought.

lord of the seventh, and so on,[43] then we have erased such distinctions and we have wandered from the delineation process itself.

Victor calculations become more problematic, the more complicated they are. In my own view, a weighted victor calculation with serious problems is William Lilly's, which is a variation on a victor among places.[44] Lilly throws dignities, house placements, direction of movement, speed of movement, solar phase, relationship to benefics or malefics, and relationships to fixed stars, all into one table indifferently. For example, in Lilly's scheme a planet will either gain or lose 2 points for the following reasons: being in its own bound (+2), being in the ninth (+2) or eighth or sixth (-2), being swift or slow (+/-2), or being in a favored relationship to the Sun (+2). But it is easy to see that these conditions have nothing in common that could be described meaningfully by the number 2.

A different (and to my mind more reasonable) approach is that adopted by Hermann in *Search* III.1-2. First, Hermann separates the evaluation of dignities from the ranking of houses (and also from the other conditions, like the relationship to the Sun or direction of movement, and even the dignity a planet has in its own place). Second, he does not simply count up the dignity points, but notes whether a planet gets its points primarily from the more important dignities (like domicile and exaltation) or from the less important ones (liked triplicity and decan). In this way, differences between the planets' features are still somewhat preserved, and one's professional judgment is more involved in the process.

In my Introduction to *PN II*, I argued that the use of weighted victors was probably an invention of Arabic-speaking astrologers in the late 8th or early 9th Centuries AD. For while 'Umar al-Tabarī does speak of victors over natal topics (see *PN II*), he is not specific about any numerical method; and according to Abū Bakr (again, in *PN II*), a 9th-Century contemporary in Baghdad named al-'Anbas had claimed to have adopted weighted victors in express imitation of 'Umar. And so, I suggested that either al-'Anbas or a

---

[43] For example, if such a planet were only the victor because of a multitude of points from lesser dignities usually ignored in much normal delineation (such as bound, triplicity, and decan), and had no obviously important rulership over, or location in, the usual places indicating marriage.

[44] *Christian Astrology* Vol. I, p. 115. Lilly is trying to determine the relative strengths of the planets among each other. But this same victor is also identified by him as the lord of the whole nativity (Vol. 2, pp. 531-32): an example of a numerical horary victor crossing back over into natal delineation.

similar figure had introduced weighted victors into nativities. I wish to modify my former view here, in light of *Search* and its Appendices. I now believe that weighted victors were indeed inspired by natal texts such as Ptolemy's *Tetrabiblos*, but their formal use originated in the combined practices of thought-interpretation and answering questions, even as early as the *Yavanajātaka*.[45] It was only in the late 8th or early 9th Centuries that certain astrologers formally reintroduced such victors back into natal astrology from their proximate origin in thought-interpretation and questions. 'Umar might have enabled this transfer out of horary into nativities, since he was well-known as a horary astrologer; but again, while his thought and horary material does use weighted victors, his natal material expresses no preference as to how to find them. At a minimum, 'Umar's instructions imply nothing more than Ptolemy's single-count victor,[46] or perhaps a generic preference for "whichever of the many significators is the best of the bunch." And so, it is very possible that an avid reader of 'Umar's works could have seen a demand for victors in his natal material on the one hand, and a description of weighted victors in the horary material on the other—and simply brought the two together. Therefore, I still believe that the use (or common use) of weighted victors was indeed introduced into natal work during the late 8th or early 9th Centuries, but the origin of weighted victors themselves goes back further, to early thought-interpretation and questions.

In *Search* and its Appendices, we can generally find four types of victor-significators, used in various ways:
- The significator of a *thought*, and sometimes also for an *object* hidden in the hand.
- The significator of the *querent* and/or an explicitly-stated *house topic*.
- The victor over the *whole chart*.
- The longevity *releaser*.

---

[45] See the reference to numerical methods in the *Yavanajātaka* above.
[46] See Appendix H below.

Following is a tentative table of the victor-significators described or mentioned in *Search*:[47]

Attributed to:	Victor/Sig.:	Citation:
Al-Rāzī/Māshā'allāh	Thought	*Search* I.3.1
Dorotheus	Thought	*Search* I.3.2
Unknown	Thought	*Search* I.3.3
Māshā'allāh	Thought	*Search* I.3.4
Hermes	Thought	*Search* I.7; App. G
Dorotheus, Antiochus, Valens	Thought	*Search* I.9.1; *OHT* §2 (App. C); cf. *Skilled* I.9.2 (App. A); cf. App. J
Hermes/Māshā'allāh	Thought	*Search* I.9.2; *OHT* §2 (App. C)
Indians #1	Thought	*Search* I.9.3; cf. *OHT* §2 (App. C), App. J
Indians #2, Hephaistio #4	Thought	*Search* I.9.3; *OHT* §2 (App. C); *Apotel.* (App. H), App. J
Indians #3	Thought	*Search* I.9.3, App. J
(Māshā'allāh)	(Thought)	(*Search* I.9.4)[48]
Dorotheus, Hermes	Thought	*Skilled* I.5.2 (App. A)
Valens/Māshā'allāh	Thought	*Skilled* I.5.2 (App. A)
Persians/Romans	Thought	*Skilled* I.5.2 (App. A)
Māshā'allāh	Thought	*Skilled* I.5.2 (App. A)
'Umar al-Tabarī	Thought	*Skilled* I.5.2 (App. A)
"Al-Kindī"	Thought	*Skilled* I.11 (App. A)
Valens	Thought	*Skilled* I.11 (App. A)
Hermes	Thought	*Skilled* I.11 (App. A)
Unattributed	Thought	House-specific advice (App. A)
Sahl bin Bishr	Thought	*On Quest.* §13.18 (App. B)
Māshā'allāh #1	Thought	*Thought* (App. C)

---

[47] This is not wholly exhaustive, as sometimes Hermann or others will add extra details to a method already described, and attribute them to unnamed persons. Or, sometimes a method in one source seems extremely close (but not identical) to a method in another. Finally, sometimes the texts are not absolutely clear as to whether they are seeking the significator of a chart as a whole, or over the matter, or whether these are the same thing.

[48] I put this in parentheses because Hermann or his source is mixing up a number of views Māshā'allāh attributes to *others* in *OHT* §2.

Māshā'allāh #2	Thought	*Thought* (App. C)
Ptolemy	Thought	*OHT* §6 (App. C)
Ibn Ezra	Thought	Apps. G, J
Argafalau	Thought	App. I
Book of Tamedas	Thought	App. J
Others #1	Thought	App. J
Others #2	Thought	App. J
Hephaistio #1 and #2	Thought	App. H
Hephaistio #3	Thought	App. H
Argafalau	Object in hand	App. I
Book of Tamedas	Object in hand	App. J
'Umar al-Tabarī	Affair/chart	*Search* II.4.4[49]
Māshā'allāh	Chart	*Search* III.1.1
Ptolemy	Chart	*Skilled* I.5.2 (App. A)
Dorotheus, Hermes	Chart	*Skilled* I.5.2 (App. A)
Valens	Chart	*Skilled* I.5.2 (App. A)
"The Philosopher"	Chart	*Skilled* I.5.2 (App. A)
'Umar al-Tabarī	Chart	*Skilled* I.5.2 (App. A)
Ibn Ezra #1	Chart (natal)	App. F
Ibn Ezra #2	Chart (natal)	App. F
Porphyry/Antiochus	Chart (natal)	App. H
Abū 'Alī al-Khayyāt	Querent?	*Skilled* I.9.2 (App. A)
Al-Kindī	Querent	*Skilled* I.9.2 (App. A), *Forty Chaps.* Ch. 3.2 (App. E)
(Generic)	Querent, question	*Search* II.4.5
'Umar, Māshā'allāh	Querent, question	*Skilled* I.9.1 (App. A), *Judges* §0.4 (App. D)
'Umar al-Tabarī	Question	*Skilled* I.9.2 (App. A), *Judges* §0.3 (App. D)
Dorotheus	Question?	*Skilled* I.11 (App. A)
Sahl bin Bishr	Question/chart	*On Quest.* §1.9 (App. B)
Al-Kindī	Topic	*Skilled* I.9.2 (App. A), *Forty Chaps.* Ch. 3.1 (App. E)

---

[49] But this might really be a version of al-Kindī's *Forty Chapters* Ch. 3.2 (Appendix E below), also described in *Skilled* III.6 (Appendix A below)

Māshā'allāh?	Topic	*Search* III.1.3
Ptolemy	Topic	*Tet.* III.4 (App. H)
Ptolemy	Topic	*Tet.* III.5 (App. H)
Sahl bin Bishr	Prediction	*Search* II.5 (*passim*)
(Generic)	Long. releaser	*Search* III.2
Al-Kindī	Long. releaser	*Forty Chaps.* Ch. 3.3 (App. E)
Porphyry/Antiochus	Long. releaser	App. H
Al-Rijāl	Degree	*Skilled* I.10 (App. A)
Al-Rijāl	Degree/house?	*Skilled* I.9.2 (App. A)
Ptolemy	Degree	*Tet.* III.3 (App. H)

Figure 4: Victor-significators in *Search* and its Appendices

§4: Thought-interpretation and the history of horary

The obvious antiquity of the practice of thought-interpretation (*Yavan-jātaka*, Hephaistio) means that we must reappraise our notions of the history of horary astrology. Many people believe that full-blown horary astrology (in the sense I have described it) is one of the oldest branches of astrology, and it is logically possible that as soon as rules for planetary configurations and natal interpretation were published by some early figure—Nechepso, Petosiris, someone—certain astrologers stepped right in to set up practice much as William Lilly or Guido Bonatti did, receiving requests about explicit questions like lost pets and the outcomes of wars.

But we cannot accept this interpretation based on the evidence at hand. For one thing, we have already seen that certain older texts are preoccupied first with identifying thoughts and only secondarily on their outcomes and answering explicit questions. For another, some of the material ambiguously straddles the divide between thought-interpretation, thought outcomes, and explicit questions. In Appendix H, Hephaistio provides three examples of his Lot of Fortune approach to foretelling thoughts. He describes his third example as indicating that what the man wants "will be found to be utterly pointless." Here is the ambiguity: is Hephaistio making a purely *descriptive* statement about the thought, namely that "the client is engaged in a pointless affair"? Or is Hephaistio describing the thought as "involving affair *X*," and then offering a separate *prediction* about the man's action, namely that "it will be pointless?" The first possibility would be pure thought-interpretation, while the other would involve the blurred area between predicting thought outcomes and answering explicit horary questions. I am not sure we can ever really know what the answer is for Hephaistio—if indeed he thought about it in this way at all.

Third, some of the more important horary texts with long pedigrees are actually adaptations from earlier electional and natal material.[50] As an example of the latter, consider Dorotheus's *Carmen*. We know from other sources (such as Hephaistio) that Book V of *Carmen* was primarily on elections; but in 'Umar's Arabic translation of the 6th Century Pahlavi version, Book V is said to be on "questions" or "inquiries" (Ar. *masā'il*), and certain portions of the book are written as though they are questions about *whether* and how something will happen, not about how to construct an election. Again, in *Search* there are two examples of Māshā'allāh adapting natal material from *Carmen* to thought-interpretation.[51] Finally, material from *Carmen* on thieves and hidden things gets passed on to people like al-Kindī in his *Forty Chapters*, but now put fully into explicit horary-style forms.[52]

And so, what the written record *does* support is the following:

- Early familiarity with thought-interpretation (between the 2nd and 5th Centuries), along with other material resembling horary questions or elections, but perhaps only as dealing with the *outcomes* of the previously-determined thoughts.

- 6th-Century rewrites of electional material in *Carmen* into a more recognizably horary style, and early Arabic material on thought-interpretation or questions which is a rewriting of natal material.

- Arabic horary manuals of the 8th century (but surely based on much older books in Pahlavi), some of which handle significators of thought in addition to answering questions, but sometimes deal only with what is now an independent horary-style practice, no longer obviously resembling natal or electional material.

After this early Arabic period, it seems that—al-Rijāl's summaries notwithstanding—thought-interpretation declined in importance or simply got absorbed into horary practice. In some cases it was probably overlooked

---

[50] See *Carmen* V generally, as Pingree pointed out (1997, p. 47). According to Pingree, important Persian reworkings of Dorotheus took place in the 6th Century.

[51] See *Search* Ch. I.8, and the view of Māshā'allāh in *Skilled* I.5.2, using the squares of the Moon.

[52] See *Forty Chapters* Chs. 6.10, 7.3, and 8.4.

entirely: Sahl's references in the early sections of *On Quest.* are very easy to miss,[53] and references in John of Spain's translations to a significator of an "intention" can easily be mistaken for the quaesited matter itself. In other cases, the overwhelming number of references to significators of all sorts can lead one to overlook specific significators of thought. But probably many astrologers simply didn't see the point in thought-interpretation, and dismissed it as an extra and unnecessary step. Nevertheless, I can think offhand of six vestiges of thought-interpretation and its associated victors:

(1) Consultation charts, examining especially the Ascendant in order to identify the client's state of mind or issue before a reading. The "considerations before judgment" in horary[54] would be an extension of this.

(2) The use of victor-tables for planetary strength in horary, to identify the "strongest" planet in the chart, which will help give insight into the matter.[55]

(3) The survival of the Hermes chart about the sick mother (see *Search* I.7 and *Thought* in *WSM*) up through Leopold of Austria's use of it in the 13th Century: this was reprinted at least through the end of the 15th Century (see Appendix G).

(4) Leopold of Austria's late use of his own and others' thought-interpretation methods (Appendix G); Leopold got some of his material from ibn Ezra, whose reports of thought-interpretation were reprinted in Latin as late as 1507 (see Appendix J).

(5) Dream interpretation rules found as late as Lilly's *Christian Astrology* (drawn from Sahl's *On Quest.*), in which the astrologer describes the content of the client's dream. To me this still counts as thought-interpretation because Sahl (and Bonatti) claim that some configurations can also show whether the client has forgotten the dream—that is, whether the memory of it even exists in the client's thought.

(6) Māshā'allāh's puzzling chapter on the longevity releaser in the midst of his horary work, *On Reception*. In his 1998 translation,[56] Robert Hand

---

[53] As I will suggest below, I suspect that *On Quest.* (like many early horary works) was about answering questions that arose *after* identifying the client's thought: therefore there was no need to discuss thought-interpretation in them, since it was already assumed to have taken place.

[54] For example, a very late or very early Ascendant is supposed to indicate something about the timeliness of the question and the client's efforts. One may find such considerations in *Christian Astrology* pp. 121-23.

[55] But I also believe that these victors were then transferred into natal work from their prior official position in thought-interpretation and horary questions.

[56] Hand 1998, pp. *ii* and 48. My own translation is available in *WSM*.

reasonably wondered whether this chapter might not be an interpolation from a later author. I believe we are now in a position to answer why this chapter appears in such horary work: it is precisely because traditional authorities had recommended using the longevity releaser in all charts, as a general significator of the chart or of the thought. Explicit instructions like this can be found below in *Search* III.2 and *Forty Chapters* Ch. 3.3 (see Appendix E below). So, the inclusion of the longevity releaser is not an aberration, but an inherited part of thought-interpretation and the use of victors, dutifully passed on but puzzled over by astrologers like us centuries later.

§5: Summary of the argument

Let me sum up my current view on the role of thoughts and victors in traditional astrology, based on the material above:

(1) Early astrologers took something of a divinational approach to client work, in which they wanted to determine the "thought" of the client before the discussion began. In some cases they assumed the client already knew what he wanted to ask about,[57] but in other cases they may have assumed that the chart would reveal what the client *needed* to know, or even how the astrologer was supposed to focus the client's attention or his own analysis. Thought-interpretation did exist alongside, and possibly predated, more explicit horary astrology.

(2) Inspired by some statements in Hellenistic natal astrology,[58] they sought various ways to identify the most important planet or significator in the chart (normally called a "victor"), which would reveal the thought, and in some cases its outcome.

(3) Likewise inspired by these ancient texts,[59] they began to use certain numerical methods as a way of identifying the victor-significator of the thought.

---

[57] For example, in Appendix G, Leopold suggests that the interpretation of thought is needed when the client *does not want* to state his question. Likewise the "Indians" in *OHT* §2 (Appendix C).

[58] For example, the victors of Ptolemy and Antiochus/Porphyry in Appendix H, and the relatively standard ways of finding the longevity releaser: see the appropriation of *Forty Chapters* Ch. 3.3 in *Search* III.2.

[59] Note Ptolemy's way of assigning individual counts to dignities and solar relationships in Appendix H.

(4) In addition, Persian astrologers (among others) adapted older natal and electional material to the form of questions and thought-interpretation, so that this branch of astrology involved rules recycled from the others.

(5) Again, inspired by traditional texts,[60] these astrologers applied the concept of victors to topics themselves, so that one might finally have victor-significators of thoughts, of an entire chart, and of an individual topic (such as wealth or parents).[61] In this way, both thought-interpretation and explicit questions employed victors in ways that had been rare in earlier natal treatments.

(6) But during the early Arabic period (mid- to late 8th Century AD), certain astrologers who commonly used numerical victors when dealing with thoughts and questions, began to apply them to natal interpretation itself—which had not been mainstream practice in Hellenistic astrology.

(7) Through processes not yet fully understood, three things seem to have happened: (a) the formal role of thought-interpretation declined and virtually disappeared; (b) the use of victors came to be applied largely to nativities rather than to horary questions; (c) horary practice focused more on default house rulers and their interactions than on finding separate victors of the querent or quaesited or the chart as a whole.

§6: A proposal on the original use of thoughts in questions

So far, we have seen some of the history and scope of thought-interpretation and victors. But we have not yet clearly addressed two matters: the practical and theoretical relationship between thought-interpretation and questions, and why thought-interpretation might have arisen in the first place.[62]

I propose that the purpose of thought-interpretation was to define the proper scope of the relevant questions, providing the basis for further discussion and defining the right horary question. That is, the significator of thought must be used *alongside* the specific house lords (and Lot, *etc.*), because the thought and the question are related as universal and particular. For example, if the significator of thought indicates the topic of marriage, then

---

[60] Again, see Ptolemy's victor for a topic in Appendix H.
[61] See especially *Search* III.1-2, the al-Kindī excerpts in Appendix E, and ibn Ezra's victor for the chart in Appendix F.
[62] I am grateful to Chris Brennan for discussing the following ideas with me.

the astrologer should begin to probe the client about relationships, using the various features of the significator of thought (and the other marriage significators) to identify various issues needing attention. After exploring the client's relationship situation, the client and astrologer define the question to be answered. Of course, in many cases the identification of the thought, the discussion, and the answer, will be part of one continuous consultation and chart analysis.

This proposal has several features and advantages:

(a) It works especially well in a divinational model of horary consultation, where the *chart* (like Tarot cards, or whatever) identifies what the client needs to know, what really matters. Thus the significator of thought acts as an anchor to the consultation, a common ground, *the reason why you are really there.* And so, on this model, the significator of thought diagnoses a worry or concern that has a meaning for the client's life, even if it is not the first thing the client is thinking of.

(b) Identifying the thought also acts as a kind of consideration before judgment in explicit horary questions. For, while it helps steer the parameters of discussion and provides some context, it also acts as a check on the client's honesty or clarity. In *Judges* §0.1, Māshā'allāh makes the following statement:[63]

"But if anyone made a question in order to test [the astrologer] or in order to scoff, the effect and end of the affair in no way leaves the proper intention untouched—but he would not even know how to form any question, or how to assert what he is retaining in his mind, and how to reduce anything [to a particular topic], with care."

What I believe Māshā'allāh is saying here (through Hugo's translation), is that the significator of thought will reveal the discrepancy between what the scoffer says and what is really going on in his mind, and that a scoffer— because of his insincerity and mental laziness—will not be able to take the matter to the next step, going from a general thought to a particular question. Note that, unlike later ways of checking the "radicality" or rootedness or sincerity of the chart (such as comparing the lord of the hour and the lord of the Ascendant by triplicity),[64] using the significator of thought is *internal* to

---

[63] See also *OHT* §2, in Appendix C below.
[64] See for instance *Christian Astrology* pp. 121-23, and Bonatti's *BOA* Tr. 5, Considerations 7 and 143, and Tr. 6 (Part 1, Ch. 1).

the whole consultation process itself, and is not an *extra* technique on top of identifying the thought or matter. In fact, just as Lilly and other astrologers still read charts after absorbing information from the considerations before judgment (even if the rules say the chart should not be read), so the use of the significator of thought is also an invitation to investigate and search further—it is not a way of ending discussion.

(c) My proposal helps explain why traditional authorities used the significator of thought along with the other lords, or rather how to explain the fact that the significator of thought exists in the same chart as the other significators: because *they are all part of the same thought*. Again, Sahl uses the victor over the question as a whole in addition to the lord of the Ascendant (and so on); al-Rijāl prefaces almost every house with a discussion of how to know if the thought falls in that house, and then proceeds immediately to the questions about that house; the *Yavanajātaka* jumps right into discussing outcomes after identifying the kinds of thoughts pertaining to them; and Hephaistio has us identify the thoughts of people who are inquiring into some undertaking, which is then further explored.

(d) My proposal also draws out an explicit parallel between this kind of interrogational practice and that of nativities, annual natal predictions, and mundane astrology: namely, using a chief planet or victor to summarize the meaning of the chart, and to which the other features are in some sense subordinated: the longevity releaser in a nativity,[65] the profected lord of the year in annual predictions, and the mundane lord of the year or the significator of the king in mundane ingresses. Such a parallel could have been explicitly on the minds of those who pioneered these practices, helping to explain why the use of the longevity releaser in questions is maintained through at least the 9th Century (al-Kindī). It also suggests why alternatives to the releaser were sought, because only a few places are allowed to act as the longevity releaser, effectively limiting the variety of possible thoughts. Thus, instead of only finding the victor *among* the candidate releasers, we find a proliferation of victors *over* the releasing places.[66]

---

[65] The releaser especially is subject to primary directions (or "distributions") through the bounds, because it is supposed to sum up the life force of the native.

[66] See *Search* III.1.1-2, *Forty Chapters* Ch. 3.2 (Appendix E below), ibn Ezra's victor (Appendix F below). Another alternative using natal practice would be the view attributed to Māshā'allāh but drawn from *Carmen* I.10.14, on the squares of the Moon (see *Skilled* I.5.2 in Appendix A below).

If I am right, then we can attribute the loss of this model to several things mentioned before: the ease of overlooking references to significators of thought, the popularity of horary manuals written separately from instructions for significators of thought, and the notion that they represent a bothersome and unnecessary extra step: this is especially true if one has already advanced to finding a victor for the querent, since it will be tempting to use that as the indicator of thought instead. Indeed, in some of the texts here, it is a bit unclear whether we are looking at a significator of thought *using* the Ascendant, or the victor over the Ascendant as a *substitute* for the significator of thought. These facts imply that our late Persian sources no longer knew the real difference between, and way of linking, thoughts and questions, because they leave us no such instructions on how to connect them. In practice they may have started with a significator of thought, which would then *naturally* lead to discussing a certain horary topic; but what had begun as a conscious and explicitly justified relationship between thoughts and questions, could have settled down into a routine that gradually shed the distinct significator of thought altogether.

Although we seem to be able to trace the link from elections to thought-interpretation and questions through our texts, we are still missing the main motivation for using thought-interpretation as a preliminary for elections or questions at all (such as Hephaistio suggests).

It could be that a divinational meeting of client and astrologer was considered both conceptually and experientially prior (even if not historically or textually prior) to the asking of a specific question, for reasons which parallel statements by Sahl and Bonatti about elections:[67] namely, before an effective election may be designed and take place, we must first know whether or not the client's life actually supports the action involved. But how can we know if the life supports it? There are two possibilities: either we examine the client's nativity itself, or we examine a valid (or "rooted") horary chart on the subject of the election (such as, "will I be successful at action X?"). After determining the general possibility of success, the astrologer then crafts an election specifically tailored to the horary chart or nativity which has confirmed it.

If my proposal above is correct, then the combination of thought-interpretation and thought outcomes (or some kind of horary analysis upon a thought-interpretation) could be the proper preliminary to casting an actual

---

[67] See for instance Sahl's *On Elections* §§ 1-5c (in *WSM*) and my Introduction to Bonatti's *Book of Astronomy*, §E.

election chart or advising a specific undertaking. This idea draws on some ancient notions of the logic of action. In traditional philosophy, actions are partly explained by showing that some broad motivation (universal), combined with specific, suitable opportunities (particular), yields a concrete individual action—much as police speak of a general motive and a matching, suitable opportunity yielding a crime. If I am suitably hungry (universal), and am presented with *this* food (particular), the likely result is eating. This relation of universal-particular can be expressed astrologically in several ways:

	Universal	Particular	Action/outcome
Nativities	Nativity	Annual revolution	Annual outcomes
Inquiries	Thought	Question	Answer
Elections	Auspicious configurations	*Nativity/annual outcomes, or answer*	Successful undertaking

Figure 5: Suggested role of the logic of action in astrology

Look at the "Nativities" row of the table: we can express annual events and outcomes as a result of combining the nativity (universal) with its annual modifications through profections, transits, and directions (particular).[68] In client inquiries, the thought or its significator (universal) is made particular through the more narrowly-defined question and its significators, yielding a concrete answer. To understand what I mean by the third line, let me offer an analogy. Suppose you want to take a vacation, and you hear about low-priced tickets for flights on a specific date. In the most general sense, it is "a good time to travel" on that date. But that is generically true for *everyone* (universal): it might not be good for *you* (particular). Perhaps you have no vacation time left, or you have conflicting obligations. Just so, when someone came to the astrologer for an election, it was not enough to pick generically good transit dates: traditional authors wanted an assurance that such generically good configurations (universal) would indicate success for *you* (particular). And so, they looked at the nativity (or the annual predictive outcomes) or a suitable thought-interpretation or horary chart, to see if the undertaking would be successful (particular): favorable general conditions with an unfavorable client chart will not yield as successful an undertaking as when the client's nativity or well-rooted horary chart is also favorable. And so you can see that while annual outcomes and specific answers by them-

---

[68] This is precisely the relationship described in *PN III*.

selves can be considered as concrete combinations of a universal and a particular in their own right, each of those combinations may also itself play the special role of particularizing the generic conditions of success in an election (see italics in the table above).

If so, then the thought-question combination can form a conceptually and practically necessary stage in developing valid elections, *when* used as an alternative to nativities and their annual revolutions. As such an alternative, it could be seen as conceptually and experientially *prior* to elections themselves, since it is based on the initial, open-minded, divinational experience of the meeting between client and astrologer. Nevertheless, my proposals do not tell us when the thought and question techniques or rules for explicit horary questions were *actually* developed in relation to nativities and elections.

§7: Hermann of Carinthia

Hermann was from the European region of Carinthia (modern German: *Kärnten*), which in medieval times covered southern parts of Austria and the northeastern shores of the Adriatic Sea, around Slovenia and Croatia. Not much is known about his background and early life, but he was probably educated in northern France, and we do know somewhat more about his professional and personal relations. Between 1138 and 1143—his most productive period—he lived in the area of southern France and northern Spain. We do know for a fact that in 1141 he was with his friend and colleague, Robert of Ketton[69] in the valley of the Ebro river in Spain; between 1141 and 1143 he was in and around León, working for Peter the Venerable (abbot of the famous French monastery of Cluny); in 1143 he was in Toulouse, and in 1144 probably in Béziers (France), based on some comments by his student, Rudolph of Bruges. He claimed the famous Thierry of Chartres as his teacher.

Hermann produced some important translations of Arabic into Latin, as well as an original philosophical work of his own. For our purposes, we can divide his work and relationships into three groups:

First, there is the Arabic background to Hermann's work, and his contribution to Christian-Islamic interactions. By living in the areas he did, Hermann would have had ample exposure to Arabic and Arabic literature. In

---

[69] Ketton is (or was) in central England. Robert was the archdeacon of Pamplona.

France, there were Arabic-speaking communities in Montpellier, and both southern France and northern Spain had shared scholarship and contacts. Indeed, in Spain, Muslims still constituted a large part of Aragon's population even after the Christian conquest in 1087, and certain Muslim powers did not surrender until as late as 1140, when Hugo of Santalla (another colleague of Hermann's) began work around Zaragoza and Tarazona on a surprising discovery in natal and predictive astrology, the so-called *Book of Aristotle*.[70] While Hermann was translating astrological works on the Ebro, he was hired by Peter the Venerable to translate Islamic religious works: this must have been both for intellectual as well as polemical purposes. While Robert of Ketton produced the first Latin translation of the Qur'an, Hermann worked on two other works of apologetics and legends (see below).

Second, there is Hermann's earliest and most important interest: astrology. In fact his first translation was a rendering of Sahl bin Bishr's book on mundane revolutions (1138), and by the end of his translation period he had produced further mundane works, *Search*, and the earliest translation of Abū Ma'shar's work on natal solar revolutions—not to mention Abū Ma'shar's influential *Great Introduction* (*Gr. Intr.*). All of this was in addition to other mathematical works which were also supportive of astrological study (see below).

Hermann's closest association was with Robert of Ketton. Their relationship was not only collegial but deeply personal, and Hermann's numerous addresses and references to Robert are so effusive that to my mind the relationship was evidently rather homoerotic, if not actually sexual.[71] In speaking about Robert, Hermann makes the same reference to Aristotle's one-soul-in-two-bodies theory of friendship that St. Augustine does in his own *Confessions*; but whereas Augustine uses his unnamed friend's death as a further occasion to speak about himself, Hermann's devotion is focused on Robert.

---

[70] In 2009 I translated this work as part of *PN I*.

[71] Hermann speaks of Robert as his "unique and distinguished partner," his "most devoted Robert," that only Robert is "a special and inseparable sharer of all my cares, and through all the partner of my impulses and deeds," that Robert is his "soul," that their lives are "undivided, our minds are the same, and we share completely the same soul," and even makes Minerva say that from the beginning she had made one man from both of them. See Low-Beer pp. 21-22.

In addition to Robert, Hermann also worked with Hugo of Santalla. All three men labored on astrological translations in the same area at the same time, and indeed the *Book of the Three Judges* (later expanded to become the *Book of the Nine Judges*) was a collaboration between them. Hermann uses Robert's translation of al-Kindī for the relevant portions of *Search* (rather than Hugo's),[72] but by the time of *Judges* it seems that many of the earlier portions by Hermann or Robert have been reworked by Hugo alone. Hermann must also have relied on Hugo's translation of *On the Secrets of Nature* by Bālīnūs, since *Search* attributes several views to him under the name "Appollonius."

The third phase of Hermann's output overlaps with his translation of *Gr. Intr.*: namely, an original work of metaphysics and cosmology entitled *On Essences*.[73] In *Gr. Intr.*, Abū Ma'shar draws on elements of Aristotle, Neoplatonic thought, and other influences, to establish an astronomically-oriented Aristotelianism that justifies astrology. In fact, Lemay argues that important doctrines and elements of Aristotle might have re-entered the Latin West precisely through scholars' reading of Abū Ma'shar. Hermann was inspired by Abū Ma'shar (though not following him exactly), and began to develop his own cosmology in tune with other developments in 12th Century academic thought. The classical *quadrivium* had made astronomy just one of its four disciplines, but Hermann re-distributed mathematics and astronomy: he assigned mathematics (number, proportion, measure) to the movements of the stars, and their effects to the physics of both the upper and lower worlds—the upper world dealt with formal causes, while the lower world dealt with material causes. Astrology was therefore made into a centerpiece of learning about ultimate reality.

Hermann also adapted material from the late Roman Boethius and his own teacher Thierry of Chartres, making physics more important than mathematics: this change was partly due to his understanding of Arabic thought (including the Arab al-Fārābī) and comments in Aristotle's *Metaphysics*,[74] where Aristotle puts physics between mathematics and theology. But Hermann also structures his book according to ultimate principles and essences in non-sensible aspects of reality (such as cause, movement, place,

---

[72] I have used Hugo's translation of al-Kindī as the primary basis for my English *Forty Chapters* (2011).
[73] This was translated into English by Burnett in 1982.
[74] *Met.* 1026a6-19.

time, "bearing,"[75] and so on). So, as with much medieval cosmology, there is something of a background in Plato's *Timaeus*, but the details of physics come from Aristotle.

Following is a list of known works by Hermann, all of which are translations from Arabic (apart from his *On Essences*):

1. *On the generation of Muhammad* (legends about Muhammad), 1141-43.
2. *The teaching of Muhammad* (a dialogue between a Jew and Muhammad, in which the Jew is converted), 1141-43.
3. Sahl's *On the Revolution of the Years of the World* (on mundane astrology), known in Latin as the *Fatidica* ("Prophetic Sayings"), 1138.[76]
4. Abū Ma'shar's *Great Introduction* (1140).
5. Abū Ma'shar's *On the Revolution of the Years of Nativities*.[77]
6. *The Search of the Heart* (after 1140).
7. *Liber Imbrium* (the "Book on Heavy Rains"), on weather prediction.[78]
8. Khwārizmī's astronomical tables (lost).
9. Ptolemy's *Planisphere* (Toulouse, 1143).
10. Lost works on the function of numbers and finding a square root.
11. Euclid's *Elements*.
12. Theodosius's *Spherics*.
13. *On Essences*, an original work of metaphysics and cosmology (1143).[79]

---

[75] *Habitudo.*

[76] I will produce an English translation of this in 2012 for the mundane portion of my *EMA* cycle (see Appendix M).

[77] Hermann refers to this in *On Essences*, but his version has not yet been identified. I have translated another, incomplete 13th Century Latin version as *PN III* (2010).

[78] I will produce an English translation of this in 2012 for the mundane portion of my *EMA* cycle (see Appendix M).

[79] See the Bibliography for Burnett's 1982 translation and commentary.

§8: *The Search of the Heart*: structure, special features, glossary

This translation of *The Search of the Heart* is based largely on Sheila Low-Beer's 1979 edition, which was not a critical edition, but a provisional version drawn from five manuscripts. In creating my own translation, I have made some changes and relied on a number of other sources which Hermann uses, including Sahl's *On Times*, *On Hidden Things*, al-Kindī's *Forty Chapters* (the Robert of Ketton translation) and excerpts from *Judges*. I have also supplemented the text with numerous Appendices.

The Low-Beer edition was structured in approximately four parts. (1) The first part was actually a summary of Hermann's own translation of Abū Ma'shar's Lot calculations in *Gr. Intr.*, followed by a short passage on ascensional aspects or ascensional directions. The rest of the book was divided somewhat uncertainly between material on (2) thought-interpretation, (3) more horary-style questions on hidden objects and planetary configurations and timing, and (4) calculating victors and the releaser for the whole chart, with extra advice on delineation.

But the Lot material is not at all used in the rest of *Search*, and there is internal evidence that the core of the book was in two parts—interpreting thoughts on the one hand, and the more standard horary approach to objects, configurations, and timing on the other—with probably the last material on victors and delineation being a separate work or appended later. So, I have omitted the material on Lots, put the passage on ascensional aspects in Appendix K, and structured the book as follows:

Book I: The Consultation and Understanding Thoughts
Book II: Descriptions, Treasure, Configurations, Timing
Book III: Victors and Significators of Charts & Topics

Most of the Book and Chapter headings are my own, usually for the sake of clarity. My title for Book I is based on explicit statements by Hermann (at the beginning of Book II and in Ch. II.4.3), that Book I is on *consilio querentis et cogitatione*: "the querent's consultation and thought." I have also changed the order of some of the passages, following clues within the text itself.

Following are a few notable features of *Search* and Hermann's approach:

1. Whole-sign houses from the Lot of Fortune. In Ch. II.4.5, Hermann explicitly endorses using whole-sign houses from the Lot of Fortune, as an aid to understanding topics. For example, in questions about wealth and livelihood (2nd house), Hermann suggests looking at the second sign from Fortune as well. References to Lot of Fortune-based houses are rare enough in Hellenistic astrology, and much more so by the medieval period, so this reference is a welcome sign of older doctrine being preserved.

2. *Quadrant-based houses, secondary significators.* In Chs. I.3 and II.4.5, Hermann explicitly endorses quadrant-based houses, but without describing a specific house system (e.g., Porphyry, Alchabitius Semi-Arcs). At first (Ch. I.3), Hermann notes that the "proper place" of the cusps is in the whole signs we would expect—such as the Midheaven falling on the tenth sign—but that it is a serious error to simply assume whole-sign houses: for although a planet might fall into the rising sign, it might actually be in the twelfth or second quadrant-based house instead.

Later (II.4.5), Hermann clarifies his view so as to account for certain signs and their lords as secondary significators. That is, he uses quadrant-based houses as already stated, but he also uses the lord of the whole sign (or "proper place" mentioned above) as a kind of secondary significator, *provided that* some part of that sign falls into the quadrant-based house. For example, suppose the Midheaven falls on the ninth sign, so that part of the tenth sign (the proper place of the 10th) falls into the 10th quadrant-based house: in that case, it would be all right to adopt the lord of the tenth sign—in addition to the lord of the Midheaven, which is on the ninth sign—as another significator for matters of reputation and profession. But if the Midheaven fell onto the eleventh sign, then nothing of the tenth sign would fall into the 10th house region at all, and so in that case the lord of the tenth sign would be irrelevant.

Hermann's view is very similar to the later view of Lilly and Morin. For Lilly and Morin tend to ignore whole signs altogether, and will allow any sign falling into the house region (and its lord) to be a co-significator. So, if the Midheaven fell onto the eleventh sign, and part of the twelfth sign were in that region, Morin would allow the *twelfth* sign and its lord to be co-significators with the lord of the *eleventh* sign, in matters of the *tenth house*. But Hermann is only interested in using the lord of the "proper place" or whole-sign house as a co-significator, *if* it falls into the quadrant-based region of the same name.

3. *Use of natal material; Māshā'allāh's translation of Dorotheus.* As already mentioned before, *Search* (and other horary works) do show clear signs of

adapting natal material for questions and thoughts. Four examples in *Search* and the Appendices should illustrate this. (1) In *Skilled* I.5.2 (Appendix A), al-Rijāl credits Māshā'allāh with a certain view on finding the significator for a chart: but this view closely resembles *Carmen* III.1.10-14,[80] suggesting that some version of Māshā'allāh's translation of *Carmen* enjoyed new life in the context of thoughts and questions. (2) In *Search* Ch. I.8, the "first book" of Māshā'allāh is credited with certain views on identifying someone's social status—but really, this sounds like certain statements in the first book of *Carmen* (specifically, *Carmen* I.10): again, it suggests an ongoing access to and appropriation of Māshā'allāh's translation. (3) Third, the attributions of house strengths to Māshā'allāh and Dorotheus (Chs. I.3.4 and III.1.1) is yet another indication that Dorothean statements about the advantageous or busy places were being used—with a pointing system—for finding the victors in thoughts and questions.[81] In this case, the differences between Dorotheus and Māshā'allāh may be due to manuscript differences, or even a conscious decision on Māshā'allāh's part to re-assign the points. (4) Lastly, Hermann's appropriation of *Forty Chapters* Ch. 3 is a use of natal material for questions, since al-Kindī recommends using the longevity releaser and its *kadukḫudhāh* in all matters and their inceptions or beginnings. (Of course, the use of Ptolemy's releaser is also found in *Skilled* I.5.2.)

Speaking of authorities used by Hermann, following is a list of those real or legendary writers explicitly cited or at least used in the text. Hopefully, in the future we will be able to identify all of the sources:

- Abū 'Ali al-Khayyāt,[82] student of Māshā'allāh (source unknown).
- Abū Bakr Muhammad bin Zakariyā' al-Rāzī (ca. 865-925 AD), the famous Persian physician and polymath.
- Al-Kindī, from his *Forty Chapters*.
- Bālīnūs (or "Appollonius"), probably from Hugo's Latin translation of his *On the Secrets of Nature*.
- Hermes.

---

[80] Recall that only 'Umar's incomplete translation of *Carmen* into Arabic has survived; Māshā'allāh's only survives in little bits.
[81] Note that when we follow Hermann's advice in III.1.1 and do not count the house points along with the dignities, then the appraisal of houses becomes less about adding up points as about understanding the preferred *rank* of the houses, which is undoubtedly what Dorotheus would have preferred.
[82] Called variously *Alkamaz* and *Albukeiz*.

- Jirjis (also called Zymus, Georgius). Source and identity unknown, although Jirjis also appears throughout *Judges*.
- Māshā'allāh, from his *On Hidden Things* (attributed), and probably his translation of *Carmen*.
- Sahl bin Bishr, from his *On Times*, *Fifty Judgments*, *On Quest.*, and *Introduct.* (see *WSM*).
- 'Umar al-Tabarī, primarily from 'Umar's horary material also found in *Judges*.
- Various unnamed Indians and Persians.

Finally, as in recent translations, I would like to offer a short list of technical terms that reflect Hermann's translation style (a more complete glossary of terms may be found in *ITA*):

- **Aversion.** Being in the second, sixth, eighth, or twelfth sign from a place. For instance, a planet in Gemini is in the twelfth from, and therefore in aversion to, Cancer.
- **Bearing** (Lat. *habitudo*). In *Search*, any kind of planetary configuration as described in Ch. II.4.2 (cf. *ITA* III).
- **Binding, being bound** (Lat. *ligo*). Equivalent to a planet being connected by degree (e.g., within orbs) to another planet, as opposed to merely aspecting it by sign or being assembled with it in the same sign. For assembly, whole-sign aspects or regards, and degree-based connections, see *ITA* III.5-7, respectively.
- **Destruction** (Lat. *exitium*). Equivalent to being in the sign of detriment.
- **Disposition** (Lat. *affectus*). I am not entirely happy with my translation here. Normally, disposition evokes "dispositors," namely the lords or rulers of something; or, it suggests the pushing or committing of disposition (really, "management": see *ITA* III.18). But in Hermann, *affectus* or disposition really refers to planetary relationships and configurations—in other words, all of the **bearings** of the stars, along with planetary strengths and weaknesses.
- **Fortune.** Normally, one of the two benefic planets (Venus, Jupiter), but perhaps a planet such as Mercury or the Moon if in a good condition.
- **Infortune**. Normally, one of the two malefic planets (Mars, Saturn), but perhaps a planet such as Mercury or the Moon if in a bad condition.

- **Leader, leadership** (Lat. *dux, ducatus*). For the most part I have translated this as "significator" and "signification," as a more accurate translation of the Arabic. The Arabic means to indicate by pointing, so as to lead one's attention to something. I normally try to avoid using Hermann's and Hugo's terminology for this, so as not to lead to confusion.[83]
- **Partner** (Lat. *particeps*, from Ar. *ṣāḥib*, "associate, owner"). Usually, one of the lords of a place. But sometimes it seems to mean a planet in some configuration with another, and so having a partnership with it; or even a planet in a place, which therefore becomes a partner of the lord of that place, in indicating that topic.
- **Remote** (Lat. *remotus*). Normally, equivalent to being cadent, but in some cases perhaps equivalent to being in **aversion** to the Ascendant (that is, being in the twelfth, eighth, sixth or second signs from the Ascendant).
- **Sovereignty** (Lat. *regnum*). Equivalent to exaltation.

---

[83] This use of "leader" by Hermann forms an exception to Lemay's claim that Hermann wants to avoid Arabic sentence structure. For the Arabic would say that a planet "leads to" or "has an indication over" something, and Hermann's Latin does indeed sometimes replicate this phrasing. Hermann also had another reason for such phrasing: because if the astrologer is engaged in a *search*, we want to be *led to* the answer. See §1 above.

BOOK I: THE CONSULTATION & UNDERSTANDING THOUGHTS[1]

Chapter I.1: By what means the path of judgments comes to be

The path of the judgments of the stars is wholly divided into two parts: one is that of the questions of a birth or even of annual [predictions];[2] the other, that of counsel and the thoughts of men and a concealed thing and the proper quality of persons.[3] For just as nature has created diverse things, so the observation of astronomy leads to an understanding of them by a dissimilar method [for each], a treatment of whose types[4] follows. And so:

[1] The first thing for us [to consider] is how Māshā'allāh relates it: the nature of the stars and planets must be observed (to the extent that this category demands it).[5]

[2] Next, as Hermes lays it out, one must follow up with how much pertains to their accidents.[6]

[3] Finally, by what search the significator of this whole art can be chosen,[7] and at the same time we will sneak in [how] its assistance [may be] applied.[8]

---

[1] I have derived this title from Hermann's own text, since the beginning of Book II explicitly states that Book I is on this topic. *Consilium* can mean "consultation" (as I have it here) as well as "advice, counsel, deliberation, intention."

[2] That is, nativities and the revolutions of years. This topic is covered fully in *Persian Nativities I-III.*

[3] This second branch of astrology is precisely the topic of *Search*, though this sentence does not clearly state the difference between thoughts and questions proper: for that distinction, see Ch. II.4.1.

[4] That is, the specific types just mentioned: Book I deals with thoughts, and Book II with objects and persons (along with more strictly horary approaches, timing methods, *etc.*). Book III will deal with methods for determining victors or chief significators over an entire chart and a particular topic.

[5] See Chs. I.2-I.2.4, and I.2.6.

[6] See Ch. I.2.5.

[7] See Chs. I.3-5, I.9-10. I will omit this boldface designation below, because the chapters are not continuous and it might cause confusion.

[8] See Chs. I.6-8, I.11. I will omit this boldface designation below, because the chapters are not continuous and it might cause confusion.

Chapter I.2: On the natures of the signs, houses and planets

[1] Therefore the principal [significations][9] of the signs are twelve, of which certain ones are allotted the nature of [each individual triplicity]:

Chapter I.2.1: Objects signified by the signs

Fiery Signs	
♈	Everything engraved, polished, and tempered in fire, as are precious metals like gold and silver and what is like these.
♌	Bright and planed [gems] and those which are of great value: as is hyacinth,[10] emerald and that kind—unless the Sun or Mars are joined as significators, for then [Leo signifies] copper or iron.
♐	What is more low-quality in this category, as are gypsum, bricks, tiles and earthenware, and what is like these, tempered by fire.

Airy Signs	
♊	First to men, then to animals of a light and small body; hands and feet or feathers.
♎	[Beings] whose feet are different and of diverse form,[11] part of whose color [is] different from [other] parts, of heavier animals.[12]
♒	Vile things, as are four-footed things in the waters or living in dung[13] (that is, things creeping on the earth).

Earthy Signs	
♉	Higher trees whose fruits are handed over for use.
♍	Those which require irrigation,[14] like crops, flax,[15] cotton and vegetables.
♑	Thorny trees, thickets,[16] orchards, edible reeds,[17] and pastures.

---

[9] *Principalia.*
[10] Or yellow zircon, which appears in igneous rocks.
[11] This probably means, "whose feet are different from the upper limbs."
[12] I confess I am not sure what kinds of animals this would include.
[13] Or, "muck" (*stercoralia*). This probably includes both pigs and insects such as flies.
[14] Or, good watering (*irriguum*).
[15] I.e., for linen.
[16] Or, "brushwood" (*virgulta*).
[17] *Arundinetum victus* (tentative): from *harundo*, "reed," and *victus*, "food, nourishment."

Watery Signs	
♋	Among aquatic animals, those like crabs, turtles, and that kind, unless the Moon is equally in a watery [sign]: for then it signifies frozen or boiled water, as is salt or sugar and what is like these.[18]
♏	Much wateriness and every heavy liquid and commixture, such as mud, [what is] curdled, or anything massed together,[19] and that type.
♓	The rest of the kinds of fish.

Chapter I.2.2: Limbs and regions signified by the signs

But they apportion lands and the human body in this way:

	Limbs	Regions
♈	Head & face	Persia and Babylonia
♉	Neck	[Al-Suwād, Māhīn, Hamadhān, and the cities of the Kurds who live in the mountains][20]
♊	Arms	Greater Armenia and Memphis[21]
♋	Chest	Lesser Armenia
♌	Back	Parthia[22]
♍	Belly	[Jarāmaqa, Syria, the Euphrates, al-Jazīra, and Persia following Kirmān][23]

---

[18] Hermann must mean things that are crystalline or boiled in water to draw them out (such as when sugar cane is boiled).

[19] *Commassatum.*

[20] Adding from *ITA* I.3.

[21] That is, "Egypt," here and below.

[22] *ITA* I.3: the lands of the Turks.

[23] Reading with *ITA* I.3 for Hermann's *Furaa*, probably a transliteration for "Euphrates."

♎	Flanks & thighs	Rome and thence to Africa, thence to the boundaries of Memphis
♏	Groin	The countrysides of the Arabs
♐	Buttocks & hips[24]	Monastic areas and places of prayer[25]
♑	Knees	Valleys and the Moors and India
♒	Shins	Farmers[26]
♓	Feet	Aracoa[27] and from Rome up to Syria

Chapter I.2.3: Significations of the houses

Then it follows that:

The east:	The life of a man and [his] mind and body
Second:	The possessions of a man, and [his] livelihood, & assets
Third:	Brothers and sisters
Fourth:	Parents, an estate,[28] and the ends of things
Fifth:	Offspring, heralds, gifts
Sixth:	Slaves, the sick, beasts
Seventh:	Betrothals, sexual intercourse, adversaries, controversies
Eighth:	Death and dread
Ninth:	Travel, dreams, wisdom, law
Tenth:	Dominions, kingdoms, and trades
Eleventh:	Supremacy,[29] monies, hope
Twelfth:	Enemies, prison, and beasts of burden[30]

---

[24] Including the thighs.

[25] *ITA* I.3: "Baghdad and al-Jibāl, Isfahān, places of the Herpads and fire-worshippers." I have read "monastic areas" for *Search*'s "Cenobia," under the assumption that Hermann means places of cenobites, viz., monks who live communally.

[26] *ITA* I.3. reads: "al-Suwād toward the mountains, and Kūfa and its parts, and the rear of the Hijāz, and the land of the Copts of Egypt, and the western region of the land of Sind, and it has partnership in the land of Persia."

[27] Uncertain. *ITA* I.3. reads: "Tabarīstān and the northern region of the land of Jurjān, and a partnership in Roman [lands] up to Syria, and it has al-Jazīra and Egypt and Alexandria and the sea of Yemen."

[28] Or, "farm" (*fundum*).

[29] *Regnum*, normally Hermann's word for "exaltation."

[30] *Iumenta*. This helps to clarify the attribution of large animals in the twelfth: it is not so much that they are large, as that they are beasts of *burden*, which is a theme of the twelfth.

Chapter I.2.4: Regions signified by the planets

But concerning the proper qualities of the stars, these things must be said:

	People & things	Regions
♄	Old men and common people	Mountains,[31] wintry places[32] and earthy and rocky places
♃	Socially important people,[33] judges, and friends	Media, Persia, Babylonia
♂	Arms and militias	Syria
☉	Princes and kings	Rome and Anicosea[34]
♀	Women, foods, drink, expensive clothes	Arabia (with Mars)
☿	Possessions, merchants, books	India
☽	Heralds, commissions,[35] and mothers	Parthia and Armenia

---

[31] Or specifically, the Alps (*alpes*).
[32] Lit., "Ireland" (*Hiberniam*).
[33] *Praelatos*, which could mean simply "prelates."
[34] Possibly Khurāsān: see *ITA* V.4.
[35] That is, people commanded (*mandata*) by an authority to perform a special function.

Chapter I.2.5: Solar phases and planetary motions

[2] Which, since the natures of the stars are in a certain way put under the whole circle, there is a variety of accidents by means of [their] change in place; [and] by means of the various applications amongst themselves, there is an alteration of outcomes. As a matter of fact, for this reason:

Eastern [planets] are in charge of youths and the newness of things; western ones, the contrary.[36]

Retrograde ones, complications and reversals; direct ones, the contrary.[37]

Those lofty and adding, increase; pressed down and subtracting, made low.[38]

In their own dignities, strong; foreign,[39] weak.[40]

Chapter I.2.6: Senses ruled by the planets[41]

Senses	
♄ ♃	Hearing
♂ ♀	Smell
☉ ☽	Vision
☿	Speech

---

[36] See also *ITA* II.10.3.
[37] See also *ITA* II.10.4.
[38] *Detrimentum.* See also *ITA* II.1 and II.4. This paragraph has to do with planets in their apogees or perigees, and probably planetary speed.
[39] Or, "peregrine."
[40] See also *ITA* I.8.
[41] Note that touch is not represented here: the planets are really indicating orifices in the head: the ears, nostrils, eyes, and mouth.

Chapter I.3: Finding the significator of thought[42]

These things having been observed, it is first necessary that the east be established most exactly, and the pivots of heaven made firm so that there could be an exact discernment of the places of the stars. For sometimes [it happens that a star] occurs within the pivot of heaven [while the pivot is] in its own proper place,[43] or it falls into the ninth or in the eleventh; but once these are distinguished it sometimes happens that a star placed in the east[44] is in the second or in the twelfth [quadrant-based house], which is not an insignificant error. Therefore, if this happened, it will comply with the majority [of cases].[45]

These things having been put in order, then the whole industry of the art is taken up by the choosing of the significator of the matter. Once it has been found, then at last it is appropriate for the suitable testimonies to be applied[46]—[but] not by judging immediately before all testimonies of the significator are fully understood, and its counsels examined in detail. [Rather], the place of its principal significator (both the natural and accidental one)[47] should be carefully and soundly [examined] first, and both its nature and accidents should be examined in detail. Then the rulerships, applications and separations; then also its place, strength, and manner. When these have been diligently and fully looked at, there is nothing which could overwhelm a cautious mind.

---

[42] The methods in this chapter are based on the Ascendant and its lord, perhaps on the principle that the rising sign shows all matters, including questions, emerging from out of darkness into light (Sahl, *Introduct.* §3).

[43] Namely, in the tenth sign.

[44] That is, the rising sign.

[45] Most of this paragraph is extremely dense and Hermann has omitted some operative verbs for stylistic purposes. But Hermann or his source is indeed endorsing quadrant-based houses. The paragraph up to this point reads: *Hiis conspectis, primum necesse est oriens certissime constitui, cardinesque caeli firmari, ut locorum stellarum certa possit esse discretio. Nonnichil enim est inter caeli cardinem proprio in loco consistere aut in nonum aut in undecimum incidere; hiis enim in discretis plerumque accidit stellam in oriente locatam in secundo esse aut in 12o, cuius non est levis error. Id igitur cum acciderit maiori parti concedetur.*

[46] See Ch. I.3.5 below.

[47] I am not quite sure whether this refers to a natural and accidental significator, or to its "natural" and accidental place (such as by rulership or location).

Chapter I.3.1: Finding the significator (al-Rāzī/Māshā'allāh)

As al-Rāzī teaches, as we are following him: After the east was established by degrees and minutes, and the rest of the domiciles put in order, and also the degrees and points of the stars made firm, then at last I search first for the place[48] of the significator, according to the opinion of Māshā'allāh (which must be followed).[49] Nor, as Māshā'allāh says, is a significator fit unless it is either the lord of the east, or of the sovereignty of the east, or the first lord of the trigon of the degree of the east, or [of the luminary of] its sect,[50] or the lord of the hour. Others[51] add [to this] from the lord of the decan and from the lord of the bound.

Which if all of these were adverse, and none among them were fit,[52] and the question were diurnal, the Sun will have to be consulted; if nocturnal, the counsel of the Moon should be applied, or the lord of the Lot of Fortune. Which if all of these were adverse, so that (of all of them) none were fit, let [these] be left aside, [and] let us embrace the Moon by day and night, wherever she is in the places.

Chapter I.3.2: Finding the significator (a "Dorothean" Lot-like method)

But the opinion of Dorotheus[53] is that the number of degrees should be taken up from the degree of the lord of the hour to the degree of the lord of the east, and the whole [number which is] counted will begin from the degree of the Sun (with the degrees of the Sun being added [to the beginning of the sign]),[54] or from the pivot of the Midheaven, namely assigning 30° to each

---

[48] Reading *locum* for *loco*, as the object of *indago*.

[49] Reading *prosequendam* for *prosequenda*, to modify *sententiam*.

[50] *Haizehu.* Hermann is probably drawing on Māshā'allāh's mainly lost translation of *Carmen*, since Dorotheus is famous for his promiscuous use of triplicity lords. The lists of possible significators in *Thought* (Appendix C below) do include the sect light (the Sun in the day, the Moon in the night), but not the triplicity lord.

[51] The Indians mentioned in Ch. I.9.3 below and in *OHT* §2 (see Appendix C).

[52] For fitness, see Ch. I.4 below and *ITA* IV.1-2.

[53] This is probably a pseudo-Dorotheus.

[54] This is a standard medieval way to make the counting out of Lots easier. See the example in *ITA* VI.1.1. Put more simply, the Lot being described here is taken from the lord of the hour to the lord of the Ascendant, and is projected from either the Sun or Midheaven. But my sense is that this calculation has gotten garbled. In Ch. I.11.2 below, the calculation is switched (measuring from the lord of the Ascendant to the lord of the

sign: therefore, where the number left off, [the rulership] will be bestowed between the lords of its sign and its bound. Therefore, the one which appeared familiarly,[55] and to whom many testimonies were conceded, will no doubt obtain the signification.

Chapter I.3.3: Finding the significator (a proportional dignity-house method)[56]

However, we can also find the significator in this way: that the portions of the stars' dignities would be computed, and the one to whom they conceded more, were it [also] established better, will obtain it.

But the [initial] distribution of portions of this kind is: the lord of the east claims 18; the lord of the sovereignty 13 (provided that it is eastern in that degree);[57] the first lord of the trigon, 10; the lord of the bound, 6.

With these distinctions having been applied, one must observe that the number of parts is whole [if the planets are] in the pivots; outside the pivots, [they are] diminished in this way: while they were in the third or ninth or fifth or in the eleventh, they retain one-half; in the four averse places (in the second, sixth, eighth, twelfth), one-third.

These things being accurately examined, the one to which they conceded more parts, and were better established, that one will no doubt obtain the signification.

---

hour), and the projection from the Midheaven is part of a different Lot described in Ch. I.11.1.

[55] *Familiarius*. This refers to how well a planet aspects and from what kind of place: see Chs. 1.3.4 and I.6.1.

[56] This method seems to be based on the Dorothean "advantageous" places, which include the Ascendant and all signs aspecting it, except for the third (which is still considered a good place, but the weakest of all); those places in aversion to the Ascendant are not considered advantageous. In the diagram, all places configured with the Ascendant (including the third) have either full or half strength, and the places in aversion have one-third. But see another version attributed to Dorotheus and based on *Carmen* I.5, in Ch. III.1.1 below.

[57] This sentence might actually mean, "if the degree of the east *has* a lord of the sovereignty [exaltation]."

Lords of Ascendant	Points
Domicile	18
Sovereignty/exaltation	13
Primary triplicity lord	10
Bound	6

Figure 6: Ruler strengths for the proportional dignity-house significator

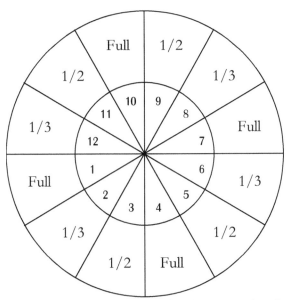

Figure 7: House strengths for the proportional dignity-house significator

Chapter I.3.4: Finding the significator (Māshā'allāh)[58]

But among all things, says Māshā'allāh, one must see which one would have more dignities in the east: that is, with 5 belonging to the domicile, 4 to the sovereignty, 3 to the bound, 2 to the first of the lords of the trigon, 1 to the decan.

Lords of Ascendant	Points
Domicile	5
Sovereignty/exaltation	4
Bound	3
Primary triplicity lord	2
Decan	1

Figure 8: Ruler strengths for Māshā'allāh's significator

But it is plain that the one which had more in the east, and were stronger and placed more intimately, will obtain it. The one which is in the east (as Māshā'allāh teaches)[59] has 12 parts; in the tenth it has 11 parts; in the eleventh, 10 parts; in the fifth, 9 parts; in the seventh, 8 parts; in the fourth, 7 parts; in the ninth, 6 parts; in the third, 5 parts; in the second, 4 parts; in the eighth, 3 parts; in the twelfth, 2 parts; in the sixth, 1 part. And this [arrangement of houses] is according to Dorotheus,[60] but most people [prefer the pivots to the rest, in order].[61]

---

[58] See another, more lengthy presentation of this in Ch. III.1.1 below. The difference between this version and that in III.1.1 seems to be that this one identifies a significator for the querent personally (because it is derived from the lords of the Ascendant). But in III.1.1, one calculates a compound victor or significator for the entire chart, using the lords of the places of several traditional releasers (the sect light, Ascendant, Lot of Fortune, and the pre-natal lunation).

[59] But see a slightly different version attributed to Māshā'allāh in Ch. III.1.1 below.

[60] *Carmen* I.5, which however does not assign actual points.

[61] Using the wording from III.1.1 below, for "but most people do not put the pivots." An example of preferring the pivots would be al-Kindī, in *Forty Chapters* Ch. 13 (§461); also Abraham ibn Ezra, in his determination of the victor of the chart (see Appendix F below).

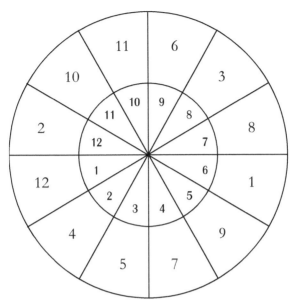

Figure 9: House strengths for Māshā'allāh's significator

Chapter I.3.5: Applying the other testimonies[62]

Then, the appropriate testimonies should be applied: namely those of the lord of the hour, and the lord of the day; also by day the Sun, by night the Moon, and the Lot of Fortune. For all of these which construct the path [of judgments] increase the indication of the significator.

---

[62] Applying the testimonies was stated as a task at the beginning of Ch. I.3 above. It might be a reference to statements such as al-Kindī's on how perfection of a matter is made more certain: see my Introduction to *Forty Chapters*. Or perhaps we are to see which of these other things is most closely connected to the significator, as in Ch. I.6.

Chapter I.4: "Integrity" and "evenness"[63]

The significator being discovered in such an order and in this way, and the testimonies being made firm, the [1] "integrity" of the significator and [2] its "evenness" must be looked at:

[1] For integrity is that it would be in its own domicile or sovereignty or trigon or bound, or decan or degree or domain.[64]

[2] But evenness is that it would be either in the east or in the pivot of heaven or the setting or the pivot of the earth, neither scorched nor under the rays, nor in its own fall, nor retrograde, nor joined to the infortunes, nor opposed [to them], nor in their tetragon.

For, if [the significator] were established thusly,[65] one will not have to examine the others which prevent this. Which if the aforesaid things were less, and there would be an enemy preventing it, placed in the way which was said, it is necessary [that the] one[66] most in charge should fulfill the role; but if the tenor of that significator is not sound, then the testimony of the Moon must be brought to bear, unless perhaps she herself obtained the signification: for then her testimony is doubled.[67] For which reason [one should] principally embrace her,[68] provided that she would hold onto the rulership of the east or [its] sovereignty or trigon,[69] and especially with her being received and the others less fit.

---

[63] As this chapter shows, it is not enough to simply win by rulership points *over* a place or by house rank, but the significator should ideally be in one of its own dignities and in a good condition, as well.

[64] Normally, domain means that in a diurnal (day) chart, diurnal planets are above the earth and nocturnal planets are below it (and in a nocturnal chart, that nocturnal planets are above the earth and diurnal ones below it), with the planet also being in a sign of its own gender. For more, see *ITA* III.2.

[65] That is, if it were both integral/whole (in a dignity or its domain) and even (in a strong house and not harmed in the ways mentioned above).

[66] From here through "not sound," reading for *praepotens impleri; sin autem sanus sit ducis tenor.*

[67] See a description of this in Ch. I.6.1 below.

[68] Reading *Qua causa [necesse] est* for *quae causa est.*

[69] See also Ch. I.6.1 below.

Chapter I.5: How many impediments of the Moon there are[70]

But the impediments of the Moon which would prevent [her] signification in this,[71] are five in number—[and] if she is so overwhelmed, it is necessary that she have signification over thefts and fugitives, [and] in concealed places that are dug [in the ground], and over controversies.[72]

Therefore, the first impediment is for her to be under the rays.

The second, in the opposition [of the Sun].

Third, being bound [by degree][73] to the infortunes.

Fourth, to be in the domiciles of infortunes or [their] bounds, or assembly [with them by sign], or next to the Head or Tail.

Fifth, not to be regarded by her own lord, or to advance [while] solitary.[74]

---

[70] See also the fuller list I have appended from Sahl's *Introduct.*, in Ch. II.4.3 below.

[71] See the end of the previous subchapter.

[72] That is, the Moon is often the default significator in such cases: see *Forty Chapters* Ch. 5 (controversies), Ch. 7 (thefts and fugitives) and Ch. 35 (hidden treasure). This must also mean that if all the other significators are unfit, and the Moon is impeded, then the Moon is the significator *and* the matter involves something like these topics.

[73] *Ligatam.* Following *ITA* III, I now translate these applying aspects by degree as being "connected."

[74] That is, emptiness of course (being void in course): *ITA* III.9.

Chapter I.6: What the significator means

The meaning of the significator is wholly divided into three parts: [1] one is when it directs its course [while] solitary, applying to none, none to it.[75] [2] Another, if it were strongly with others.[76] [3] [The third, the circumstances of the question.][77]

Chapter I.6.1: By place, when alone

[1] Therefore, whenever the significator were in the [following places], solitary, a regard to none, the thoughts of the querent are:

In any pivot[78]	Similar to [the pivot of the east below].
In an advancing [place]	About some matter coming into his hands.
In a remote [place]	About something concluded or past, or which went out of the querent's power.

In the east	About himself or about his own proper matter or proper business.
The second	About a close relationship,[79] about a possession or profit, or underofficials and that type.
The third	About brothers and kin, neighbors, and visions.
The fourth	About parents, about a farm, villages,[80] products of an estate, burdens, the knowledge of old things, and one harshly imprisoned. For the pivot of the earth is the most strict prison, but the sixth and the twelfth, not so much.

---

[75] See Ch. 1.6.1 below.
[76] See Ch. 1.6.2 below.
[77] See Ch. 1.6.3 below.
[78] Or, "angle." Hermann follows al-Kindī by calling planets in angles (or pivots) "pivotal," succeedent places "advancing," and cadent places "remote" (*Forty Chapters* Ch. 1.2.3). But Abū Ma'shar classifies both angles and succeedents as advancing (*ITA* III.3-4).
[79] *Familiaritate*, specifically about household relationships, people close to hand. I omit *locatus* ("placed") as being redundant, since the whole table refers to the place of the significator.
[80] Or the neighborhoods, quarters, or blocks of a city (*vicis*).

The fifth	About offspring, and the monies of the parents, the friend of a friend,[81] the brother of a brother.
The sixth	About a slave, a sick person, four-footed beasts, fathers or paternal cousins, a friend of the mother,[82] or an uncle.[83]
The seventh	About partnerships, spouses, adversaries, the grandfather or someone like him, controversies between [the querent] and a woman, especially if the seventh is a feminine [sign].
The eighth	About the assistants of spouses, and death and the assets of the dead (that is, what is leftover), ancient things, a fugitive or things stolen.
The ninth	About progress[84] or a journey, a dream, a man of the law (whether [secular] law or papal [law]), a herald acquainted with divine offices, the brother[85] of a friend, a slave of the parents.
The pivot of heaven	About the wisdom of the trade professions, a peasant, about the king or a client of the king, or a mother-in-law or a stepmother.
The eleventh	About friends or those connected to[86] a trade, or the underofficials and expenses of kings, or the offspring of [romantic] partnerships or of the stepchildren of adversaries.[87]
The twelfth	About sufferings, enemies, the stupid, friends of the trade professions, slaves of spouses, about a lost thing or a fugitive or a thing taken in a robbery.

---

[81] Where the third signifies friends, and the fifth is the third from it. The third is sometimes associated with people who are esteemed, and intimates (see for example *ITA* I.13 and *Forty Chapters* Ch. 9.3 §337, and Ch. 12.2 §446).

[82] Where the fourth signifies the mother (as a parent), and the sixth is the third (friends) from it.

[83] The brother of a parent: the third from the fourth.

[84] Or, "setting out" somewhere.

[85] This does not make sense to me based on the derived houses. But I can imagine a friend of a friend (the eleventh from the eleventh) or the spouse of a friend (the seventh from the third, where the third is a friend).

[86] *Complicibus.*

[87] Omitting *4* as a misprint.

And so,[88] since so many and such diverse things are in[89] those same domiciles, a decision over matters is sought through the counsel of the significator. For example, to the seventh belong spouses, exchanges,[90] adversaries. If therefore the lord of the seventh were Mars, the question comes to be concerning controversies and enemies; if Venus, about a spouse and joy; if Jupiter, about exchanges and partnership; and thus the significator's counsel discerns the blending of all the signs and domiciles.[91]

Nor must the nature of the place be overlooked: such as if the lord of the third were in the fifth, the question comes to be about the children of the brother or sister; and the discernment about this is, if the third is male or its lord male, the offspring of the brother are in question; if female, those of the sister. And one's judgment must be brought to bear in all things, nor should one depart from the testimony of the Moon. For the Moon, bordering on the regions of heavenly things, [also] obtains a signification in the world of lower things.

However, this should be noted, with the place of the significator being preserved: if the Moon regards its place,[92] the judgment is most firm, especially if the Moon were a partner[93] of the significator's place; which if [the situation] were less [than this, it is] weaker.

But it must be known that if the Moon is either the lord of the east or of [its] sovereignty, or of [its] trigon or bound or face, strong, placed intimately,

---

[88] There is some ambiguity in this paragraph, because Hermann uses both the place of the significator and the lord of that place in order to isolate the topic. Hermann could mean that (1) the significator itself isolates the subtopic through its presence *in* the house (such as if the significator were Mars, and he were in the seventh)—but that would make his statement about Mars being the *lord* of the house, incorrect. Or, he could mean that (2) the significator simply shows the general array of topics by its location, but the lord of that house is the one which isolates the subtopic (for instance, if the significator were in the seventh, and Mars were the lord of the seventh). Or Hermann is referring to (3) the house of the chart which the significator rules and is either in or aspects best—such as if Mars were the significator, and he ruled and was aspecting the seventh. Or perhaps (4) Hermann is mixing up various methods, so that while it is important to narrow down the topic, no single method is represented in this paragraph. But see also the Hermes example in Ch. I.7 below, which does in fact use the domicile lord of a house and *its* location, as well as—maybe—the significator's location.

[89] Reading *insunt* for *inficit*.

[90] Reading *cambitiones* for *captiones* (tricks), since it is meant to relate to Jupiter below.

[91] In other words, the nature of the lord narrows down the possibilities inherent in the house meaning.

[92] That is, the place of the significator. See a bit more about this at the end of Ch. I.6.2 below.

[93] This most likely means "a ruler."

she herself will obtain the signification. Nor must the testimony of the partnering stars[94] of the east be omitted.

And thus far, the things which have been said are appropriate to a solitary significator, when it neither applies to any, nor does any [apply] to it. Then, let us pursue this difference in signification according to the applications.

Chapter I.6.2: The significator in combination with others

[2] To the generality of the teachers of this profession, it seemed that whenever the significator is found in its own fall, it is a plain sign of a theft or captive or lost thing.[95] But in passing over from [one] sign to [another] sign, of motion in place or a road.[96]

Whenever the lord of the east or of the second occupies the fourth (or conversely), [the thought is] about a farm or buried money and which has appeared so far,[97] and with the rest [of the houses] in this manner.

The significator with the Tail or Head in the fourth or fifth, about buried money.[98]

The significator with the Head, in its own sovereignty or the tenth, about the king. In [its own] domicile, it is a judgment about the search for treasure.

With the Tail, controversy or enchantments, especially if Mercury testifies. Nor [is it] otherwise [if] the significator [is] with Venus, regarded by Mars.

But the significator applying to the lord of the eighth or third,[99] judges about death or dread.

The significator standing towards retrogradation is a sign of a traveler returning. Standing toward direct motion, it is a sign of the matter that he would move forward.

The significator with Saturn, regarded by Mercury, or with Mercury [and] regarded by Saturn: thoughts[100] and enchantments; and thus [also if]

---

[94] That is, of the other rulers of it.
[95] See Ch. I.5 above.
[96] See for example *Forty Chapters* Ch. 6.5.5, §§205-06.
[97] Reading *et* for *aut*. This is probably a reference to Ch. II.2.3 below (see *Forty Chapters* Ch. 35, §640).
[98] This sentence originally appeared at the end of the last section, but it evidently belongs here.
[99] This should probably read, "fourth."
[100] *Cogitationes.* Perhaps, "worried" or "negative" thoughts?

scorched. Nor does it bring it about otherwise with respect to spirits, in the bounds of Mercury or Saturn.

The Moon with the significator indicates speech or controversies. Nor [is it] otherwise [if] the significator is conjoined to Mars.

Whenever[101] the lodging-place[102] of the significator [is] a fiery sign, regarded by Mercury,[103] it indicates with respect to alchemy; [a sign] of human form, about a fight. And if Mars [is] in that place, [and] the east a domicile or sovereignty of Mercury (or a place of which he is a partner,[104] and Mercury the significator in that place), regarded by Mercury, it gives a question about books or about a shaped thing or about some wisdom [or] a thing manufactured by an artisan.

And in this way we follow up with the powers of the rest of the stars, in terms of the quality of the places. Provided that the significator obtaining their dignities applies to them, or they to it, the signification is thus wholly firm. For if the significator applies to another, or another to it, one must immediately inspect the application and separation: that is, the one to whom it applies, or which one to it, or which one would be separated from it, or it from which one. For the one which applies to the significator (or the significator to it) accompanies its nature and accidents. And if another [applies] to the significator, and the significator to the other, one will have to presume upon the one which was closer to the east—but it is that it should be conveyed between each in this manner: for the one which appeared as the lord of the east or the second (or before it in order),[105] that one will be truly nearer. For if it were the lord of the east, he bears a question about himself and his own affairs. But [if it were the lord] of the second (since it is close to the east), about possessions and income[106] and underofficials. Of the third, about brothers, neighbors, relatives, visions, and that type.

And we should carry out the rest of the things in this way, in order, by the method which was stated, always with the partnership being brought to bear, both with the significator and with the one applying or the one to which it is applied. But if the Moon applies to that star or regards it, the signification is

---

[101] In this paragraph, there are certain missing words and errors which make the exact conditions unclear.
[102] That is, the sign.
[103] Reading *signum igneum fuerit, Mercurio respectum* for *signum igneum Mercurii respicit.*
[104] That is, if he is a different type of ruler.
[105] *Vel deinceps ante alium.* Hermann means, "whichever one rules [or is in?] the house closest to the east."
[106] Or, "livelihood" (*quaestu*).

certain, and the testimony of the planetary partner of the east [is] firm—by the method which was stated with respect to the Moon.[107] This [planet] therefore, if it regarded the significator in a friendly way, or it applied to it, making the testimony firm, it denies error. And in this manner we follow up with the judgment of the significator and the application of the witnesses, namely about that matter which fell into question.

Chapter I.6.3: On the two circumstances of a question[108]

[3] There remain the two circumstances[109] of a question, which we weigh carefully from the reciprocal dispositions[110] of the significator: the first is [3a] the motive and cause of the question, the second [3b] the result and end of the quaesited matter.

[3a] One must wholly observe the star to which the significator applies (or [another star] to it), [and discover] from which of the stars it is being separated.[111] For this is the cause and beginning of a question, [and] its nature and accidents lay bare the cause most exactly.

[3b] Lastly, the one to which the significator applies (or it to the significator): it must be noted to which of the stars it would apply. For this wholly explains[112] the results of matters (in terms of [the star's] nature and accidents), [and] will dictate the end of things most exactly.[113]

---

[107] In Ch. I.6.1 above.
[108] Except for the quote from al-Rāzī below, this is evidently drawn from *Thought* (see Appendix C below).
[109] Literally, the things which "surround" the matter in time and effect: that is, what precedes and motivates the question on the one hand, and what follows it.
[110] *Affectibus.* As Hermann explains immediately below, this refers to the applying and separating connections between the significator and other planets.
[111] Normally one would expect to examine only the *significator's* separations, but Hermann might be trying to include cases where Saturn is the significator. As the slowest planet, Saturn does not separate from others, so in such cases Hermann must be recommending the separations of whatever other planet is applying to him. Of course we should not omit the fact that the Moon's separations and applications are also important: see *Carmen* V.5.24-27.
[112] Reading *explicit* for *excipit.*
[113] See also Chs. I.8 (second paragraph), I.11, and II.4.5.

Here occurs something which al-Rāzī said: firstly, the significator of the thought must be observed, then its lord and its nature, and equally its place, and it is necessary to respond immediately to the question.[114]

Chapter I.7: An example from Hermes[115]

An example of matters. First, for general consideration[116] we introduce a question judged by Hermes ([which was] later displayed by many astrologers), which al-Rāzī and Jirjis[117] used, just as was shown in their treatises. For the east was Taurus, in 10°. Venus in Cancer (her trigon), 15°. The Moon in Libra (in none of her dignities), 10°. The Sun in [Cancer. The Lot of Fortune in][118] Sagittarius, in aversion to the lords of the Lot of Fortune.[119] Saturn in Leo, in none of his own dignities.[120]

Therefore, Venus appeared as the significator of the question.[121] [Then he examined the Moon's separation and application, because she is the domicile lord of Venus.][122] The Moon [is] separated from Saturn, [and] had been

---

[114] Omitting an apparently redundant and ungrammatical *locique naturae.*

[115] As Hermann points out, this chart appears in many works. It is attributed to Māshā'allāh in *Thought* (see *WSM*), which I take to be in John of Spain's Latin. It is attributed to Hermes in Leopold of Austria's *Compilatio* (Appendix G below). A comparison of Hermann and Leopold suggests that Leopold used Hermann's text. I have made some corrections based on the translation in *Thought* and Leopold's version below, but until we find a good Arabic source in al-Rāzī or elsewhere, certain points about the method will remain unclear.

[116] *In medium.*

[117] *Zimus.*

[118] Adding with Leopold.

[119] If I am correct about the original chart, then this is not true: for even if the Lot were in Sagittarius, Jupiter is in Aquarius, which is indeed configured to the Lot by a sextile; but the Lot should actually be in Aquarius, which is opposed to its lord.

[120] Below Hermann reports that Saturn is in the first degree of Leo, which suggests (due to possible inaccuracies in the planetary tables) that he might actually have been at the end of Cancer.

[121] The version in *Thought* claims that Venus is the significator because no other planet is as strong as her in place. The third house is not a particularly strong place, but perhaps it is because she is the primary triplicity lord of Cancer, and is also the lord of the Ascendant. Leopold's rules suggest that we revert to the Moon because Venus (as the lord of the Ascendant) is burned by the Sun (see Appendix G).

[122] Adding based on John's and Leopold's versions. See above (end of Ch. I.6.3), where al-Rāzī says to look at the significator and its lord, and the lord's place. But I suspect that al-Rāzī says this simply because the chart description talks about it, and not because of a separately-discussed method. See al-Rāzī's or Hermes's own explanation in the last paragraph below, and Ch. I.6.1 above, which says the domicile lord of the significator helps to narrow down the signification of a house.

bound[123] [to him] from the sixth, by which he judged that the question was about an infirm mother (because the Moon is in charge of mothers).[124] But the Moon is being separated from Saturn (which is the cause of the infirmity), [so the infirmity] is cold and dry. And because Leo occupies the stomach of the human body, it shows it is in the stomach. Since Saturn is in its first degree, it shows the infirmity is near the mouth of the stomach. Therefore, these are the matter and cause of the question.[125]

But the end of the quaesited matter[126] is examined in this manner. Therefore, [since] the Moon obtained the signification of this thought, one must inspect the one to whom she applies. Because she applies to a strong Venus, [who is also] receiving [the Moon], he gave the opinion that she will be healed. But there were 5° between the Moon and Venus, which, because it was in a convertible [sign], was stated as being toward five days. For if the Moon was occupying a firm [sign], toward five years. If double-bodied, toward that many months.[127]

But if she were applying to Saturn instead of Venus, we would have said she was going to die toward so many days. But conversely, if [the lord of the significator] had been Venus instead of the Moon, the question would have been about some woman of his clan.[128] If Saturn, about the father. If Mercury, about a child. If the Sun, about the king.

---

[123] Reading *ligata erat* for *ligetur*.

[124] This suggests that since the significator (Venus) is in the third, the thought is about kin; and because her domicile lord (the Moon) indicates mothers, it is about the mother; and by the Moon being in the sixth, it is about a sick mother. The problem is that the significator—Venus herself—ends up receding into the background.

[125] The "first circumstance" of a question, from Ch. I.6.3 above.

[126] The "second circumstance" of a question, from Ch. I.6.3 above.

[127] See *Forty Chapters* Ch. 2.6, and Ch. II.5.3 below, at the end of the first house. Movable (or convertible or "cardinal") signs standardly indicate the quickest times (hours, days, weeks), common (or double-bodied or "mutable") signs months, fixed or "firm" signs years. But these times must be evaluated according to the type of question (as al-Kindī explains).

[128] Especially because of the location of Venus in the third (kin).

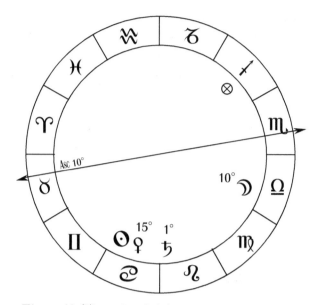

Figure 10: Thought of sick mother, from Hermes

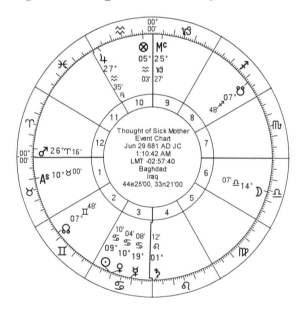

Figure 11: Likely chart for Hermes's example[129]

---

[129] One glaring problem with this being the original chart, is that the Moon is not actually applying to Venus as is required. Instead, their degree positions are reversed.

But if Venus had held onto the seventh, it would have been about betrothals. If Mercury, [about a letter or wisdom.][130] [And if Mercury were in
the seventh],[131] about the son of a sister provided that he were male; while
female, about the daughter of a sister. And for this purpose one must
observe regarding the lights: for the Sun is male in the day, [but] female by
night; the Moon conversely so. But if Jupiter had held onto the ninth in this
manner,[132] the question would have been about a dream. If Mars [had been]
in the seventh, about a controversy. And in this manner we achieve a
judgment of the accidents of the lower world, according to the counsels of
heavenly things.

For al-Rāzī said in this question: since I had seen the east to be female and
its lord female and in a female [sign], the question would plainly have been
about a woman. But since the lord of the lord of the east was the Moon, in
the fourth from [Venus, the lord of the east], and [Venus was] in the
domicile of brothers, [and the Moon was] applying to [Venus], being
separated from a Saturn which was holding onto the fourth (which belongs
to parents), I took the question as certainly coming to be about the mother.
And because mothers belong to the Moon (who applies to the lord of the
sixth from the sixth itself), it demonstrated she was infirm; and because she
was being separated from Saturn, (from whom there is harm), and [she
applies to Venus],[133] it shows she will be healed. And so al-Rāzī commented
on the question in this way.

---

[130] Adding with John.

[131] Tentatively adding, as it is the only house which makes sense. That is, with Venus in
the third (as in the example), but if her domicile lord were Mercury and in the seventh
(the fifth from the third): the child (Mercury, derived fifth) of a sister (Venus, third).
Neither John's nor Leopold's versions include this sentence.

[132] Probably as the significator, and likewise for Mars in the next sentence.

[133] Adding with Leopold and John.

Chapter I.8: On the person of the querent

And so, with these things being handled in detail, the person of the querent comes very much into the judgment.

And first, if what it is going to convey to us is advantageous or not. For
whenever, for any querent, the fortunate ones [are] free [and] possess the
tenth and the east (or at least the eleventh or the second), bound [by
degree][134] to the lord of the eleventh in a friendly way, with reception, it is a
promise of advantage. If not, less so.

Then the four dispositions[135] of the mind of the person must be had. One
must have discernment about the [1] art, [2] fortune, and [3] bodily manner,[136] with only the [4] querent's frame of mind being introduced with
respect to the occasion of the question:[137]

[4] But whenever, for any querent, the lord of the east and the Moon were
in their destructions,[138] it grants a judgment that he has been forced by a
powerful impulse and has come to the question reluctantly. Now therefore,
to the extent that the fortunate ones possess or regard the pivot of the
tenth[139] in a friendly way, they predict he is reasonable.[140]

[1-2] But if, meanwhile, the infortunes possess the tenth, provided that it
is their domicile or sovereignty, it indicates he lives by manual arts. Here, if
the lord of the east were in its own sovereignty, [it indicates] the person of
the querent (or the one about whom it is asked) is a king. If in [its own]
domicile, a great man. If in [its own] trigon, rich; in the bound and decan,
less. In fall and destruction, it is the contrary. And the Moon would agree
with each.[141]

[2-3] Here we must insert what Māshā'allāh wrote in [his] first book:[142] for
whenever, in a nocturnal question, the Lot of Fortune holds onto the twelfth,

---

[134] This probably includes both by assembly in the same sign and connections from other
signs.

[135] *Affectus.*

[136] *Tenoris.*

[137] The rest of this chapter gives some indications for these types of information.

[138] That is, "detriment."

[139] Reading for "the tenth pivot."

[140] *Sensatum.* I take this to mean that he is eager and willing to engage both the issue and
the answer.

[141] That is, if she were in fall or detriment.

[142] The following material is more likely drawn from Māshā'allāh's own (largely lost)
translation of Dorotheus's *Carmen*, since they match or resemble 'Umar's version as well.

[and] the Moon the sixth, while the lord of its bound[143] would equally be foreign,[144] the one who gives the question is a male or female slave, particularly if the Moon should hold onto a masculine sign but the east [is] a feminine one. But if the question were diurnal, and the Sun in a feminine sign, but the east masculine, it nevertheless brings forth a slave.[145] The Moon with the Lot of Fortune in the sixth or twelfth, regarded by Saturn or Mars, brings it about that the master of the question is sick or corrupted by poisons or bribes.[146] Which if Jupiter or Venus are regarding, [then] not at all.

[2] Whenever[147] the first of the lords of the trigon of the east would regard it from an adverse place,[148] and the Moon from the opposite, or an infortune [would regard] the Sun and equally the Moon in the twelfth, it means that the querent's parents belong to an alien power, and that he himself has an obligation to foreign servitude.[149] Which if Jupiter regarded by a trigon, it means either he is going to be ransomed or is going to be liberated at no cost. If however Mars regarded a Moon applying to Saturn, it designates he is going to die in that condition. Nor otherwise does it denote a slave if Saturn regarded a Moon applying to Mars, or she were with an infortune in a pivot.

Nor however should one overlook the testimony of the Lot of Fortune in the meantime.

---

[143] Probably the bound of the Ascendant (cf. *Carmen* I.10), but perhaps the cusp of the 6th.

[144] That is, "peregrine."

[145] See *Carmen* I.10.17.

[146] *Beneficiis.*

[147] The first part of this paragraph is very much like *Carmen* I.10.23: "If you find the lord of the triplicity of the Ascendant cadent and you find the Moon [with] a malefic opposing it and the Sun in an evil place, the native's parents are slaves."

[148] But the "adverse" places in Hermann are those in aversion from the Ascendant, and so cannot aspect them. Hermann's source probably reads more like the *Carmen* excerpt in the footnote above.

[149] *Tam parentes quaerentis alienae potestatis produnt quam ipsum alienae servitutis debitum.*

Chapter I.9: Other opinions on identifying the thought

Chapter I.9.1: The thought according to "Dorotheus"[150]

Dorotheus[151] judges this kind of question in a certain other simple manner, [and] commands that the Lot of Fortune in particular should be observed: which if it were in the east, the question comes to be about himself and his own matter; in the second, about commerce or about [something] deposited [for safekeeping]; in the third, about a brother, friend, and movement in place or a lost thing; in the fourth, about a matter [already] concluded or old and ancient; in the fifth, about offspring or a donation;[152] in the sixth, about troubles of the body, the spirit-possessed and the imprisoned, or shipwreck and that type; in the seventh, about betrothals, a woman, controversies; in the eighth, about a dead person and his things left behind (as inheritances are); in the ninth, about a road,[153] books or prophecy; in the tenth, about wisdom, sovereignty, or a high matter, or the king; in the eleventh, about the clients of the king; in the twelfth, about banditry or a rebellious slave.

Which[154] if it were in a four-footed sign, [it is] about a four-footed [animal]; if in a human one, about a man; and if in a fiery one, about fiery things; if in an airy one, about airy things.

And[155] the lord of its bound must be applied everywhere in this manner: which if it were male, [it is] about a male; if female, about a woman. Which if it is Saturn, about an old man or a slave; Jupiter, about gain; Mars, about banditry and fights; Venus, about riches and sensations;[156] Mercury, about a

---

[150] Note how these three paragraphs mirror Hephaistio's paragraphs on the Lot of Fortune, persons signified by the planets, and types of signs (Appendix H). Could this material—either here or in Hephaistio—originally have been from Dorotheus?

[151] The view attributed to Dorotheus here is the same as that attributed to Dorotheus, Antiochus, Ptolemy and Valens in *OHT* §2 (see Appendix C). See also Hephaistio's Lot of Fortune method in Appendix H.

[152] Reading *donatio* for *dotio*.

[153] Or more likely, a journey.

[154] This part is missing from *OHT*.

[155] This part is missing from *OHT*.

[156] *Sensato*. Normally this medieval word (derived from *sentio*) would refer to someone sensible or wise, not normally a signification of Venus. I take it to refer more to the "sensation" aspect of *sentio*.

scribe or merchant, and often the wisdom of diverse counsel;[157] the Sun, about the king; the Moon, about an effeminate man.[158]

Chapter I.9.2: The thought according to Hermes[159]

But the opinion of Hermes in this affair is that one should discover the strongest among the significators (either [1] the lord of the east or [2] the one receiving its management),[160] and the kind of thought will be in accordance with the quality of the place from the east.[161]

No less do we choose the kind of question from the degree of the east itself: indeed [3] the star to which the degree of the east is bound, indicates the question in accordance with its place.

No less does [4] a star occupying the east [indicate it], if [the star] were not cadent from the degree of the east:[162] [the question will be] in accordance with its nature, and by the place of its domiciles[163] from the east.

---

[157] Reading *sapientia diversi consilii* for *sapientiae diversi consilii*.

[158] Omitting *subitaneo*.

[159] According to Low-Beer, what follows here and in the next few paragraphs is an interpolation only found in two of her manuscripts. But it closely matches the material in *OHT* §2 (as several parts of *Search* do), so I re-insert it here as being part of Hermann's work.

[160] That is, the one to which it applies (*ITA* III.18).

[161] That is, what house it is.

[162] That is, if it were in the first house by quadrant-based divisions, and not more than 5° from the degree of the Ascendant itself.

[163] Reading with *OHT* for *domini*. *OHT* says that the topic will be according to the domicile of its own which it aspects: so for instance if it were Venus, but she aspected Taurus and not Libra, it would be according to the house occupied by Taurus.

Chapter I.9.3: The thought according to the Indians[164]

[1] But the third authority is that of the Indians, that [one should take] the stronger one between the lords of the bound and decan of the degree of the east, and the star to which it applied.[165]

[2] But more firmly,[166] that one should observe in what sign the twelfth-part[167] of the degree of the east fell. And so, if the lord of its place or some other star were found here, the place and the star will obtain [the significa-tion]. But if a star is not in it, then the lord of its place will share it [with the place where it is]. For example, if Aries had been the east, with 12° being given, the degrees which have arisen in Aries are [multiplied at a rate of] 2 ½° through individual signs: the number is in Leo, the fifth[168] domicile.[169] Since neither the Sun nor a foreign star[170] is found there, we looked at the Sun. But the Sun was holding onto the seventh, so it was judged that the question was about a child seeking[171] a wife.[172]

---

[164] Again, following the "interpolation" in Low-Beer.

[165] Omitting *eius loci dominus obtineat* ("the lord of its place would obtain"), since it has no grammatical object and does not match *OHT*. It seems to be a mistaken phrase that has been partly copied from below. In Low-Beer's edition, it awkwardly (and mistakenly) bridges two different types of consideration kept distinct in *OHT*. See also Ch. I.3.1 for another reference to these Indian sources.

[166] See *OHT* §2 (Appendix C) for this same example, and Hephaistio (in Appendix H) for complete delineations of every possible thought based on the twelfth-parts.

[167] Reading *duodecima* for *dignitas*, with *OHT*.

[168] Reading *quinto* for *quarto*, with *On Hidden Things* and Leopold.

[169] If we divide the 12° that have arisen by 2.5, we get 4.8: we distribute the 4 to the signs in order from the rising sign: Aries, Taurus, Gemini, Cancer; the rest leaves off in Leo. One could get the same answer simply by using a table of twelfth-parts, as found in the table I have appended from *ITA* IV.6 below.

[170] The author means that since the Sun rules Leo, any other planet would be a foreigner or peregrine there. That is not strictly true: if for instance it were a nocturnal chart, then Jupiter would be the primary triplicity ruler for all fiery signs, and so would not be peregrine. But the point is that no planet at all is in Leo.

[171] Reading *querentem* for *queritantem*.

[172] The twelfth-part of the Ascendant was in the fifth (Leo), children; its lord (Sun) was in the seventh, a spouse. Thus the Sun combines the two meanings by its location and rulership. *OHT* adds: "And if the Sun had been in the sixth, I would have said that he was seeking concerning an infirm child; and so on with the rest of the twelve signs."

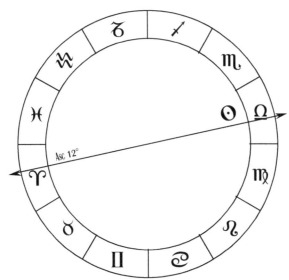

Figure 12: Second Indian method, using twelfth-parts

	0°-2.5°	2.5°-5°	5°-7.5°	7.5°-10°	10°-12.5°	12.5°-15°	15°-17.5°	17.5°-20°	20°-22.5°	22.5°-25°	25°-27.5°	27.5°-30°
♈	♈	♉	♊	♋	♌	♍	♎	♏	♐	♑	♒	♓
♉	♉	♊	♋	♌	♍	♎	♏	♐	♑	♒	♓	♈
♊	♊	♋	♌	♍	♎	♏	♐	♑	♒	♓	♈	♉
♋	♋	♌	♍	♎	♏	♐	♑	♒	♓	♈	♉	♊
♌	♌	♍	♎	♏	♐	♑	♒	♓	♈	♉	♊	♋
♍	♍	♎	♏	♐	♑	♒	♓	♈	♉	♊	♋	♌
♎	♎	♏	♐	♑	♒	♓	♈	♉	♊	♋	♌	♍
♏	♏	♐	♑	♒	♓	♈	♉	♊	♋	♌	♍	♎
♐	♐	♑	♒	♓	♈	♉	♊	♋	♌	♍	♎	♏
♑	♑	♒	♓	♈	♉	♊	♋	♌	♍	♎	♏	♐
♒	♒	♓	♈	♉	♊	♋	♌	♍	♎	♏	♐	♑
♓	♓	♈	♉	♊	♋	♌	♍	♎	♏	♐	♑	♒

Figure 13: Table of twelfth-parts

[3] The[173] Indians even pursue the significator of this craft by means of groups of nine. But this is that [the degree of the Ascendant is multiplied by 9, and the result is projected from the beginning of the rising sign, until nothing is left over.][174] But where what is left over from the east stands still, there is the ninth-part of the east: therefore that domicile judges the question. For example, if the Ascendant were [the tenth degree of][175] Aries, [the degrees of the Ascendant, multiplied by 9][176] would be led down from the [beginning of the] rising [sign] itself: the number stands still in Gemini, the third domicile, where Saturn is found retrograde. It was judged that the question was about an exile, [namely] when he would return. But since its lord [Mercury], equally with the Sun (the lord of the sovereignty of the east), possessed the tenth,[177] in the domicile of Saturn, it seemed he was an exiled king, and [so on] in this manner.[178]

---

[173] This method is not in *OHT*. I have substituted my own wording for Hermann's in some of this, because his explanation is virtually incomprehensible. For a fuller explanation of the ninth-parts, see *ITA* VII.5. But note that Hermann's presentation here is not like the usual ninth-parts. The ninth-parts are normally attributed to *planets*, whose order is based on their rulership of the signs in order from the movable sign of the triplicity. For example, in *any* fiery sign, the first ninth-part (0° - 3° 20') is ruled by Mars, since he rules the movable fire sign (Aries). Then the next 3° 20' of *any* fiery sign is ruled by Venus (for Taurus), then Mercury (for Gemini), and so on. But Hermann projects from the rising sign to yield signs that fall in houses, rather than identifying planetary rulers. The problem with using any ninth-part scheme is this: since they only include the first nine signs (whether from the movable sign of a triplicity, or from the rising sign), the types of questions are limited according to the rising sign. If Aries is rising, then the ninth-part can only include the first nine signs from the Ascendant, meaning that only questions of the first through ninth houses are possible. If Taurus is rising, then only the first nine signs from Capricorn (the movable sign of the earthy triplicity) count: ninth-through-fifth house questions. Hermann's scheme is actually even more limited, because by definition one could only ask first-through-ninth house questions.
[174] Reading for *a principio Arietis usque ad gradum orientem per singula signa 9 colligantur novenae totique numero 12 trahantur donec minus relinquatur.*
[175] Reading for *10 gradibus.*
[176] Reading for *3 novenae collectae 9 ab ipso oriente.* So, Hermann is multiplying the 9 rising degrees by nine, to yield 81°: added to the beginning of Aries, this lands in Gemini.
[177] Reading *decimum* for *decimi.*
[178] Unfortunately this combination of planets is too common to reliably suggest even the century whence it derives.

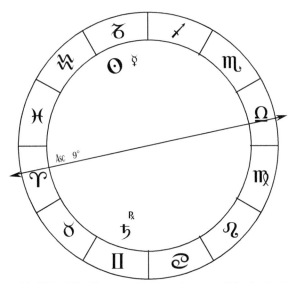

Figure 14: Third Indian method, using modified ninth-parts

Chapter I.9.4: The thought according to Māshā'allāh[179]

The fourth [opinion] is the signification of Māshā'allāh, generally mixing together all of these from the east:[180] the lord of the rising sign, the lord of the sovereignty, lord of the trigon, the bound, the decan, the ninth-part, the twelfth-part, the star to which the rising degree is bound, the star which occupied the east. Apart from the east, the Lot of Fortune with its lord, the lord of the hour, and the lord of the Sun (by day, [but] of the Moon by night]. The one which was strongest among all of these, and which many testimonies favored, that one plainly obtains [the signification].

Therefore[181] the one to which it applies (or which [applies to it]) should be observed. For if many, or many at once, are being bound to it, [the signification] is passed over to the closest one; [if] solitary, it mixes only the testimonies of its own nature, [and] particularly of the place.

---

[179] This material seems to be based on a mixture of views found in *Thought* and *OHT* §2, attributed there to a number of sources (see Appendix C).
[180] Omitting *si 9 praeter oriens 3*.
[181] See Chs. I.6.1-6.2 for the significator alone and with other planets.

Chapter I.10: Multiple questions

From[182] the beginning of the treatise up until now we have recounted the search for a significator in detail, and eagerly so; we have likewise prescribed that you choose [from among] so many and such diverse [candidates]. The reason is this: because if only the lord of the east or the Moon always held onto the signification, [then unless] no sign arose for more than one moment, nor did the application of the Moon (in which the Moon applies to some star) last longer than any one sign would arise, it would be impossible for questions about different things to come to be.

Since[183] this does not happen, they instruct that [multiple] questions should be ordered through the order of the domiciles or the application of the Moon.

But[184] one should even note this: whenever (in this signification) the testimonies of the infortunes were equal to the fortunate ones, it is impossible to avoid error.

Likewise,[185] this work is idle unless it is about the thoughts of questions: the motion of the circle leads the querent forward, with human inclination following the dispositions of heavenly things.

---

[182] This paragraph is based on Māshā'allāh's *Thought* (see Appendix C) and is meant as a *justification* for resorting to many different candidates for the significator of thought. Māshā'allāh is saying the following: "(1) Under normal circumstances, we might favor the rising sign and the application of the Moon for determining thoughts. (2) But that makes handling multiple questions and clients difficult or impossible. For if you had multiple clients over a short period, they would all show the same motive; and multiple questions from the same client would have the same results. (3) Therefore it makes sense to look at other candidates as well, such as planets in the angles, planets aspecting the degree of the Ascendant, and so on."

[183] That is, signs do not rise in a single moment, and the Moon's applications do last for more than it takes for a single sign to arise. The solution in this paragraph must come from Sahl's *On Quest.* §13.14, where he specifically states that successive applications of the Moon can be taken as significators of multiple questions. Other alternatives are given by al-Rijāl (in *Skilled* I.11), in Appendix A below.

[184] For this paragraph, cf. 'Umar in *Judges* §0.2, and *OHT* §1.

[185] This paragraph is probably based on 'Umar in *Judges* §0.2: "For the Divine power of the celestial circle, and the property of effectiveness in the hour of his question, seem to be related by a certain likeness to the intelligence and mind of those asking. [That is], I say that the motion of the circle compels the querent to ask [the question], for the human condition does not cease to duly imitate the order and progressions of the heavenly dispositions, both of the stars and the circles, as though by the chains of someone's love."

Chapter I.11: Outcomes to questions, and life questions

Finally, in this affair there are three questions which frequently come up: [1] first, whether what is sought is going to come about; [2] second, whether what is proposed is going to useful; [3] [third, about the status of life and the fortune of matters].[186]

Chapter I.11.1: Will it come about?

[1] A subdivision of the first question must be made, namely of solving [the matter of] hope and grief. First it is appropriate for the east to be established, and for the pivots to be made firm, and the domiciles to be organized, with the stellar places. This being done, one will have to compute [the distance] from the lord of the seventh up to the degree of the east, and that whole number will be led out beginning from the degree of the tenth[187] by equal degrees. Where [the final number] stood, the lords of its sign and decan will be consulted. Which if they both regarded the east, they completely ensure [the matter's] outcome. If only one, partly so; if neither, they deny [it]. And if in a friendly way, easily; if unfriendly, with difficulty. And if that significator[188] occupied the east or the tenth, quickly; if in the fourth or seventh, [it will be] slow in starting.

Then, whence the question comes to be: we will consult the significator:[189] which if it is Saturn, it indicates a farm, sowing, and an ancient matter. Jupiter: a prelate,[190] gold, silver, and copper. Mars: a fight, controversies, a journey, travelers. Venus: pleasures, jokes, and the affairs of women. Mercury: commerce, books, enchantments.[191] Either of the lights: the

---

[186] Adding based on the description of the question below. These questions resemble al-Rijāl's lists attributed to various astrologers in *Skilled* I.5.2 (not in Appendix A).

[187] But based on the specific mention of "hope," one would expect the eleventh. Indeed, the text reads *x* ("of the tenth") which could originally have simply been *xi* ("eleventh").

[188] The domicile or decan lord of the Lot-like position just mentioned.

[189] I take this to mean the significator of the thought itself (many methods for which have already been given), since the Lot-like position just described has to do with outcomes, not the thoughts themselves.

[190] A religious official, or simply someone with a high public profile (*praelatum*).

[191] Hermes Trismegistus was credited not only with teaching the arts of both writing and magic.

commands of kings. But he[192] [also] applies the places of [their] management.[193]

Chapter I.11.2: Will it be useful?

[2] The second question, namely of what is useful: one will have to count
from the lord of the east to the lord of the hour,[194] and the whole number [is
projected] beginning from the degree of the Sun. Where it left off, we will
consult the lords of its sign and bound. Which if they were both fortunate
stars, or there were fortunate stars in that place without the infortunes, the
usefulness will be complete (provided that they are free); [if] infortunes, the
contrary. If one [of the lords] is of the infortunes [and] the other one, being
of the fortunate ones, is stronger, he will obtain [the matter] by his own
powers.

But were the Lot of undertaking some effort[195] taken up from Saturn to
the Moon, [and projected] beginning from the east, the lord of the place
where the number of the degrees stood, settles [the decision about the
matter's usefulness].

Chapter I.11.3: The status of life and the fortune of affairs

[3] The third question is namely about the [3a] status of life[196] and [3b] the
fortune of affairs.

[3a] Bālīnūs solved the first part of this [question], and he measures the
bound of the east thusly: [following Hermes, he multiplies the whole by the
years of each time for a man];[197] but how many degrees came out [indicates]

---

[192] I am not sure to whom Hermann is referring here.

[193] Reading *dispositionis* for *discretionis*. That is, the places ruled by the significator will also
supply information (and especially that domicile of its own which it aspects more
strongly).

[194] This is the reverse of the method in I.3.2, which is taken from the lord of the hour to
the lord of the Ascendant.

[195] *Cuiusque studii aggrediendi pars*. This Lot's calculation is that same as that for the Lot of
authority and what a native does (*ITA* VI.2.40) and the Lot of intellect and profound
thought (*ITA* VI.2.33).

[196] This includes both longevity and the general course of life. For instance, Lilly discusses
this in *Christian Astrology* pp. 129-36.

[197] This is my very tentative translation of the following (which I find virtually incomprehensible): *ut translatio prima Hermetem totum perseipsum multiplicatum annos hominis utriusque*

life already finished; how many follow, what follows after that. But Māshā'allāh[198] proposed the star from which the lord of the east (or the Moon) is separating as the span [of time already] finished, [and] the one to which it applies what follows after that—which we will describe more fully in a translation of his book.

[3b] But the east and its lord and the Moon indicate the fortune of matters in accordance with [the client's] status.[199] For if they [are] strong and being bound [by degree] with reception to strong fortunate [stars] in a friendly way, it is a sign of complete fortune; the contrary with respect to the infortunes. Likewise it is a sign of fortune when they cross over from infortunes to fortunate ones, for the evil is changed into good; and conversely [if from fortunate ones to the infortunes]. Now, from fortunate ones to fortunate ones [goes] from good to what is better, [and] the contrary with respect to the infortunes. And even if they are being separated from fortunate ones, it is good so long as they do not apply to infortunes. If they [cross over] from infortunes [but] are not taken in by fortunate ones, it is bad. Which if they are in the middle, consisting of the strong and the weak, they denote only medium fortune. For the quantity of fortune and the span of changes is produced to the extent that the applications are, which we explain more plainly elsewhere.[200] In the meantime, [we will speak about] something else.

The first book ends. The second book, on the nature of the signs, begins.

---

temporis numeret. At any rate, the technique does seem to involve distributions through the bounds. My forthcoming translation of *Judges* will present several such methods.

[198] Probably a reference to some of the material on longevity in Ch. II.5.3 below.

[199] Or perhaps, "in accordance with the status of [their relation to the fortunes and infortunes]."

[200] One may also see Abū Ma'shar's treatment of this type of thing in *PN III*, particularly Ch. III.2.

BOOK II: DESCRIPTIONS, TREASURE, CONFIGURATIONS, TIMING

The treatment of the above volume on the querent's consultation and understanding [his] thought, has been carried out [according to] ancient authority. The sequence [of chapters] in this little book takes on the type and form of concealed things from that same authority. For after:

[1] The nature of the signs (which is laid out in the first chapter of [this] book) has been diligently examined,¹ then:

[2] The signification of the stars [are described] for the significator given by a method.² This being found,

[3] [We will examine more house significations and planetary conditions. Then,]³

[4] The dispositions⁴ of the stars must be described in order.⁵

[5] [Finally, we will examine timing methods for specific topics, based on Sahl's *On Times*.]⁶

Chapter II.1: On the nature of the signs

[1] It is necessary to discuss [1a] the fourfold nature of the signs in a fourfold way, and we will examine it first. Then [1b] we will communicate⁷ what is proper to the individual stars through individual signs. [1c] Finally, we will describe their powers [generally] and [those of] each separately.

Much of the assistance [given here] in this part on the exposition of the proper qualities of the stars, is understood [to be valid] in every secret of

---

¹ Ch. II.1 and its subchapters.
² *Quo duce qua datus est ratione.* This refers to the examples of finding concealed objects in Ch. II.2 below, but see also Chs. II.1.7-1.8.
³ Added by Dykes to account for Ch. II.3.
⁴ *Affectus.*
⁵ See Ch. II.4.
⁶ Added by Dykes to account for Ch. II.5.
⁷ Reading *communicabimur* for *commutabimur*.

astronomy. But that of the Treatise above accompanies more the *accidents* of the signs. Here we embrace more the *nature* of the signs[8] and stars.[9]

Chapter II.1.1: The stars as significators in the triplicities[10]

[1a] But [when speaking of what each planet signifies in each triplicity], one must attend generally to this: whenever the Moon regards the significator of the concealed thing, [it means] it is shiny [or] polished, like glass, marble, [or] a finished iron implement. Which if one [of the lights aspected the significator], it will [also] add to the splendor in accordance with its powers: the Sun, half as much; the Moon, one-third.

♄ as significator in the signs:	
Fiery:	The cheaper things of his kind: like clay,[11] wax, and lead.
Airy:	[Something] dead from living things, like hair, wool, leather.
Earthy:	Unseasoned[12] things and those of its kind, like acorns, grains and the meats of gourds, and wild cucumbers, and what is like these.
Watery:	Mud, poisonous snakes, and trees which die without watering.

♃ as significator in the signs:	
Fiery:	Ornaments for each sex, like hyacinth, silver, rings, belts.
Airy:	Domestic living things, clean fattened things not flying much, unless [he is] in a domicile of Mars, bound to Mars: for thus [it is] a dog or cat.
Earthy:	Clean herbs of good odor, like *paxa*.[13]
Watery:	Shiny watery things, as are pearls and that type [of thing].

---

[8] Reading *signorum* for *siderum*.

[9] I do not see an obvious distinction like this between the treatments in Book I and Book II.

[10] In Hermann these significations were arranged by triplicity, which obscures the overall meaning of the planet itself. I have arranged the significations by planet. If one compares the triplicities, one sees the following patterns: fiery signs tend to show artificial products finished by fire; airy signs, living things (animals); earthy signs, agricultural products and plant life; watery signs, things underground or in the water, or which require much irrigation.

[11] *Lutum*, "mud" as below; but below I have chosen mud because it is more watery, whereas clay is more suitable for fired object.

[12] Reading *insapidas* for *insipidas*.

[13] Unknown at this time.

♂ as significator in the signs:	
Fiery:	Arms and that sort [of thing].
Airy:	The class of wild animals and hawks, unless he was adverse[14] or retrograde or in his own fall: for thus [it indicates] a poisonous [animal].
Earthy:	Herbs of red color whose fruits are acidic (like white mustard, pepper, cole[15]), and prickly trees.
Watery:	Wild sea and saltwater animals, and things like this.

☽ as significator in the signs:	
Fiery:	Delicate gilded vessels of great luster, as are dishes and that type [of thing].
Airy:	Outgrowths of the body, like nails and hair on the head.
Earthy:	Great trees whose fruits are unuseful; unuseful lumber.
Watery:	Dried-out hay.

♀ as significator in the signs:	
Fiery:	Necklaces and women's ornaments of that type.
Airy:	Domestic living things by which we work, whose meat is used.
Earthy:	Sweet herbs with a beautiful look [and] sweet odor, like apples and citrus trees, *dot*[16] and sandalwood.[17]
Watery:	Barley, wheat, and what is of that kind of grain, flying aquatic [animals] and the rest of that kind of body.

---

[14] Probably being in the twelfth or sixth (or maybe eighth); but this could also be a misread for *adustus*, "burned/scorched" by the Sun's rays.

[15] *Eruca*, a kind of cabbage.

[16] Unknown at this time.

[17] Reading the Ar. *ṣandal* for *ẓamdal.*

☿ as significator in the signs:	
Fiery:	Hand-held instruments like little pitchers, a knife, scissors,[18] a razor, and that kind of light and delicate thing.
Airy:	Down[19] and light little birds, unless he is in a hot and moist sign:[20] for then [it indicates] moist creeping things of the waters, as are worms and that type [of thing]. Here, if Mercury applies to some star, the things pertaining to Mercury will be [more] towards the nature [of the one] to which he applies.
Earthy:	Light and delicate things, as are vases and that type [of thing], unless he is bound with others: for thus he yields to [that planet's] nature.
Watery:	Veins[21] of the earth, as are roots which are extended above the surface of the earth, [and] as [are] black stretches of land and truffles.

☽ as significator in the signs:	
Fiery:	Pearls and that type [of thing].
Airy:	Turtles and oysters and that kind [of thing], unless she is in a domicile of Jupiter:[22] and thus [it indicates] domestic fattened fowl and animals by which one labors.
Earthy:	[Tends] towards the nature of the one from which she is separated.
Watery:	[Tends] towards the nature of the one from which she is separated.

---

[18] Reading *forpices* for *forsices*.
[19] *Plumam.* Or, "feathers."
[20] This does not make sense: all airy signs are hot and moist.
[21] *Venas.* Or, "channels."
[22] But neither of Jupiter's domiciles are airy signs. Perhaps Hermann means an application with Jupiter by degree, or being in a bound of Jupiter.

Chapter II.1.2: On the kind and color of concealed things

Therefore every kind of concealed thing, whether it is new or old, and useful or unuseful or harmful, also simple or manifold, [is found in this way]:

And so, if the significator over the hidden thing is eastern, it designates [something] new; [if] western, old.

The same [planet] being bound [by degree][23] or conjoined to infortunes, [signifies] what is unuseful or even harmful; to fortunate ones, the contrary.

The same [planet] in double-bodied [signs] or joined to others, double; also, in the conjunction, if there is a commingling of nature, that kind is doubled from one thing to another, as are rings, a razor, belts, and that type [of thing].[24]

One must also know that the significator proceeding more quickly makes the matter easier; more slowly, it makes it more burdened.

Even every star holding onto the upper part of its circle[25] remains in its own nature; the lower [part] yields to the nature of the one which follows [it in the circles].[26]

Also, in its own sovereignty it designates whatever is more precious of that kind; in [its own] fall, what is more cheap.

---

[23] That is, in a connection by degree from a different sign.

[24] *Conduplatum* [*conduplicatum?*] *ex altero in alterum.* I do not quite understand Hermann's point or how the examples illustrate it. But it could mean an object in which one part or thing is inserted into another part or thing: such as a finger into a ring, a strap razor into its sheath, a belt end into the buckle.

[25] This could either be in the middle of its epicycle (in the middle of its forward movement), or in the circle of its apogee (see *ITA* II.1).

[26] That is, the one lower in the planetary hierarchy.

Chapter II.1.3: The colors of the signs

However, we borrow the color of concealed things from the significator, in accordance with the quality of the place.[27] The significator in:

♈	White color mixed with red
♉	White with citrine[28]
♊	White with red
♋	Green
♌	Red
♍	Gray
♎	Black
♏	Black
♐	Red-yellow[29]
♑	Citrine
♒	Sky-colored[30]
♓	White

Moreover, Cancer, Scorpio and Sagittarius designate things that are complicated,[31] or what the wind stirs up.

Chapter II.1.4: What each planet signifies through the individual signs[32]

[1b] Next, we will talk about what belongs to the individual planets through the signs, according to ancient experience. The place alone does not lay bare the quality and essence of a concealed thing, [but] it assists somewhat in uncovering the secrets of thoughts.[33]

---

[27] See also the colors of the quarters in Ch. II.3.5.

[28] A variety of yellow.

[29] *Flavum.*

[30] *Caelestem.*

[31] Lit., "folded up" (*complicata*).

[32] Note that the dignities are used in identifying people below: for example, planets in their exaltations and falls show elevated (or royal) people and fugitives, respectively.

[33] I believe Hermann is saying that the following lists should be read with horary questions generally. I do not thing he is saying that Book II itself is still on the general topic of interpreting thoughts, especially since in Ch. II.1.6 he seems to assume a known question about objects *without* actually finding a significator of thought (or perhaps *after* finding the significator of thought); moreover, at the beginning of Book II, Hermann explicitly says Book I is devoted to thoughts, and Book II to hidden objects.

♄ as significator in:	
♈	Ox
♉	Horse
♊	A man proposing a journey
♋	Silver
♌	Gold
♍	A corrupted woman
♎	A crowned king
♏	A woolen garment
♐	A man seeking metals and gems
♑	Grain
♒	A killed man
♓	Iron, copper, an alloy of silver and lead.[34]

♃ as significator in:	
♈	Horse
♉	Ox and sheep
♊	A man seeking a woman
♋	A king
♌	Ornaments and gems
♍	A dyed garment
♎	A talkative man and one comprehending many things
♏	Grain
♐	A rider in an army
♑	A fugitive slave
♒	A killed man
♓	Ermine worked with silk, and an abundance of wool

---

[34] *Stagnum.*

♂ as significator in:	
♈	Swords, worked belts,[35] and fiery work
♉	Four-footed animals
♊	A sweet odor, gemmed ornaments
♋	A fugitive slave
♌	A male rider striving for wars
♍	A woman looking for sex
♎	A bride taken away from [her] bridegroom
♏	A garden and trees
♐	A man slandering[36] [another] man
♑	A king
♒	Men arriving
♓	A bright garment of different colors

☉ as significator in:	
♈	A crowned king
♉	A bride in the bedroom
♊	Gold and silver
♋	Grain
♌	A man riding to fight
♍	A woolen garment
♎	A fugitive slave
♏	A thief and ornaments
♐	A severe man
♑	A woman harmed by bewitchment and taken away from [her] spouse
♒	A dead man
♓	Musk, amber, and [things with good] odors

---

[35] Probably the belt-buckle in particular.
[36] *Detrahentem*, here and below; but the word can also mean to rob.

♀ as significator in:	
♈	Four-footed [animals]
♉	A groom in the bedroom
♊	Pearls
♋	Gold and silver
♌	Grain
♍	A fugitive slave
♎	A man inquiring about a woman
♏	Treasure
♐	A woman inquiring about a male traveler
♑	A garment dyed many colors
♒	A male murderer of his partner
♓	A crowned king

☿ as significator in:	
♈	Goats and sheep
♉	Male and female horses
♊	A scribe
♋	Ornaments
♌	Odors[37]
♍	A king
♎	A woman slandering [her] husband
♏	A woolen garment
♐	Grain
♑	Treasure
♒	A man who has lost many multicolored things
♓	A king slandering a king

---

[37] Probably, "sweet-smelling" things.

☽ as significator in:	
♈	Four-footed [animals]
♉	A king
♊	Garments
♋	A farm[38] and sowing
♌	Gold and silver and pearls
♍	A woman separated from [her] spouse
♎	A woolen vest
♏	A fugitive slave; also treasure if she should hold onto the pivot of heaven or [its] opposite
♐	A man setting out on a journey
♑	Figs, barley, wheat
♒	A dead man
♓	An alloy of silver and lead.[39]

---

[38] Or, "estate."

[39] *Stagnum.* This can also mean "a swamp."

Chapter II.1.5: What the planets would signify in terms of colors and things

[1c] Now the powers of each [planet] must be investigated separately, in which we briefly cover virtually every rulership of the stars over the things of the world.

Tastes, colors, animals	
♄	Color, leaden; taste, unseasoned; wool, hair, hides, pelts, alcohol,[40] the names of a slave; of men, the Jews.
♃	Sweet water; an emerald, apple, sweet cucumbers, the names of God, the color green (whence *almumin*)[41]—that is, what belongs to Jupiter is often enjoyed in this color. Whence also it used to be the custom of the ancient Persian kings to use practice it monthly.[42] But between Jupiter and the Sun and Venus and Mercury and the Moon, there is an intimate and fraternal acquaintance.[43]
♂	Red-hot lava stones, gold coloring, a condiment[44] of green color: watercress, pepper and that sort [of thing], cabbage, mustard, thistle. Snakes, serpents, lizards, crocodiles, dolphins, and such aquatic [animals], and those virtually without hair; and hawks.
☉	Whiteness, cleanliness, luster; palm trees, resins, pine nuts; wild nocturnal deer, white sheep; great men.
♀	Living things of the sea, partridges, quail and that type [of thing]; also meat and fat.
☿	Sculpted gold, computations,[45] books of wisdom, silk, spelt, leeks,[46] legumes; topaz.
☽	[In] her own sovereignty, sweet; in [her] fall, stinky. To her belong boulders,[47] pearls, domesticated cows, white sheep, panthers,[48] great men, [*illegible*].[49]
☊ ☋	The Head [of the Dragon] is of the nature of the Sun; the Tail, of Saturn.

---

[40] *Alkohol.* Or perhaps, coal.

[41] Unknown at this time.

[42] It could also be that *viridis* ("green") is meant to designate the color of forests, so that the Persian kings made it a point to spend time in nature and the forest.

[43] I am not sure what the purpose of this comment is.

[44] Reading *conditio* for *confectio.*

[45] *Compotum*, but this might modify the golden objects: i.e., sculpted things *made out of* gold.

[46] Or, scallions and probably green onions.

[47] Or possibly, cliffs (*saxa*).

[48] Or any of the larger wild cats.

[49] *C---ini.* The reproduction of Low-Beer is faulty on this page, and I cannot tell what the word is from the Bodelian manuscript.

Types of people[50]	
♄	In the first place, a king; then a master of real estate, a preferred farmer, an actor, a medical doctor of those dying, then an oven-worker, lastly he cleans toilets.
♃	A judge of judges,[51] a hermit, seller of gems and rings.
♂	A judge, general, soldier, dyer, robber, craftsman, archer, butcher, one who collects tolls.
☉	A great king, geometer,[52] a distributor of an estate.
♀	A seller of odiferous things and ornaments, an artisan of rings, of jokes, singing, a pimp, an adulterer.
☿	A great artisan, scribe, consultant, teacher, philosopher, sculptor, master of alchemy and experiments.
☽	An associate of kings, hunter, fisher, water manager, traveler, finally one who washes clothes.

Chapter II.1.6: On the colors and tastes of the planets (Abū 'Alī al-Khayyāt)

Until now we have followed the authority of Māshā'allāh in the judgment of concealed things; now we must subjoin a certain opinion of his student, al-Khayyāt.[53] For he says the east and its lord testify to the nature and matter of a thing, the lord of the hour to the color, the lord of the bound of the east to the taste.

Therefore, a fiery east indicates regarding red-hot things; an airy one, living things; a watery one, moist things; an earthy one, vegetation (as was said before).

---

[50] The lists for each planet run from those in higher and more socially-approved stations, to lower-class and more disapproved stations.
[51] Reading *iudicum* for *iudicium*.
[52] Lit., "one who measures the land."
[53] Lat. *Alkamaz*.

And so, the lord of the hour or the lord of the bound of the east:

	Color	Taste[54]
♄	Black	Unseasoned
♃	Green	Sweet
♂	Red	Bitter/pungent/tangy[55]
☉	Shining[56]	Acidic/sour[57]
♀	White	Greasy
☿	Sky-colored	Vinegary[58]
☽	Grey	Salty

Chapter II.1.7: Number, location, place of a concealed thing (Abū 'Alī al-Khayyāt)[59]

[Concerning] which, he elsewhere takes the number from the Moon to Mercury, and one must keep [in mind] how many signs or degrees there were between [them]: if therefore the number of what was taken up were odd, what is hidden is one; if even, many.

Moreover, the lord of the east in a firm [sign], single; in a double-bodied one, double; in a convertible one, it indicates [something] manifold.

Moreover, the lord of the east being eastern, [it is] new; western, old.

And thus with the tenth and the fourth: in the upper hemisphere, [it is] above ground; in the lower one, below the ground. In the tenth, in the air.

In a convertible [sign], in a movable thing; in a double-bodied one, around the window; in a firm one, in an immovable place.

---

[54] In medieval Latin texts, the terms for all of the hot, sharp, sour and pungent tastes are often used inconsistently. See *ITA* V.1-7 for similar distributions of tastes to the planets.

[55] *Amarum.*

[56] *Glaucum.*

[57] *Acre.*

[58] *Acetum.*

[59] Source unknown at this time, but note its similarity to *Carmen* V.35.72-74. There, Dorotheus says to count from the first degree of the Moon's sign, to the degree of Mercury himself: if there is a double-bodied sign in between, then what was stolen is multiple things, including things tied together; otherwise, it is a single thing. Of course, most of the time there *will* indeed be a double-bodied sign between the Moon and Mercury.

Chapter II.1.8: On the discernment of persons[60]

Also, the discernment of persons brings some judgment in concealed things, and a demonstration of the thief or whoever it is asked about, is of no little assistance:[61]

[Saturn as the significator of a person]

So, Saturn as the significator of the thief or whatever kind of person [it is]: in a masculine sign [and] western, in his domain,[62] indicates a male: an old man, obscure, swarthy, black, silent, with a prominent forehead and head, foul [in the face],[63] easily cunning. But in a female sign and female quarter, a eunuch or old woman.

However, at the beginning of his easternness,[64] [it indicates] a boy of senile form;[65] in the middle [of easternness], a youth; at the end [of easternness], a man of the same likeness.[66]

Then, one must investigate what the nature of the signs adds to him and the other [planets]:

♄ as significator in:	
♈	An unpleasant voice, whitish and swollen eyes, prominent eyebrows, thick face and [straight][67] tip of the nose, cheeks insufficiently bearded, sparse hair on the head, large buttocks,[68] and having thin shins.
♉	A thick top of the nose, a broad forehead, a husky voice, nasty lips, sparse hair, swollen eyes, a broad back, wide feet, obscure, troubled if he is harmed by an infortune.[69]

---

[60] This subchapter is based on al-Kindī's *Forty Chapters* Ch. 6.2 (see also *Judges* §7.112), and was originally on the identification of thieves. It should be read with Ch. I.8 above.

[61] Omitting the puzzling *quod genus quanto vilius in rerum amissione, tanto carius in recuperatione rei.*

[62] See *ITA* III.2.

[63] Adding with *Forty Chapters.*

[64] Reading *orientalitatis* for *orientalis*, with *Forty Chapters.*

[65] That is, with an old man's mind or bearing (*Forty Chapters*).

[66] Omitting *huiusmodi forma proprietati saturnine* as redundant and not reflected in al-Kindī.

[67] Adding with *Forty Chapters.*

[68] *Inclunes*, undoubtedly from *clunis*, "buttocks." This area is attributed to Sagittarius below, undoubtedly because of the large buttocks and associated muscles on horses. Robert of Ketton reads "buttocks" (*nates*), while Hugo reads "kidneys" (*renes*), evidently a euphemism.

II	Average stature, a pleasant voice, good tongue, discretion in counsel, wide shoulder blades, a fitting and even beard, luxurious hair (even[70] if he were bald), cautious, cunning.
♋	Prominent black pupils, a face with little dark spots, a wide forehead, multicolored eyes, dry limbs, big feet, ugly hands, unstable in morals and mood.
♌	A grim face, deep-set eyes, flat between the eyes,[71] a broad top of the nose, wide nostrils, delicate lips, a short and thick neck, with thick arms and a medium-sized chest in the lower part, and narrow and dry ankles and a large belly, a hairy neck, bold, brash, with a deep voice, a powerful eater.[72]
♍	Of medium stature, a wide head, hairy body, and more so from above (in the arms and extremities), discerning in morals, cautious, disguising [his true feelings] with calm and peace.
♎	An oblong[73] head, with a long nose, a long neck, very black hair, delicate shins, a narrow back, elevated buttocks, long toes.
♏	Prominent eyebrows with a narrow border,[74] much hair and often a thick, and a large head, big feet, ugly hands, pale with green and grey, small eyes, a short[75] back, long shins; malevolent.
♐	Ample eyebrows, prominent eyelids, a long face, a wide nose and a mouth with swollen lips, long hair and much of it, a hairy neck, prominent buttocks.[76]
♑	A long, reddish face, soft eyes, a sharp voice, eyebrows [with sharp] borders, swarthy with thick hair, a hairy body.
♒	A square-shaped head, the face wide from above and narrow from below, a profession in water and wet things, like sailors and fishermen and those who launder clothes.

[69] In *Forty Chapters*, it is unclear whether al-Kindī means that such a man will be touched by *misfortune*, or Saturn indicates this if he is in a bad aspects with, say, Mars.
[70] Reading *etiam* with Robert for *et*. But Hugo reads this as "*unless* baldness impedes this."
[71] My best rendering of *interluminari plano*.
[72] See also Saturn in Pisces below. Medievals associated Saturn with a powerful appetite: see *ITA* V.1.
[73] Reading *oblongum* with Robert for the odd *mundum*.
[74] *Angusto confinio* (identical to Robert). Hugo reads only, "straight eyebrows."
[75] Or possibly, "narrow" (*breve*).
[76] This phrase incorrectly appeared in the Scorpio material immediately above.

♓	[If] strong [and] received by fortunate ones, he denotes a person of the class of the rich. Being unfavorable, corrupted by infortunes, it describes that he had been [wealthy] but was cast down. Gentle eyes, an ample mouth, crooked teeth, a balanced bearing in the body, silent, and an enormous eater, [even straight and flowing hair in a male].[77]

On the marks of the Moon[78]

If the Moon [were] here [in the seventh], [presiding over] the lodging-place of the significator [provided that the significator were peregrine, and] it testified to her strongly from a pivot, she adds marks to the judgments [of the significator of the person], such as are allotted in human bodies of any humor [and] any color.[79]

Which if she were so placed in Aries, he bears a mark on his head, and a beauty mark on the head or face. Taurus, possessing it on the neck. Gemini, on the shoulders and arms. Cancer, on the chest and breasts. Leo, on the belly and pubes; Virgo, on the back and sides. Libra, on the flanks and thighs; Scorpio, around the groin; Sagittarius, around the buttocks; Capricorn, on the haunches around the knees; Aquarius, on the shins; Pisces, on the feet.

But she bears this beauty provided that she is fortunate. For, corrupted, [she signifies] ugliness in those places in terms of the amount and quality of the one corrupting her, [and] in the computation of [her] adding or subtracting [in light].

---

[77] Adding with Robert.
[78] This section is based on *Forty Chapters* Ch. 6.3 (see also *Judges* §7.112).
[79] Translating somewhat freely from Robert's *quales in corporibus humanis ex quibuslibet humoribus nate quoslibet colores sortiuntur.*

Other planets as significators of persons[80]

But [the other planets] as significator[s] of the person, apart from what the nature of the sign suggests:

♃	A rounded beard, the color golden yellow, black pupils exceeding what is proper,[81] white spots on the eyes,[82] good habits, of a decent style of movement,[83] of the class of the wealthy.
♂	A red, round face, with an unfriendly mind, sharp vision, sparse hair, sharp, harsh, fickle,[84] brash.
☉	White, noteworthy, a round face, renowned, feared, divination, medicine or in some profession which cleans with water.
♀	White, a clean color, pleasing in looks, wide pupils, fitting in motion and figure, sweet, friendly, worthy hips and buttocks.
☿	A light body, sparse beard, veiny face, white mixed with citrine.

The nature of the signs adds discrete [characteristics] to these properties of the stars which were stated, just as was said before with respect to Saturn, in terms of the age and sex of the person, according to the nature of the stars and [their] accidents.

---

[80] This section is based on *Forty Chapters* Ch. 6.4 (see also *Judges* §7.113).
[81] Reading with Robert for Hermann's *parum*.
[82] *Albugines.*
[83] *Decentis tenoris.*
[84] *Levem.*

Chapter II.2: Finding treasure

[2][85] A more firm type comes under the category of concealed things, namely concealed or buried monies and treasures, whether old or recent. Since we wanted to gather this art from different writers, the disagreement in their judgments has compelled [us] rather to introduce the words of each one to the public (translated by us into Latin speech), so that [even] if Fate should lead someone more properly to the place [of buried treasure],[86] it is not annoying to try out the individual [methods], since it is not that much work.

Chapter II.2.1: The opinion of Jirjis on finding treasure[87]

Zymus, a certain Greek (whom a certain man translated into Arabic as Jirjis),[88] speaks thusly: in searching for treasure [and knowing] whether it is in a [certain] place or not, first one must note the seventh from the east, in which, if you found any of the fortunate ones in it, it is there; and the same is assured in the rest of the pivots.

And so from here, if the Sun and Moon equally regarded the east, they indicate it is inside the building. Then one must observe the lord of the hour: which if it were in the east, it is in the entrance of the building; in the tenth, in the middle; in the west, toward the western part; in the fourth, toward the northern part. Moreover, the lord of the hour being eastern demonstrates it is recent; western, old and ancient.

Here, then, if Mercury possessed the east, it indicates it is buried underground; if Jupiter, in a wall; Venus, around cradles and couches,[89] Saturn, in a stinking, obscure, and unclean place; Mars, around a foreign tenant and places of lighting fires; the Sun, in a middle place of the house; the Moon,

---

[85] This is the second topic as described at the beginning of Book II above.

[86] Hermann is expressing doubt about the methods because they disagree in some respects, but he may also mean that the methods will at least get one close, even if it is ultimately by luck or Fate that one finds the exact spot.

[87] See the corresponding passage in *Judges* §4.20. This material is attributed to Dorotheus in *OHT* §5.

[88] Lat. *Egigius*.

[89] Or, "beds" (*cubilia*).

where the porter is,[90] or around the seats of women; the Head, in a high place; the Tail, in a horrid and dark place.

If therefore the Sun and Moon equally regarded or occupied the east, they promise it will be found easily. Then the star which possesses the seventh (or [lacking that],[91] at least its lord) should be consulted: for this one wholly describes the quality of the concealed thing.

[1] Finally, the whole building or the space of the fenced-in area will be divided into four parts: eastern, western, southern, northern. That being done, see how many degrees of its sign the lord of the hour has traversed: the whole number is multiplied by twelve, and the amount produced [will be] led down by equal degrees, starting from the east: where [the counting] comes to a standstill, the sign there should be noted as to whether it is western or eastern, southern or northern, and it judges [the concealed thing] to be in that part.

[2] In short, for that fourfold part, the lord of its sign [must be examined to see] how many degrees of its lodging-place it has traveled through, [and] the whole number will be led down from that sign, beginning by [giving] 7.5° to individual signs; and where it comes to a standstill, that sign will likewise have to be noted [for what direction it indicates].[92]

[3] And that part, being divided into four parts, will be discerned [in the same way]. And the part found will likewise [be divided into] four parts. And moreover the lord of its sign: how much of its lodging-place it has penetrated will be led out.

[4] And this will happen as often [as needed] until one arrives at the place [of the concealed thing].

---

[90] Or, a gatekeeper (*in loco portario*). Perhaps in average modern houses this might simply be a closet near the front door?

[91] Adding based on *Judges*.

[92] Although the next paragraph is a bit jumbled, from here on out we simply take each dispositor in turn, and project its longitude forward at a rate of 7.5° per every 30° increment of the zodiac.

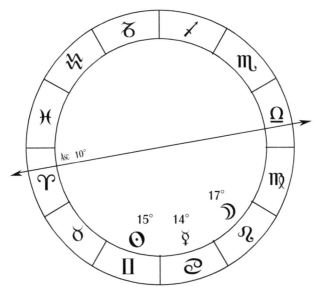

Figure 15: Jirjis on buried treasure

For example, Aries was the east, by 10°; the lord of the hour, Mercury, in 13° Cancer:[93]

[1] This number,[94] being taken [and multiplied by] twelve, and being led down from the beginning of Aries by equal degrees, stands in Virgo, a southern sign.

[2] The amount [which Virgo's] lord Mercury has traversed in Cancer is led out from Cancer at a rate of 7.5° [per sign], and it comes to a standstill in Leo, an eastern sign.

[3] Since its lord, the Sun, was in Gemini, and the degrees of its lord Mercury [were] in Cancer, [do] from thence as it was led down before, where they first fell.

---

[93] Or perhaps 14° (as I have depicted it here, from the diagram in *Judges*. Medieval texts are often unclear as to cardinal versus ordinal numbers. If we compare Hermann's description with Hugo's in *Judges*, we see that they handle the example differently. Hermann projects all distances from the beginning of signs, whereas Hugo projects them from the degree of the Ascendant or of the planet involved. This leads each of them to different results. Unfortunately, *OHT* has no example so we cannot get any help from John. My sense is that Hugo is probably right. Note especially that Hermann's description becomes garbled in step [3], which makes me think that something has happened to the text. Hugo also includes brief comments on the Lot of Fortune, which are missing here but confirmed in *OHT*.

[94] That is, Mercury's 13°.

[4] And one must repeat that as many times [as it takes] until the place itself is discovered.

Chapter II.2.2: The opinion of 'Umar on the same[95]

But 'Umar al-Tabarī the Syrian, established this skill in this manner. He says that in the first place, the intention of the querent must be discerned, to see whether or not he asks about money which he himself concealed, and afterwards he forgot what kind of place it is in (whether buried in the ground, or a fenced-in area or in the house), and he does not know the place, or[96] it is with respect to the reserves of his parents and that type [of place], or about ancient treasures.

After discerning this, the east will be put over the querent. And should he inquire about something of his own, we pursue the lord of the second. Which if the [lord of the second] were in the east, or the lord of the east were in the pivots or its own domicile, it designates that the concealed thing is [in his own home or with] his spouse or parents or his [place of] business.[97] Which if he did not have parents, [but it is in the fourth, it is] in the middle of the house or his fenced-in area. And thus with the rest in order, in the same manner.

But if the lords of the east and the second were averse to each other,[98] nor were there a transfer of light between them, nor [a planet] which collects their lights, the work is ineffective.

And we will investigate what is left behind by the parents in this manner.

But if the question is about treasures, we must first see whether or not there is anything in that place. If therefore the fortunes occupied the seventh, it testifies that something is in there. If the infortunes possessed it, it was there but has already been taken out.

And so, the star which is in the seventh indicates the quality of the buried thing.[99] If its partner[100] were a fortune, that one designates the kind of metal which the lord of the seventh does.

---

[95] See the corresponding passages in *Judges* §§4.18-19.

[96] Reading *aut* for *ut*.

[97] That is (reading with *Judges*), if in the first it will be in his own home; in the tenth, at work; in the seventh, with the spouse; in the fourth, with the parents.

[98] That is, not aspecting each other by sign. Transferring or collecting the light of planets in aversion is called by Abū Ma'shar "reflecting" their light: see *ITA* III.13.

[99] That is, once we know something is in the place (see previous paragraph).

But if [the planet in the seventh is] devoid of dignity,[101] it will share with the lord of the seventh. For if it were the Sun and it is Aries or Leo, it designates gold and precious gems; in the others, silver, crystal or glass. Mercury: coins, quicksilver, books—and so on with the rest [of the planets], according to [their] nature and disposition.[102]

[1] Then, whether or not we are going to get what we intend. For if the star occupying the seventh, its partner,[103] or the lord of the seventh [applied to the lord][104] of the east, or it to [one of them], or there is a transfer of light between them or a collection of their light, they promise he will get it. And if it is from the trigon or hexagon, quickly and easily; and from the tetragon or opposition, the opposite. An assembly [in the same sign] between each shows success, provided that it is with reception.

[2] And so, having discovered the space in which the treasure is, if one were finding the place itself, one must note the lord of the seventh to see in which part of the circle it is, between the eastern and the western [parts].[105] [2a] Therefore if [it is] in the eastern one, it is toward the east in the building or fenced-in area; if in the western one, toward the west. [2b] The same [planet] in a firm sign: it establishes [that it is] in the ground; in a double-bodied one, in the wall; in a convertible one, in the ceiling.

[3] Then one must divide the house or fenced-in place or space (however big it was) into two parts, an eastern part and a western one: and one must see which one the significator[106] occupies, and you must measure it in whatever kind of measuring [unit], namely rods or cubits or feet.

[4] That being done, one must see which decan of that sign the significator is holding onto: and with that part [of the room or house] being divided into three, it will occupy that one-third.

[5] Then [look at what] degree and third of the decan [the planet is in]: and once that number is distributed[107] from the east or west, one will finally arrive at the place itself.

---

[100] This probably means an aspecting planet.
[101] Reading *dignitatis* with *Judges* for *duritatis*.
[102] *Affectum.*
[103] *Judges* omits this; again, it is probably an aspecting planet.
[104] Adding with *Judges.*
[105] This probably means the eastern or western hemispheres of the chart.
[106] This may be the fortunate star which originally showed that there was a treasure (as al-Kindī also treats it, below). It might even be the victor over the whole chart.
[107] Omitting *ad eum numerum.*

Chapter II.2.3: The opinion of al-Kindī on the same[108]

But after the most learned Māshā'allāh, al-Kindī in this manner. He says:
[§639] If it is asked whether or not a treasure or any amount of money is buried in a place, one must establish the east and the rest of the pivots. This being done, if a fortunate one is found free [from the infortunes and] in the east [or any of the pivots],[109] it confirms that it is in there, and the amount is according to [its] robustness or weakness.

[§640] Which if it were corrupted by a strong infortune, [it indicates] it had been in there, but the whole or greater portion [of it] has already been borne away. [But if made fortunate, it is in there].[110]

[§641] Then the lord of the east and the Moon must be noted. For if there were an application with reception between them and the aforesaid significator, it promises to the querent [that it can be] gotten. If not, not.

[§642] Once these things have been looked at, straight lines cast out from the center of the whole place towards the outermost [limits] will cut the whole circuit twelve times with equal angles. When these [lines] have been drawn out, the point of the rising sign will fix the eastern point of the place.

[§643] Then, once the place of the significating star is discovered exactly, a straight line will be drawn from the center of the space to the point of [the star's] place. This being done, one must discover where the significating star[111] is, and how distant it is from the degree of the east: the distance [of the treasure] from the eastern point of the place is that much. Nevertheless, a straight line will [also] be drawn out from the center to [its] place.

[§644] Then one must discover whether it is closer to the center or the circumference. So that it may be easy, we will cut the line drawn to the place of the star, in half. And with one foot of the compass being fixed in the center, and the other occupying the point, you will draw the path of the Sun all around. One will immediately see that if the latitude of the star were southern, it indicates toward the south [and the circumference];[112] if northern, toward the north [and the center].[113]

---

[108] See *Judges* II.8-9, and *Forty Chapters* Ch. 35. Another Latin translation appears in *OHT* §7. I have added the section numbers from *Forty Chapters* so one may compare the texts: *Search* uses Robert's translation, but *Judges* (and my *Forty Chapters*) uses Hugo's.
[109] Adding with Burnett 1997, based on the Arabic.
[110] Adding with Burnett 1997, based on the Arabic.
[111] Reading with the Arabic of the *Letter* for Robert's "lord of the significating star."
[112] Adding with Burnett 1997, based on the Arabic.
[113] Adding with Burnett 1997, based on the Arabic.

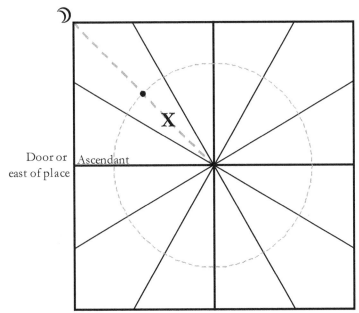

Figure 16: Al-Kindī's example of finding treasure[114]

[§645-46] Which if it did not have latitude, [it will be] on the [Sun's] path itself. After discerning this, [one must see] into what direction the portion [of latitude] declines. However many degrees the maximum[115] latitude of the star is, whatever space was in between will be cut by that many equal parts—[that is], from the middle circle toward the center or toward the circumference—

---

[114] In this example from al-Kindī's *Letter* (Burnett 1997, pp. 70-71), the treasure is in a house, and the Ascendant represents the door. The square house is divided into twelve equal parts representing the signs (§642). The Moon is the significator of the treasure, and is 45° to the south of the Ascendant, with 2° northern latitude. *Forty Chapters* has us estimate which third of the sign the planet is in (§643), but al-Kindī's *Letter* recommends using the exact degree). We draw a dotted gray line from the center of the house towards the southeast, at an angle of 45° from the Ascendant (§642-43). Then, divide this line in half with a mark (§644), and use a compass to draw a circle representing the ecliptic (the circle is actually unnecessary, what matters is dividing the line). Then, determine what the maximum latitude of the planet is, and what its latitude actually is at the time (§644-45): in this case, the Moon's maximum latitude is 5°, but she is actually at 2°. Northern latitudes will be between the mark and the center of the house, southern latitudes between it and the circumference of the figure (§645). Since she is 2/5 of the way towards her northern-most latitude, the treasure will be at a distance 2/5 of the way from the mark to the center of the house, marked by the X. Her distance towards or away from her apogee will determine how high up or low the treasure is (§647).

[115] Reading more accurately for "whole" (*tota*).

in equal sections, [according to] the portion of the whole latitude of the star [which] the present latitude was. And this is the definite place of the treasure, in whichever direction on this line (toward the south [and the circumference] or toward the north [and the center of the place]). But if the star were without latitude (as was stated), the [treasure will be] on that point dividing the line.

[§647] But the depth [of the treasure is] according to the loftiness and depression of the star.[116] For if the star is in the middle, the place of the treasure is in the middle, namely between the foundation stone or water and the surface of the earth.

[§648] Then, when choosing a fitting hour for digging it up, we will bind the Moon and the lord of the east of that hour to the lucky significator in a friendly way,[117] [and it is stronger if it they are in an assembly],[118] and we will make the pivots free of every infortune; and if opportunity allows, we will bless [them] with the fortunate ones.[119]

---

[116] This appears to mean whether the planet is ascending or descending in its apogee (ITA II.1). Burnett believes it is the star's altitude above or below the horizon (1997, p. 60).

[117] In other words, one must make sure the significator of the election chart is a fortunate planet, and is aspecting or connected to these other planets by a favorable aspect.

[118] Reading with Burnett's Ar. for "with reception." An assembly is a conjunction within the same sign (ITA III.5).

[119] Al-Kindī's Arabic reads that we will avoid accidents, but making the pivots fortunate would certainly do that.

Chapter II.3: House significations and forming judgments

Since we have described in detail what the nature of the signs[120] and planets bestows upon the judgment of concealed things, we must next investigate:[121]

[3] What their accidents would add to the judgments of matters.[122]

[4] The category of heavenly things is nevertheless supported in uncovering secrets, with respect to which we will set out certain figures of the stars.[123]

[5] Then we will apply the testimonies to the natures of the individual domiciles.[124]

Chapter II.3.1: Relation of houses to agricultural questions

[3] And so, having seen before which part of the fourfold nature of the signs[125] obtains the signification, then at last they approach the testimonies of accidents. Once the east has been established and the pivots made firm, if the portion[126] which is in charge of vegetation obtained the signification, [then]:

---

120 Reading *signorum* for *siderum*.

121 This preview re-establishes the contents already laid out at the beginning of Book II.

122 By "accidents" or accidental signification, Hermann means the (largely) house-based considerations below, including some aspects and considerations of planetary motion.

123 This refers to Hermann's long treatment of planetary configurations and conditions in Ch. II.4.1 (which was already identified as the fourth main topic of Book II, and which corresponds broadly with *ITA* III-IV).

124 This refers to Hermann's own rendition of Sahl's *On Times* below, which contains predictive material for most houses. I identified this as the fifth main topic of Book II, above.

125 See Ch. II.1.1 above.

126 *Portio.* Hermann seems to mean, "if the relevant planet and sign indicate vegetation."

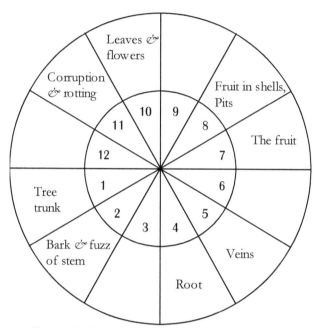

Figure 17: House significations for vegetation

Chapter II.3.2: Significators and houses for commodities

But[127] the lord of the east and its place indicates for the type and form; the lord of the bound of the east, the flavor. The lord of the Moon, the number.[128] The lord of the Lot of Fortune, the age. [The Lot] and its place, the quantity. The lord of the hour, the color. The lord of the twelfth-part of the east, the nature.

These things having been looked, at [the houses indicate the following]:

---

[127] See also the view of "Ptolemy" in *OHT* §6 (in Appendix C below).
[128] *Numerum.* But below, the lord of the Moon indicates the *matter (materiam)*.

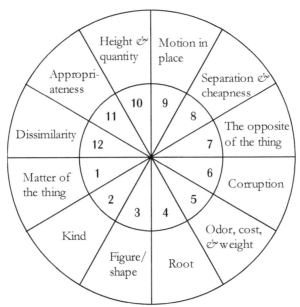

Figure 18: House significations in commodities (Hermann)

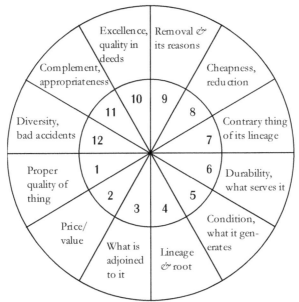

Figure 19: House significations in commodities (*Skilled* I.6.2)[129]

---

[129] Note the similarity between Hermann's and al-Rijāl's attributions: they must come ultimately from the same source.

These places having been looked at, one must be wholly eager for the advice of the lords which are safe: they bear a free signification.[130]

Chapter II.3.3: Significations in living things

But if the signification yielded to a portion[131] which indicates ensouled things, first one must examine in detail the distribution of the signs into the bodies of ensouled things, since there is a distinction of the limbs of the body amongst the stars themselves. For:[132]

♄	The right ear and the spleen
♃	The left [ear] and the opening of the stomach
♂	The right nostril and the liver
☉	Right eye (by day), left eye (by night),[133] heart, stomach
♀	The left [nostril] and the kidneys[134]
☿	The tongue and gallbladder
☽	Left eye (by day), right eye (by night), brain, lungs

Figure 20: Planetary significations in the body

But the judgments of things of this kind are: the significator[135] of the eye indicates the color of things; the significator of the ears, the voice; the significator of the mouth, the flavor; the significator of the nose, the odor; the significator of the heart, the sense; the significator of the liver, its newness; the significator of the spleen, malevolence; of the kidneys, the decoration; of the stomach, the eating [of it]; of the lung, the quality of the form; of the gallbladder, deceit.[136]

The lord of the Moon signifies the matter and nature of the thing: for it[137] indicates the body and corruption of the thing. The significator of the head

---

[130] A "safe" planet usually means that it is not under the Sun's rays, and is not in an assembly or square or opposition with a malefic (preferably not even by sign, but certainly not a connection by degree). A "free" (*liber*) signification probably means something like "positive, constructive, certain."

[131] Again, I think this simply means "if the planet and sign indicated living things."

[132] Note the similarity to *Tet.* III.13.

[133] This is probably meant for males, both for the Sun and the Moon here. The eyes should be reversed for women.

[134] In this case Hermann probably does mean the kidneys and not the buttocks.

[135] For these first few instances, reading *dux* with the rest of the list, for *dominus.*

[136] *Dolum.* But perhaps this is *dolorem,* "pain, aching"?

[137] Or perhaps, "she," indicating the Moon.

[signifies] the creature [itself] or the first part[138] of the thing. The lord of the east makes a [signification of] the chest, of the eleventh [its] beauty, of the seventh the form of the feet and the number, the [lord] of the fourth indicates the creating[139] of the feet.

Therefore, the testimonies of each kind of star must be applied in this way. For, of these places of the circle, the one in which the Moon was corrupted denotes a deformity in that place in the body.[140]

Then, too, the lords of the places must be noted, and the testimonies of each mixed together. For if the place were earthy but the lord watery, it indicates vegetation; which if one [were] earthy [but] the other fiery, metal or sulphur or that kind [of thing]. Which if one of them [were] earthy, the other airy, living things taken from the earth. But if both were earthy, they establish an earthy thing—and in this way with the rest.

One must know that whenever Jupiter and Venus agree, a signification of living things is made firm. And if the signification of Jupiter and Mars were in agreement, the signification of metals and gems is made firm. And thus that of Saturn and Mercury, in vegetation and an earthy nature.

Chapter II.3.4: What planetary conditions and motion signify

Then, whenever the signifying star is found to be retrograde, it designates the concealed thing is reduced.[141] Next, if the Moon either applies to the Sun or is being separated from the Sun, it is not[142] concealed.

The significator being eastern indicates a new, good, expensive thing; western, the contrary.

The Sun in the east, a scarcity of the thing; in the pivot of heaven, greatness and height, breadth and luster. Concerning the kind of length,[143] while it is in a sign of many ascensions[144] [it is long]; in a sign of few,[145] the contrary.

---

[138] *Capitis*, which can also mean "head, top."

[139] *Creaturam.*

[140] See also the marks of the Moon in Ch. II.1.8 above.

[141] Lit., "sent back" (*replicatum*), but it can also mean something reduced.

[142] *Nondum*, lit. "not yet." This might make sense for the Moon applying by body to the Sun (i.e., she has *not yet* entered the rays), but for a planet emerging from the rays one would expect it is "no longer" concealed.

[143] *Longorum.*

[144] That is, of right or direct ascensions. See *ITA* I.9.1.

[145] That is, of crooked ascensions. See *ITA* I.9.1.

The [Sun] in his own domicile or sovereignty or the tenth, a thing of copious quantity and great price (like if it indicates metal, it is gold or silver; if gems, hyacinth or emerald or sapphire; if vegetation or wood, that of a great price or type).

Now, a male east indicates male things; a female one, female ones, provided that the places of the lord of the east and of the Moon agree in each sex.

But the lord of the east, and the sign in which it is, designates the thing itself. Therefore, a free, lucky, [and] strong significator designates a sound and valuable thing; [but] corrupted and involved in complications,[146] the contrary. Wherefore[147] if Saturn [were] corrupted, [it indicates] a corrupted or dried out thing. But if Mars, a thing chopped up by iron or scorched by fire. But if the Head or Tail complicated [it, it indicates] a thing which has been complicated from one thing to another.

In a double-bodied [sign, something] double or in two parts.

Chapter II.3.5: More significations of objects and commodities

A moist star in an earthy sign has an indication over vegetation of the earth. But conversely, [it indicates] mud and that kind [of thing]. In an airy sign, free from the bad ones, a living thing; corrupted, a dead thing (and if [it is corrupted] by Mars, [something] tempered by fire, like a horn of leather and what is like that).[148] In a fiery [sign], touched by fire. In a watery one, taken out of water. The lord of its place has an indication for things living in the water, if it regarded the significator in an airy sign. But in a fiery one, pearls or gems from the sea. In a watery one, vegetation from the bottom of the water.[149] And in this manner the nature and condition of the stars must be mixed together.

The significator being eastern above the earth, provided that it is outside of scorching, denotes a thing commonly in the hands of men; conversely, the contrary.

---

[146] *Involutus.*
[147] Note the similarity to *Forty Chapters* §213, on the description of the thief's door.
[148] That is, a dead thing (hide, leather) worked by fire.
[149] Perhaps this includes crops such as rice.

It must be known that [the following things are attributed to the planets]:

♄	Heavy and stinking things
♃	Clean and moist things
♂	Hot things
☉	Things which appear, and which are costly
♀	Things soft to the touch [and] sweet in odor (unless she is corrupted, [in which case] the testimonies for the contrary signification must be mixed together)
☿	Light and delicate things
☽	Things that cost less[150]

Figure 21: Planetary significations in things

☉	Round, polished, beautiful, bright
☽	Round and not full, there is a fragment missing,[151] and a hole; not swarthy in color, [but] a white luster unless in the sixth or seventh, [in which case it is] obscure.
☿	Light, cheap, those of average height.[152]
♀	Clear odors, whose shape is triangular or spherical
♂	Red, dry, bigger in length than breadth
♃	Golden yellow, beautiful, tall, fleshy buttocks
♄	Black, tall, low-class

Figure 22: Further planetary significations in things and people[153]

Moreover, with a question about vegetation being understood: the significator in the domiciles of Jupiter and Venus or Mercury designates vegetation for human use; likewise ensouled things. [In a question] about red-hot things, [if it is] in a domicile of Mars, [it indicates] things tempered by fire; in a bound of Mars, beaten by hammers.

The significator in the tenth designates that the concealed thing has a covering or is surrounded by a jug, [according to][154] the figure of the star in

---

150 This either means things inherently less expensive, or at least less expensive than solar things (based on this phrase's placement in the text).
151 Or perhaps, there is only a fragment left.
152 Omitting *cuius formae pares designat.*
153 This list was originally at the beginning of Ch. II.3 above, but I have moved it here. Some of the translation is tentative, as there seems to be some serious garbling. *Sol quidem rotundus, levigatus, pulcher, lucidus. Lunae: rotundae nec plene fragmen inest et foramen plene minime in colore fusco nitor alba nisi in 6a et 7a obscura. Mercurius: levis vilis cuius formae pares designat medios stantes. Venus: lucida odora cuius figura triangula aut in speram. Mars: rubeus siccus longo, maior lato. Iupiter: flavus pulcher longus inclunis canus. Saturnus: niger, longus, vilis.*

the tenth. But its creation and form [is indicated by] the nature of the eleventh.[155] The significator in the fourth [indicates] a thing within another thing, determined in that same way.

The place of the significating star [indicates] the weight of the thing: earthy ones [indicate] heavier [things]; after this the watery ones; less so the airy ones; the fiery ones are most light. Also, the firm [signs are] heavier; convertible ones, lighter; double-bodied, middling. Moreover, the domiciles of the superior stars [indicate] in accordance with how they follow each other: [superior planets are] heavier, the inferior ones lighter, in order.

But al-Khayyāt claimed[156] he had tested a certain thing: the bounds of Mars in the watery signs designate tiles and brickwork. And so, the Moon being regarded here by Saturn, in some dignity of his,[157] [indicates] brickwork or smashed tiles.

But the tenth sign measures length and breadth; then the east, average [size]; the west designates something small. So, stars in the tenth or after the tenth are in charge over the length of a thing; but in the remote [places] or in the fourth, its shortness.

With the Sun regarding Saturn, Mars in an earthy sign designates something painted gold and red. Mars regarding Saturn [indicates] something of what has been buried, or something like a dead thing. The Tail with the significator in a firm sign [indicates] a stick or broken board or something putrid. In an earthy sign, an earthy nature; in fiery signs, like brickwork and broken tiles; nor [is it] otherwise in the degrees of the east. The Sun in airy signs indicates wool or hair; in earthy signs, vegetation [and] cloths of diverse color. [Cloths] of Venus are bright white cloths; those of Mars, red; those of Saturn, cheap and black.

Therefore, one must know that from the degree of the east to the pivot of the earth is the color red; from the pivot of the earth up to the west, dark; from the west to the pivot of heaven, green; from thence to the east, white.

But the quadrants of the circle measure the increase and detriment of a thing.[158] For there is a quadrant of the circle from the beginning of the east up to the end of the third, from the end of the third up to the end of the

---

[154] Reading *secundum* or *iuxta* for *ad.*
[155] I take this to be the meaning of *nam creatura eius et forma ad naturam ✕*.
[156] Source unknown at this time. But cf. *Forty Chapters* Ch. 6.6, which lists significations for the bound in which the Moon is.
[157] Or perhaps, "hers."
[158] See the diagrams in *Forty Chapters* Ch. 1.1.2, and *ITA* I.11, for quarters and ages.

sixth, from the end of the sixth up to the end of the ninth, and thus from the end of the ninth up to the east. [The quadrants from the lowest point of heaven, through the Ascendant, and up to the Midheaven, are the ascending quarters];[159] the rest are descending.

As therefore the branches of a question are diverse, so the diverse accidents of things are investigated from diverse places: so that from the whole circle, the whole substance of anything may be established.

Chapter II.3.6: Broad indications of success or failure

A retrograde [planet] complicates a matter, burning corrupts it.

So long as fortunate ones are conjoined with infortunes, we will have to resort to the one which is stronger. If therefore the fortunate one is stronger, it will come to be after losing hope; if the infortune, it will be stained after there is hope. But fortunate ones conjoined without impediment wholly perfect a matter. But unfortunate ones similarly[160] adapted [to each other],[161] wholly stain something that was hoped for. But[162] the Moon and the lord of the east resolve the fear: which if the infortunes preceded [them] by the second degree, there can be nothing to fear. If [still] bound [by one degree] or they are applying, it is dangerous.

Even every question: if it is about accidental things, and the lord of the east or the Moon were bound [by degree] to a star placed in a pivot, and it is received there without corruption (neither burned up nor retrograde), and [nor] is it in the remote [places] by motion, [the matter] arrives to its effect. Therefore, a star reading the counsel[163] of the lord of the east or of the question, without barring, if it regarded its own domicile, assures the

---

[159] Filling in based on *ITA* I.11.

[160] Reading *similiter* for *summe* "very much, intensely."

[161] I believe Hermann means, "if malefic planets are conjoined without impediment." But this would read better if he had said, "if unfortunate ones *in a poor condition* were similarly adapted [to each other]."

[162] See Sahl's *Fifty Judgments* #4 (in *WSM*), and Bonatti's 16th Consideration. By the "second degree," Sahl means that they are separating and are now in different degrees. For example, if their exact connection happened in the fifth degree of some sign, then once the separating planet is in the sixth degree, there is a qualitative difference in the separation.

[163] That is, "receiving the management." See *ITA* III.18. This paragraph assumes that the planet receiving the application of the lord of the Ascendant is the lord of the place/topic we are interested in, such as the lord of the fourth for real estate.

outcome before one's own eyes; which if it did not regard it, and there was a commingling between the lords of the east and the one reading [the counsel], without barring and a corrupting influence, it comes to be after losing hope.

Chapter II.4: Planetary configurations and answering questions[164]

Chapter II.4.1: Introduction and preview

But every question of astronomy is generally divided into two: for it is either in thought, or in speech. But apart from the context[165] of virtually every kind of question, what is demanded in [each] circumstance is the *where* and the *what* of the concealed thing. But [given these] two ways, [if] it is expressed in speech, the second [matter] is rarely necessary [to state].[166]

Therefore, apart from how much we have described [about this] in its own place, [we] are furnishing the following treatment of what is held in common [between the two types of question]. The things common [to both thoughts and questions by voice] are seven in number,[167] of which:

[1] As the nature of everything is, the first one deals with whether it will come to be.

[2] The second, whether as a whole or in part.

[3] Third, if in part, what part.

[4] Fourth, how it will come to be, in what place.[168]

[5] Fifth, where.

[6] Sixth, whence.

[7] And then seventh, the final end of the matter. Which if [the matter] is denied, whatever it is of the other party which impedes it.

---

[164] It may be instructive that Hermann inserts 'Umar's list of planetary configurations and strengths here, after distinguishing between thoughts (Book I) and spoken questions (Book II): it suggests that the interpretation of thoughts was a much more basic procedure, and that the full array of planetary configurations only appeared for full-blown horary questions.

[165] *Circumstantiae.* This may be a reference to the two "circumstances" or "contexts" of a question from Ch. I.6.3 above, or else it is just a general statement by Hermann.

[166] This sentence is extremely compressed, but I feel fairly confident about my translation: *Voce enim duobus modis exprimitur secundum raro necessarium est.* I believe Hermann means that if the client asks an explicit question, then you rarely need to look into *what* the missing thing is—because the client will tell you. But for matters which are only in thought, the astrologer does not know what the object is up-front.

[167] These questions do not get addressed until Ch. II.4.5 below (and even then, not fully). The list recalls al-Kindī's in *Forty Chapters* Ch. 7.1, and similar lists attributed to several authorities in *Skilled* I.5.2 (not included in Appendix A below).

[168] *Quoto loco.* I am not sure how this differs from the next question, "where."

Therefore, ʿUmar al-Tabarī follows this order, after Hermes, Dorotheus, Ptolemy, and Māshāʾallāh, to whose work we add nothing necessary from the others.[169]

Chapter II.4.2: On the fifteen bearings of the stars[170]

[4][171] For contemplating this, ʿUmar bin Farrukhān [al-Tabarī] counted fifteen[172] necessary bearings of the stars: advancement, retreat, application, separation, transfer, collection, barring, reception, recompense, solitude, a gift of virtue, gift of nature, gift of counsel, strength, weakness.

[1] ADVANCEMENT is to be in a pivot or after a pivot.

[2] RETREAT is to be in the remote [places].

[3] APPLICATION[173] is [the motion] of a lighter one to a heavier one, [and] it is two-fold: namely by rays and by body, of which [the former] is called "binding"[174] and the [latter] "conjunction."[175] It is more firm [if] in the same bound,[176] [and] most firm in the same degree.

[4] When they withdraw from it, it is called SEPARATION.[177]

[5] TRANSFER is if, between two stars, there is a third separated from one [and] it applies to the other.

[6] COLLECTION is if many [stars] do not apply to each other, but they do so to a heavier one.

[7] BARRING is if some planet either applies to another [from another sign] or is assembling with it [in the same sign], when another [planet] intervening in the middle, more quickly attains it: cutting off the rays of the one, it intercepts the light of the other.

[8] RECEPTION is if one [star] applies to another from its own sovereignty or domicile or the rest of the like dignities.[178]

---

[169] *Cuius operi nonnihil ex aliis quoque necessarium adiungimus.* I believe this means that there *are no* other necessary considerations in other authors, hence he does not need to reference them.

[170] For this section, cf. *ITA* III-IV.

[171] This was the fourth topic as defined at the beginning of Book II and in Ch. II.3.

[172] In *TBN*, ʿUmar is reported as having fourteen. There must be different ways of understanding this list.

[173] Or, "connection" (*ITA* III.7).

[174] A connection by degree from another sign.

[175] Or, "assembly" within the same sign, particularly within 15° (*ITA* III.5).

[176] See *ITA* II.6.

[177] Or, "disregard" or "diversion" (*ITA* III.8).

[9] RECOMPENSE is when one applies to another from fall or retrogradation.[179]

[10] SOLITUDE[180] is the treading of a planet without the application and separation of others.

[11] A GIFT OF VIRTUE[181] is if a star applies to another from its own dignity with reception, such as the Moon [applying] from Cancer.

[12] A GIFT OF NATURE[182] is if it is from the [dignity] of the one to which it applies, such as to Mars from Aries.

[13] A GIFT OF COUNSEL:[183] with applications of this kind, they persuade the effecting of the matter: like if the lord of the east applies to the lord of the question, or [the other way around], provided there is no barring between them.

[14] There are ten kinds of strength of the stars:[184]

[14a] That it takes up a position [regarding] the east in a familiar way.[185]

[14b] Being in their own dignities.[186]

[14c] Being direct.

[14d] Being free of the assembly and regard of an infortune [from the square or opposition].

[14e] Nor are the stars [connecting to stars which are] remote or averse,[187] or placed in their own fall; nor is [a star itself] in its own fall.

[14f] Being received.

[14g] Being eastern [of the Sun, for the superior planets; but western or rising after the Sun, for the inferiors].

---

178 This is probably "pushing nature" (below called "a gift of nature"), or what I call "classical" reception, in *ITA* III.15 and III.25.

179 See *ITA* III.24 and *Forty Chapters* Ch. 2.1.6.

180 Or, "emptiness of course" (*ITA* III.9).

181 Or, "pushing power" (*ITA* III.16).

182 Or, "pushing nature" (*ITA* III.15).

183 Or, "pushing management" (*ITA* III.18).

184 This list may or may not have originally been 'Umar's, but it is virtually identical to Sahl's in *Introduct.* §5.14. It combines elements of what were later distinguished as the "good fortune" and "power" of the planets (*ITA* IV.1-2). I add clarifying comments in brackets based on Sahl's list.

185 Sahl specifies the angles and succeedents, provided they are not in aversion to the Ascendant.

186 Sahl includes the joy.

187 That is, "cadent, or in aversion to the Ascendant."

[14*h*] Being [in their] domain,[188] that is, diurnal ones in the day, nocturnal ones in the night, and male ones in the male parts of the circle,
female ones in female ones.[189]

[14*i*] Being in a sign of its own nature.[190]

[14*j*] Being in the heart, with a strong Sun.[191]

[15] Also, ten weaknesses:[192]

[15*a*] Being remote and averse.[193]

[15*b*] Being retrograde.

[15*c*] Being scorched.

[15*d*] Being assembled with the infortunes or being bound to them
[from a square or opposition], nor being received.

[15*e*] Not being free of the [besieging of the] infortunes.

[15*f*] Being in its own fall.

[15*g*] Being separated [and] removed from a receiving [planet], [or]
applying to a [planet] in aversion [to the Ascendant].

[15*h*] Being a foreign [planet].[194]

[15*i*] Being next to the Head or Tail.

[15*j*] Being impeded in itself, such as if it were in its exiles.[195]

---

[188] *Haiz.*

[189] Sahl divides this up into two different kinds of strength.

[190] *In signo connaturali.* Sahl says: being "in a fixed sign."

[191] Sahl does not specify that the Sun must be strong, but he does believe planets become strong if they are in the heart; he also points out that benefics in the heart have their good increased, while malefics in the heart have their malice decreased.

[192] Again, this is virtually identical to Sahl's list in *Introduct.* §5.15. In *ITA* IV.3-4 these items are distinguished into lists of the "impotence" and "misfortune" of the planets.

[193] That is, being both cadent and in aversion to the Ascendant (being in the sixth and twelfth).

[194] That is, "peregrine" (*ITA* I.9).

[195] Reading *exiliis* for *exitis.* Sahl explains that he means the sign of detriment.

Chapter II.4.3: Impediments of the Moon[196]

A keen observance of the rest of the impediments of the Moon can be borrowed either from the 5[197] which were laid out in the first book on thoughts, or the 10 which are in the translation of Sahl bin Bishr, or the 11 which we have enumerated in our commentary on the [*Great Introduction* of] Abū Ma'shar.[198]

Concerning the faults of the Moon, specifically the ill condition of the Moon in every matter and every beginning;[199] and it is in ten types:
[First,] if the Moon is ignited under the Sun by 12°, and she is not passing the Sun, and after it.
Second, if the Moon is in the degrees of her descension (which is Scorpio), or connecting with a star in *its* descension.
Third, if the Moon is in the opposition of the Sun, within 12°, not [yet] reaching the opposition.
Fourth, if she is assembled with an infortune or regarding it from a square, or an opposition, or enclosed between two infortunes, [both] separating [from and going towards] an infortune.
Fifth, if she is with the Head or Tail in a sign, [with] less than 12° between them.

---

[196] I have appended Sahl's list from the Arabic in *Introduct.* §5.16, after the introductory paragraph by Hermann.

[197] Reading for "ten," since in Ch. I.5 only five are listed.

[198] From *Gr. Intr.* VII.6 (Hermann is referring to his own translation). This list can be found in *ITA* IV.5.

[199] This suggests both questions and elections.

[Sixth, if she is in the twelfth sign from her own domicile],[200] and that is in Gemini; or she is in the last degrees of a sign, which is the bound of an infortune.

Seventh is if she is cadent from the stakes[201] or is connecting to a planet which is falling from the stakes.

Eighth, if she is in the ignited path: and that is the last [part] of Libra and the first [part] of Scorpio.

Ninth, if she is wild and is empty in course,[202] not connecting with any of the other planets.

Tenth, if she is slow of movement: and that is when she is decreased from her average course, or is in a decrease of light (and [that is] in the last of the month).

Figure 23: Sahl's impediments of the Moon (*Introduct.* §5.16)

---

[200] This has to be reconstructed from the Latin version.
[201] The pivots or angles.
[202] See *ITA* III.9-10.

Chapter II.4.4: Finding the significator for the overall issue ("'Umar")

In[203] the first place, it is appropriate that the significator of this whole affair be investigated (whose name is the "victor"), which (as it seemed to ['Umar] al-Tabarī) is chosen from five places. For it will be either [1] the lord of the east, or [2-3] either of the lights, or [4] the Lot of Fortune, or [5] its lord.

Among all of these, it is plain that [we must] take the one which appeared stronger and whom many testimonies supported. But if perhaps the testimonies for all, and all those which pertain to the matter, were equal, we should embrace the one which had a more powerful strength (as was stated above).[204]

Chapter II.4.5: Answering the seven questions[205]

[1:] Whether it will come to be

And so,[206] with this principal significator (which they call the "victor") being found in this way, then an observation of this kind must be applied to the two significators over the domicile of the east and of the question

---

[203] Hermann seems to want us to choose the best *from among* these places (and not the one with the most dignities *over* them), but it does not seem to be from 'Umar (whether from *Skilled* I.9.2 in Appendix A below, or *Judges* §0.3 in Appendix D below). In fact, it seems closest to a practice of al-Kindī's, which is recounted in *Skilled* III.6, and which I describe in my Introduction to *Forty Chapters* (§4, topic 8, method 4). Al-Kindī transforms his victor for the whole chart in his Ch. 3.2 (which takes the most authoritative planet *over* the releasing places) into a significator of the chart or topic as a whole, using the best *among* the releasing places—with the difference that he substitutes the lords of places like the Ascendant and Lot of Fortune for those places themselves, so that he may use only planetary significators. On the other hand, it is also possible that Hermann had and knew 'Umar's own book on thoughts in Arabic (see my Introduction above), but that this particular method did not get used in *Judges*.

[204] Probably referring to the list of planetary strengths in Ch. II.4.2 above.

[205] Unfortunately, Hermann does not seem to address all of the questions individually, but I have added headings for the passages which clearly do.

[206] This paragraph could be an extremely abbreviated adaptation of the material in *Judges* §0.4 (see Appendix D below), but it also sounds like it could be drawn from Sahl's *On Quest.* §1.9 (in Appendix B below). In that passage of Sahl's, the significator of the question as a whole is treated separately from the relationship between the significators of the querent, quaesited, and that of the Moon. In the paragraph here, Hermann seems to take the significator (attributed to 'Umar above) as indicating the *issue as a whole*, while the relationship between the significator of the querent and that of the quaesited shows its *outcome.*

(namely that of the querent and of the quaesited). For if there were an application or transfer or collection between them, without corruption and barring, they establish the outcome of the matter. Which if there were less [than this], and the Moon were mixed together with one or the other of the significators (as was said), she fills up the position [as the victor]. And if this did not exist with an appropriate advancement and reception, and with respect to [their] motion, and that type [of thing], they deny the question.[207]

Once the victor is found, [the following things] agree with the testimonies of this kind of affair: the domicile of the question and its lord, and the places of the lord, but [also] where the partnering stars in the domicile of the question are: such as Jupiter [for] livelihood, Saturn [for] parents, Mars [for] journeys.[208]

For if (as was said) there were neither an application nor transfer nor collection nor reception between the significators, and either the significator of the querent or the partnering star happened to be found in the domicile of the question (or conversely)—if it were so, it imprints[209] the matter as being established.[210] So that for livelihood, [we look for] the lord of the Ascendant[211] or Jupiter to be in [the second]; or for a kingdom, [we look for] the lord of the Ascendant or the Sun to be in the tenth; and [so on] in this manner. Conversely, for livelihood that they establish the lord of the second or Jupiter in the east, [but] for a kingdom the lord of the tenth or the Sun— but not if that place is its fall, or the lord of the question is scorched there.

One must also apply the Lot of Fortune (which is the "Ascendant of the Moon"),[212] and the second sign from the Lot for livelihood and its domicile; the third, for brothers, and in this manner through the order of the circle.[213]

Therefore, this significator[214] applying to the partner-star [when it is] positioned in the place of the question, brings about the matter, and [also] if

---

[207] A troubled sentence: *Atque si nec id cum convenientia accessus et receptione fuerit, sitque de motu idve genus, quaestionem negant.*

[208] In other words, we must examine the general significators in various questions, and consider them as "partners" of the matter.

[209] Reading *infigit* for *inficit.*

[210] Thus there are four types of perfection: a straightforward connection (in the same sign or by aspect), transfer of light, collection of light, or by location in a key house.

[211] Reading *orientis* for *secundi* and *decimi* ("second," "tenth") here and immediately below, since Hermann just described the lord as being the one governing the querent.

[212] A common designation for the Lot: see for instance 'Umar's use of this phrase in *Three Books on Nativities* (in *PN II*), Ch. I.4.1.

[213] This is a clear appeal for whole-sign houses derived from the Lot of Fortune.

[214] Probably the lord of the Ascendant or whatever planet signifies the querent.

the lord of the question is applying to the partner-star placed in the east—unless it is an infortune [which is] neither receiving nor made fortunate, or drawn into a misfortune of this kind: [namely] being retrograde or scorched or cut off[215] in body.

But in every affair, it is appropriate for the Moon to be brought to bear as a partner.[216]

It is likewise [appropriate for] the domiciles to be distinguished throughout the whole circle. For if it should happen that one domicile is divided into two, we will seek the leadership from two: such as if the tenth should fall into the ninth, [we seek the leadership] from the ninth and the tenth, but not so if [it should fall] into the eleventh.[217]

[2:] *Whether as a whole or in part*

Once[218] this reasoning [over] whether it would come to be has been had, next in order [we must determine] whether it would happen as a whole or in part. But these three significators pertain to this work: namely the Moon [and] the lords of the east and of the question.[219]

And so the Moon, being very much the partner of the east, and thus [also being] the partner of the lords of the domicile of the east and of the question, [if she is being] corrupted in a pivot, it denies the matter as a whole.

But while she is equally with the lord of the east and of the matter, it testifies [to its success].

Both [of the lords] being sound, brings about the matter as a whole—which if one of them is corrupted in a pivot, it stains approximately half [of it]; in the other [places], less so.

Nevertheless the Moon (being a partner of the east), or the east [itself], being feminine (except for Virgo and Capricorn), while the question is nocturnal, and the Moon (being in a pivot or being very much a partner of the question) being corrupted by scorching or an unlucky and retrograde star,

---

[215] *Secta.* I believe this refers to a connection with the infortune by body (rather than by aspect).
[216] *Participem.*
[217] See my Introduction §8 for an explanation of this.
[218] Cf. *On Quest.* §1.8.
[219] Probably a reference to Sahl's *On Quest.* §§1.4 and 1.8.

stains part [of the question]. But while she is devoid of [the lord][220] of the east, nor in the domicile of the question nor in a pivot, while the affair is [also] not nocturnal, the Moon's corruption does not harm.

Also, the lord of the east being corrupted, stains the matter according to the greatness of the corruption.

And the victor-significator being corrupted in a pivot stains the whole thing; after a pivot, half; in the remote places, one-third.

Also, the infortunes in the pivots reduce the matter and threaten the querent (and more so Mars in the day, Saturn in the night).

But the lord of the east or the Moon being corrupted in a pivot, stains twice as much; in a succeedent, half; in a remote [place], one-third.

And so, the outcomes of matters must be judged in this way, in light of the nature of the stars and [their] counsels,[221] even the places in which they are, [and] also the domiciles of their own which they principally regard.[222]

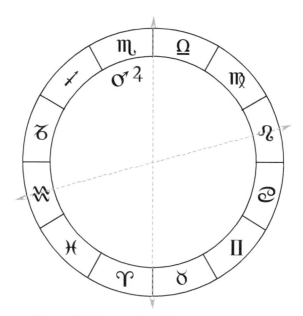

Figure 24: A question about things sought

---

[220] Adding tentatively. Otherwise, it would read, "devoid of the east," which could indicate being in aversion to the rising sign.

[221] That is, their managements (primarily, how they apply to and separate from one another).

[222] This is a common-enough principle in medieval horary, as I mention in my Introduction to *Forty Chapters*.

An example of matters:[223] the east was Aquarius, the tenth Scorpio. Jupiter was holding onto the pivot [of the tenth] equally with Mars. The second, which is the domicile of livelihood, was Pisces, which Jupiter was regarding. But the eleventh[224] was Sagittarius. Therefore it was indicated for the querent that he would get the things [he] sought, and it would be through the hands of great men (namely judges and generals and that type [of person]).

---

[223] This chart is puzzling even apart from the fact that its source is unknown (at this time). Its placement here, and the comments about Pisces and Sagittarius, suggest that it is meant to illustrate Jupiter's ability to draw on the significations of the domicile he sees (Pisces, the 2nd house)—and yet wealth or livelihood is not specifically stated as being the goal. Is it a 10th-house question? What about Saturn, who rules the Ascendant? The only thing I can be sure of is that the "judges and generals" derive from Jupiter and Mars, respectively.

[224] Reading for "ninth."

[7:] Outcomes and causes (based on Sahl)

Then,[225] let us inquire into the quality of the outcomes, according to the kind of applications and receptions of counsel.[226] For, provided that they apply to each other by friendly figures, they promise easy outcomes, and thus [too when] received; by unfriendly [figures], the contrary, and thus [also if] not received.

And so,[227] provided that the significator of the person applies to the lord of the question, [it will come about] by his own effort; conversely, by [the effort of] the other party. But a transfer [indicates it is] by mediators. Collection, by the hand of someone putting it together.

Whence also it happens that [when] we have learned the cause of the matter, we consider the movement and source in terms of those same significators. For it was stated[228] that it comes to be either by application or transfer or collection or the fitness of the stars' places. Therefore, we produce the cause of the matter from these four categories:

For if it happens by application, we consult the applying one: which if it is being separated from another, or another applies to it, its nature and accidents lay out the cause of the matter, or from what [signification][229] belongs to its lord. And in this manner with respect to the transferring and collecting [planet]. But if it is by means of the fitness of the stars in the places, that establishes the outcome.

Moreover, we produce the cause from those [planets] from which they are separating, or from the domiciles of their own which they regard, or from their lords.[230]

---

[225] Cf. *On Quest.* §1.5.

[226] Again, this simply means receiving the "management" or application of another planet (see above).

[227] Cf. *On Quest.* §1.6.

[228] Again, the four types of perfection mentioned at the beginning of Ch. II.4.5 above. But these may also be found in *On Quest.* §1.4.

[229] *A qua…dominus ipsius.* It could also be "from what house of its own [it aspects]," reading *a qua [domo] ipsius [aspicit]*.

[230] That is, the dispositors.

Chapter II.5: Timing techniques (from Sahl's *On Times*)[231]

Chapter II.5.1: Basic indications of times

[5][232] From the beginning of [this] treatment we have [only] briefly re-solved the rest of the circumstances of a question in astronomy, in order, as was proposed, [and] as was required. But in order that any [of these] may be fully explained in [these] treatments, next we must inquire into the time at which anything which is hoped for (or feared) will be, and the definite hour when anything is going to come about.

Sahl bin Bishr handles this type [of issue] fully in a separate book,[233] [but] much diversity in the signification of matters accompanies certain particulars [in it].[234] Therefore in our work [here] we will discuss what of each [topic] seemed appropriate [to us]. For Sahl says that [just as] there is [1] an altera-tion of the figures of the stars, and a [2] changing status of the circle, [so there is] a variety of outcomes in the lower world:

[1a] But the alteration of figures is in two parts: namely by longitude and by latitude. By longitude, [that] a star is now eastern, now western; by latitude, now southern, now northern. And the Moon is eastern up to the opposition, [and] from thence she is western up to the assembly [with the Sun].

[2] Also, the changing of the circle is in four parts according to oth-ers.[235] But according to Māshā'allāh (to the extent that it pertains to this affair), it is in two parts, ascending and descending. Ascending, from the degree of the fourth up to the degree of the tenth [on the eastern side of the chart]; and thus descending from that to the degree of the fourth [on the western side of the chart].

---

[231] This whole chapter is based on Sahl's *On Times*, also translated by me from John of Spain's Latin, in *WSM*.

[232] This is the fifth topic defined at the beginning of Book II and in Ch. II.3.

[233] That is, in *On Times*.

[234] All Hermann means is that there are many different opinions for the timing methods and each house topic. He mentions this again in Ch. II.5.3.

[235] This must be either the quadrants divided into the four cardinal directions (*ITA* I.11), or Ptolemy's division of the quarters into eastern and western (*Tet.* III.5). For Ptolemy, the eastern quadrants are from the Ascendant to the Midheaven, and the Descendent to the *Imum coeli*; the other two quadrants are western.

[1b] And[236] there is another alteration of the figures of the stars in [their] course: from [their] assembly with the Sun to the first station, from the first station to the opposite of the Sun, from the opposition to the second station, [and] from this up to the obtaining of the [conjunction of the] Sun [again]. [But] 'Umar adds:[237] from the top of the orbit[238] to the middle; from the middle to the opposite; and thence again to the middle; thence [again] to the [top of] the orbit.

[1c] There[239] is even [another] alteration: arriving at the places of the circle, either by the body of the stars or the rays, and thus "directing": that is, the leading of the degrees of the stars, signs, and Lots through the circle to those places by individual equal degrees or ascensions, by means of individual years or months or days and hours. So that it might be plain, one must discern (as Sahl did)[240] between firm, double-bodied and tropical signs, and so [also] between signs of light and heavy stars, and so [too] the ascending and descending part of the circle. For if the significator occupies a tropical sign, the directing of the degrees are days; in double-bodied ones, months; in the firm ones, years. But in signs of light stars, days or months; in those of the heavy ones, months or years. And thus the ascending part and descending part [indicate faster and slower times, respectively].

But 'Umar takes it in a fourfold way: that a star would be [a] in the ascending part of the circle; [b] eastern; [c] proceeding quickly; [d] received by [a star] proceeding quickly [and] freely. Which if all of [these conditions] existed at the same time, the directing of the degrees would be hours; but if one of them were missing; days; if two, months; if three, years.

---

[236] See *ITA* II.10.

[237] Here and below, the 'Umar source is unknown at this time.

[238] *Absidis.* I take this to mean the motion of a planet in its epicycle, which again determines its direct and retrograde motion and stations.

[239] This is from the last paragraph of *On Times* §1, and from §2.

[240] *On Times* §2.

Chapter II.5.2: Converting configurations into time

Sahl[241] divides this whole leading [of a degree] which they call "directing," in seven ways:

First, that how many degrees there were between the one applying and the one receiving,[242] should be counted as being so many hours or days or months or years, as was said [above].

Secondly, that the one applying should reach the degree and minute of the one receiving, by body; or conversely, that [the other] should attain it by body.[243]

Thirdly, how many degrees there are between their bodies (either by equal [degrees] or by ascensions of the climes), should be counted as being so many days, by individual [degrees].

Fourthly, how many signs there are between the one receiving counsel[244] up to the east, or conversely, should be counted as being so many months by individual [signs].[245]

Fifthly, how many degrees there are from the beginning of the east up to the rising degree, should be counted individually as days.[246]

Sixthly, what portion of the ascensions were applying, should be counted as being so many days or months or years.[247]

Seventhly, so that once significator of the space of time has been discovered,[248] how many lesser years it had should be computed as being so many hours, days, months, or years.[249]

---

[241] *On Times* §3.
[242] John reads, "by light or by body."
[243] That is, by transit in real time.
[244] That is, receiving the management, the slower planet.
[245] This is like a profection.
[246] John does not list this item.
[247] John does not list this item. This seems to mean that if there are (say) 10 ascensional times between the two key planets, this could mean 10 days, months, or years (depending on the context).

Whenever [the significator of the time] is found in a double-bodied [sign], each agrees that the span [of time] must be doubled.[250]

It is appropriate that this significator [of time] be investigated first. As [Sahl] bin Bishr says in the book *On Times*,[251] not every star is fit for this duty, even though it [may be] strong: if it did not have testimony in the question, it is not at all relevant. And so, first the Moon must be consulted, then the lord of the east, then that one (of the lords of the east and of the question) which receives the counsel of the other, or a star to which either of them is applying. Among all of these, the one which [was] stronger [and] pertained more to the question, will obtain the signification of this affair. But if the testimonies of each were equal to the rest, nor was it possible for the victor to be chosen easily, we should embrace that one of the lights which regarded the east in a more familiar way.

The[252] significator being found in this way, one must discern a [primary] direction with it. For if the one conferring and receiving the counsel[253] were both ascending, eastern, and quick, the degrees of the application are hours or days; but slow and western and descending, months or years. But if they were mixed, [it signifies something in the middle—therefore, set up the time like that].[254] For from the east to the tenth are hours, from the tenth to the seventh, months; from the seventh to the fourth, years; from the fourth to the east, days. To these must be conveyed the testimony of the places, in terms of the three-fold division of the signs,[255] and the domiciles of each

---

[248] In John's version (§3) the significator is identified as being the best of the following: the lord of the Ascendant, the lord of the matter, the planet receiving their management, the luminaries, or the planet receiving the management of the Moon.

[249] For the planetary years, see *ITA* VII.2.

[250] At this point I have omitted a puzzling and apparently incomplete section not in *On Times*, which suddenly changes the subject to a question about longevity. It reads: "Corrupting the releaser, and an eclipse or infortune, *summa transacta nutritura* [?] multiplied by twelve, counts the years of the native. ['Umar] bin Farrukhān al-Tabarī relates that he has tested [this] countless times. For, he said, the Moon was *paciens* [*petens?*] to the Tail, and there were 3° between the Moon and the Tail; [multiplied] by 12, they made 36 years (namely, of the native's [life])." I cannot seem to find a source text in *Skilled* or in *Judges*.

[251] See *On Times* §3.

[252] See *On Times* §3.

[253] That is, "pushing and receiving the management." John's Sahl is assuming the significator is either the lord of the Ascendant or of the quaesited matter, and wants to see where each of them is.

[254] Adding with John's Sahl, as Hermann does not complete his thought.

[255] The quadruplicities, mentioned above.

rank of the stars,[256] and [balance these against your] expectations about the producing of outcomes.[257]

But apart from these, there are certain other determinate spans [of time]. For the Moon, being in the place of the question, [and] being bound [by degree] to a lord which is regarding the place of the question, establishes the matter on that very day. 'Umar[258] adds that the Moon, [being] in the place of the question or a strong place, [being bound by degree] to a partner of the question (such as being in a domicile of Jupiter [in a question] about livelihood),[259] brings about the matter; and if she is being bound to the lord of either the east or the question—provided that it regards the place of the question or applies to one regarding it—it will be accomplished on that very day.

But Sahl makes the observation that whenever we measure a span [of time] as being less than a [lunar] month, by no means should it be made firm until the circle of the Moon is completed in the meantime.[260] For the same reason 'Umar even relates that whenever the Moon was a partner of the question, a span of time greater than a month should be limited while she travels through all places of the circle and the stars. Since she is a partner in virtually every signification, perhaps she would reach such a place that attaining the outcome would be necessary: such as if she would touch the domicile of the east or the question, or the degree of one lord or another, or the lord of the east itself or of the question [would do so]. Or even the Sun: for the entrance of the Sun into the quadrants of the circle changes the seasons and accidents of the world with certain successive, lawful outcomes, so that just as in the way that the Moon enriches the laws of the body, so the Sun invigorates the overall condition of the soul.

Therefore, every class [of indications for times] should be enumerated:

---

[256] Whether the lord of a sign is a superior or inferior planet, mentioned above.
[257] Reading in the spirit of John's text, to complete the odd *id de productionibus proventuum expectationibus.*
[258] Source unknown at this time.
[259] Livelihood is a 2nd-house signification, in the sense of the money and materials used to actually support one's life—it is not the same as profession and mastery, which is a 10th-house signification.
[260] Sahl means that we should watch the Moon's transits, because they might indicate the outcome before any other symbolic method we are using: during a lunar month, the Moon will have transited everything in the chart.

[1] For every alteration of the figure of the victor measures the [time] spans of outcomes, so that if the question is [posed while the victor is] eastern, [it is until the victor] becomes western, or conversely; and [if it is asked while] it is direct, until it becomes retrograde, and the contrary; [or if it is asked while] it is free [of the Sun's rays], [then] until it is scorched and so on; [or if it is asked while the victor] is a foreigner,[261] until it reaches its own dignity.

[2] Fortunate ones assembling in the place of the question even define the hour of the outcome, or [even] the one receiving counsel[262] arriving there.

[3] Also, the Sun as the partner of the question reaching the east, and thus [also] the Moon and the lord of the east, if they apply to a fortunate one or a star-partner of the question—because that is a sign of an effect.

[4] The degrees of applications measure an outcome—equal degrees, I say, or of ascensions by clime—first less, then more.[263] Therefore, these are the determinations [of time] which are not changed. For the ways arranged above are distinguished into hours, days, months and years.

---

[261] That is, peregrine.
[262] That is, the one to which the key significators are applying (i.e., pushing their management).
[263] I believe this means that one should assume that the units of time will be smaller, and only assume greater units of time if the event fails to manifest after the smaller units expire.

Chapter II.5.3: Timing for individual house topics

Since there is such diversity [of possibilities] in this business of topics, in order that they not be [too] few in number (by being listed in a spotty way), let us pursue all of them without limit, and let us finally investigate the [part] of this signification which pertains distinctly to the individual domiciles of the circle.[264]

1ˢᵗ house

At the hour of a question about life, on the span [of time] to which the east makes a claim, three places must be noted: namely [1] the east and its lord, [2] the Lot of Fortune and its lord,[265] even [3] the [most recent] assembly or opposition [of the luminaries]. Among them, the one which appeared stronger and which had more testimonies, will obtain the job of being the victor.

And so, we lead this place forth as a releaser, to the assembly of the infortunes by degrees of the ascensions of the clime,[266] and wherever the direction (that is, the leading [forth of a degree] of this kind) reached, is the mortal year—unless the rays of the fortunate ones intervened. And if the rays of the infortunes strike the bound of the distribution from the opposite or a tetragon, this intervention [of the rays of the fortunate ones] does not [necessarily][267] bring profit.

Whence [the opinion of] Māshā'allāh: he says the lord of the east should be observed (and more so the Moon, since[268] she is in front of the lord of the east). Which if both or one [of them] applied to the infortunes or approached being scorched [by the Sun], the number of the degrees between

---

[264] *Quoniam tanta rerum huius negotii diversitas est ut nec pauca numero, si sparsim dentur, firme amplecti possint, omniaque prosequi vix finitum, quid ex hoc ducatu singulis per circulum domiciliis discriptim attineat deinceps investigemus.*
[265] John's Sahl omits this.
[266] In other words, by primary directions (whether Ptolemy's proportional semi-arcs or by ascensional times).
[267] Adding with the sense of John's text. That is, a square or opposition from the infortunes might be more powerful than the mitigating aspects from fortunes.
[268] Reading *cum* for *dum* ("while"). If we read *dum*, the meaning would be that if the Moon is nearer to the infortunes or the Sun, we would prefer her. But I think Hermann is saying that the Moon is more clearly a significator of the physical body, so she is preferred. At any rate, John's text expresses no preference, so the statement is probably Hermann's and not Māshā'allāh's at all.

them and the infortunes or the scorching should be collected. Which if the lord of the east were in a firm sign, they are years; in a double-bodied one, months; in a tropical one, days. Therefore, the degrees of the application which came out from the lord of the east measure the life.

2nd house

Questions of the second, such as: in how much time we may get what we sought in terms of livelihood and that kind [of thing]. The number of the degrees between the significators count the intervening days, months, or years. [Or, see when] the lord of the second enters into the east or its own domicile[269] (or the lord of the east [into] the second),[270] or one would get to the other by body.[271]

3rd, 4th houses

But in questions about the third and fourth, the same method of this type applies.[272]

5th house

But in affairs of the fifth, if it is asked at what point some pregnant woman is going to give birth, we will first note the lord of the seventh; this being determined, we will count how many signs are between it and the degree of the fifth, as being so many months, [and] how many degrees as being so many days: the birth is completed at the endpoint of these.[273]

---

[269] Namely, the second domicile.

[270] This parenthetical comment is only in Hermann.

[271] That is, when the lords of the east and of the second would be corporally joined. But John's Sahl reads, "or [the lord of the second] will be joined to the benefics." Also, I have omitted a strange sentence fragment which appeared at this point (and is evidently part of some editorial remark by Hermann): *ut nihil pigeat tribus id terminis interclusum praescribi.*

[272] That is, look at the lords just as with the second house.

[273] But John's version measures from the lord of the fifth to the degree of the seventh, not from the lord of the seventh to the degree of the fifth as Hermann has it here. On the other hand, *Skilled* I.47 measures from the lord of the fifth to the degree of the fifth. It is probably best to side with John's reading if one sticks with Sahl's approach; but al-Rijāl's makes sense, too.

6ᵗʰ house

In questions of the sixth, the counsel[274] of the Moon should in no way be overlooked. Which if she were corrupted, she will be led forth[275] to the degree of the corrupting infortune or to the degree of the eighth. If she reaches the infortunes before she arrives at that degree, one must have fear [of his death before she arrives at the degree of the eighth].[276] If that infortune were Saturn, the degrees of the applications are months or years; if Mars, they are months or days, in light of the nature of the strength [and quickness of the place][277] and the nature of the illness—and this is where a judgment about death would be given. But in the book of judgments about health, we discussed the critical days.[278]

7ᵗʰ house

For the affairs of the seventh, such as if it is asked until when the fear of war and invasions should be postponed,[279] the Moon should be consulted. First, when she is opposite [the Sun], it accelerates. But if the Moon were distant from [completing her] application [to him at the New Moon] by 20°, it slows down. But it accelerates if she is with stars in her own domicile, and more so if she is regarded by the Sun. And thus: with the twelfth-part of the Moon in the east or in the tenth, or with the Sun or its[280] lord, or a star recently eastern, [it will be quick].

But Hermes[281] determined the period of a war already begun. He said if the lights regarded each other from a trine, nor [were they] in aversion to the east, they accelerate the end [of the war]; but by a tetragon, they slow it down, and thus [also] if they regard each other from the opposite.

---

[274] That is, her application or to whom she pushes her management.

[275] That is, "directed."

[276] Reading with John's Sahl. Hermann reads it the other way around: "If she reaches the degree of the eighth before she would be joined to an infortune arriving at that degree, one must have fear."

[277] Adding with John's Sahl.

[278] Instead of this sentence, John's Sahl says, "And you should not neglect the degree of burning" (combustion). At any rate, Sahl does discuss critical days in his *On Quest.* §6.2, and they will be covered in *Judges* as well.

[279] In other words, when a war will begin and it is time to be afraid.

[280] This could be the Sun's domicile lord or the lord of the east.

[281] John's Sahl reads "Theophilus."

One must also note the Lot of Fortune, and at the same time whether there is a planet with Mars [in the same sign] or in his tetragon: which if [each] were pretty much made fortunate, it relieves it and quickly resolves it; if unfortunate, the misfortune draws out the fervor of the war and makes it worse.

Also, Hermes discerned the period of victory. For he said if Saturn and Jupiter were quick, they accelerate it (namely, for that party [of the conflict] to whom they gave their judgment);[282] slow, they put it off.

And thusly [also] with respect to controversies, insofar as it pertains to that affair. But what this category [of judgments] bestows upon betrothals can be copied from the opinion about the second [house], if the matter demanded it.

8th house

[Judgments about the eighth house were already handled in the questions about longevity and illness, above.]

9th house[283]

For[284] questions about the ninth, such as if it is asked about the return of someone who has set out [on a journey]: first, the Sun[285] must be consulted. If at [the time of the] departure he regarded an infortune from the tetragon or from the opposite, or he were conjoined to it [in the same sign], it prolongs the journey and slows down the return. But applying to fortunate ones accelerates it. Which if he applied to fortunate ones after an infortune, it prepares danger in the journey, but afterwards it saves [him] and scales back [the danger]. [But if he applied to infortunes after the fortunate ones, he will find good things and then delay.][286]

---

282 John's Sahl reads, "for the one of them in whose clime Mars was." But I am not even sure what John's Sahl means.
283 Some of the sentences in this section differ significantly from John's version, and should be compared with his.
284 See *On Times* §9.
285 John's Sahl has the lord of the Ascendant and the Moon, which is a significant difference. Based on the material in *On Quest.*, it would be best to stick with John here.
286 Adding based on John, even though John is still speaking of the Lord of the Ascendant and the Moon.

But the Moon measures the [period of] staying and determines the return. Which if she occupied the east at [the time of] departure, it prolongs his stay, and more so with Saturn or in his bound.

If therefore the Sun appeared free at the departure, it puts off the return until he reaches the tetragon or opposition of his [original] place, or he returns to the same place. But if [he were] corrupted by the infortunes, we will consider the corrupting [planet]: which if it were Saturn and either he was the lord of the east or appeared in the ninth, it slows down the return for virtually his whole round-trip, or at least for so many months or days. But Jupiter and Saturn retrograde in a pivot slows down the return. The rest [of the stars] are easier in this affair.[287]

But[288] Māshā'allāh says that when measuring the return of someone who has set out, one must compare the Moon and the lord of the hour. If the one of them which appeared stronger, occupied the ascending part of the circle,[289] one must count the degrees between it and the east. If therefore the lord of the hour were stronger, how many degrees there were determine the return as being so many hours; but if the Moon, the number of degrees should be divided by 13: therefore, however much the division was, they bring back the one who has set out in so many days.[290] If[291] however they held onto the descending part of the circle, the degrees determined before [should be] likewise collected together: if the lord of the hour appeared stronger, they are days; if the Moon, they are divided by 13 [to yield] months.

Which if both were less fit, so that the lord [of the Ascendant][292] obtained the east in a more powerful way, it defers the return until it reaches either the east or the tenth. But if the lord of the east were weak and in aversion [to the Ascendant],[293] and the Moon strong, [and] she is joined to the east with

---

[287] That is, they do not slow down the return as much.

[288] See *On Times* §10. The Māshā'allāh source is unknown at this time.

[289] That is, between the degree of the IC and that of the Midheaven, on the eastern side of the chart.

[290] Since the Moon's average daily motion is about 13° in the ecliptic, dividing the degrees by 13 yields the number of days between the time of the question and her transit to that place itself. If she is between the Ascendant and Midheaven, it is the time until her transit *to* the rising degree; if between the Ascendant and IC, it is the time *since* her transit to that degree.

[291] This sentence actually makes more sense than John's version.

[292] Adding *orientis*, and making *oriens* the object of *obtineat*. This sentence does not quite appear in John's version, but makes more sense than John's sudden transition.

[293] *Averso.* This reading is confirmed by John, who specifically says "was not aspecting the Ascendant."

much testimony, placed in a familiar way—provided that she regards her own domicile—the degrees collected in the aforesaid manner (between her and her domicile) determine the return.

Concerning writings,[294] even if it is asked when they will arrive. First, Mercury must be noted: which if he were in the east or in the twelfth, already about to enter into the rising sign, or the Moon is applying to him or to the lord of the east, or Mercury [were] the lord of the east or very much a partner of the east, we will say it is going to arrive when Mercury either applies to the lord of the east or reaches the east (if he were nearby). But if the Moon applies to Mercury, it will be when she reaches him by [her] body or she reaches the east. Which if the Moon would transfer [light] from Mercury to either the degree of the east or to its lord, we will say that it is [when] she reaches the one to whom she conveys [that light].

10th house

For the affairs of the tenth, there are many operations of this type. One must observe the hour either of [1] the elevation of kings or princes or prelates, or [2] of [their] entrance into any dignities or offices or professions, or at least [3] of their question pertaining to this affair.

And with the east being established at that same hour, and the pivots being established, one will have to see if some star occupies the east or the tenth, with testimony. Which if it would be scorched in a pivot, it prepares the end of [his] rule in those duties, nor [is it] otherwise [with] their lords. One must even fear it whenever a star found in the tenth reaches the lord of the fall of the tenth, so that it regards the lord of the tenth at the same time. But the scorching of the one which occupies the east must be measured as being more [important] than [the scorching of one] in a pivot.

But if each of the places were empty, one should turn to the Sun [in a diurnal chart]. If he applied to Saturn or to Mars in a pivot, [the end of his rule] must be measured as being when he reaches that place. But if he applied to Jupiter or Venus, [it will be] when Saturn reaches either his[295] place or to the opposition or tetragon of the place. If however the Sun were in the remote [places], and more so in the ninth or twelfth, with testimony, [it will be] when Saturn or Mars reach that place or the opposite of the place.

---

[294] See *On Times* §11.
[295] According to John's Sahl, this refers to the Sun.

But we follow the Moon by night just as we do the Sun in the day. With her, one must first see if she is either applying to the Sun or separating from the Sun: it hands over the term of the kingdom or job to the solar counsel, as was said about him [before]. But if she is neither applying to the Sun nor separating from the Sun, it terminates the job or kingdom within one year. Nor is it otherwise if the lord of the sovereignty of the solar lodging-place were unlucky. Then, one must see to what star the Moon is applying: which if she were corrupted by either the infortunes or scorching, the degrees of the application prescribe the term. But if the Moon is not received, and the lord of the sovereignty of her lodging-place were corrupted, it terminates it within a year unless the lord of the lodging-place is clean and strong. Which if the Moon is received, it will be until the infortunes reach the degree of the one receiving [the light].

These things having been examined in detail, if the east of the elevation or entrance [into the new duty] were of the signs of the superior stars, while the lord of the Moon leads to[296] the end of the year, the years will have to be turned, which they call a "revolution of years."[297] Therefore if an infortune returns to[298] the tenth, or the lord of the east would be burned up in the tenth, it denotes he is going to die in his kingdom or dignity. If however [an infortune returned to] the second, it corrupts his possessions. But in the tenth, his work; in the eleventh, his rents;[299] in the east, his dependents.

This having been looked at, the attending stars[300] must be observed. Which if strong ones obtained the pivots, they give their own lesser years or months: such as if Saturn were in the east or the tenth with testimony, received, he gives 30 years. If therefore it were a cycle of the year,[301] if the significator or the lord of the east is being scorched in a pivot, it is a sign of corruption. [But] if Saturn is strong while [he is] the lord of the year, it does not establish [the end of the person's rule] until the cycle of the year is

---

[296] John reads this as though it is the lord of the Ascendant; by "leads to," he evidently means it "signifies that" the person will be in that position for at least one year.

[297] That is, we will have to track solar revolutions to determine when the person's authority will come to an end. The reason for this seems to be that the superior stars indicate longer periods of time, so it is important to track them over time.

[298] John's Sahl reads, "retrograde in," here and in the following statements.

[299] The eleventh is the second from the tenth, thus the revenue he gets in virtue of the position itself.

[300] Hermann adds, "which they call fixed." But John reads "planets," which must be correct since the fixed stars do not grant years in the way Sahl is about to describe.

[301] That is, a "revolution of the year." Like Hugo of Santalla, Hermann uses *conversio* ("cycle, turning") to refer to the revolution.

corrupted; but his testimony and strength [would be] receding. [In this case] Saturn, as I said, placed as before, gives 30 months. Then the cycle of the year must be noted. Which if it would be corrupted by scorching or the infortunes, if the one who is in charge of the management[302] were retrograde in a pivot, it is a threat of sudden corruption.

But Jupiter in the east or in the tenth with testimony, [grants] 12 years. But Venus in the same place and clean and received, 8; not received, [that many] months. Which if an infortune were returning to its place within those years or months, there will be a corruption and weakening of the kingdom.

Now, if Mercury is in the east or the tenth with testimony, strong, powerful with reception, he gives 20 months. And so, turn the year:[303] and if you found him weak, he gives 5 months. And if he is being scorched in a pivot, and the lord of the tenth is being involved with an infortune [by body] or its rays, it is the end of his rule.

But if Mars were in the east or in the tenth, if he would be scorched in a pivot within 15[304] months, it is the end of his rule. Therefore, turn the year.

And if the Moon were clean and received, with testimony, she gives 24 years.[305] Which if she had no testimony, she gives 25 months. One must note the star to which she conveys [management]: which if it is being scorched in a pivot, it ends; but if it is not being burned up [but were still] in a pivot, and were received, it will indicate its years or so many months.

If however the Sun (being placed in this manner) received the testimonies of the stars, it will last for a year. And if [the testimony] were very much, he gives 19 years; corrupted, 19 months. And so every assisting star, if it is not confounded by being scorched in a pivot nor harmed by an infortune when the year is turned, it saves [the kingdom] up to its rulership[306] [in terms of years or months]. [If] the contrary, [there will be] confusion and loss.

Then, just as in a birth, so for those who are made lofty: a profection[307] will be moved forward for individual years by individual signs, [to see] where the lord of its sign (which they call the sālkḫudhāy) would be applying, its status and its manner, [how it is] mixed with the lord of the tenth of the east

---

[302] That is, the profected lord of the year.
[303] That is, look at the solar revolution.
[304] Reading *15* (the number of his lesser years) for *16*.
[305] This must be under the assumption that she was important in the first year, which would mean she has 24 years left in her complete, 25-year bestowal.
[306] Reading *dominium* for *dominum*.
[307] *Aleptyphe.*

of the year,[308] [and whether] their lords agree in [his] destruction.[309] Once this is done, if the lords of the east of the year and of the tenth apply to each other, they make the kingdom firm. And thus [also] a free Moon conveying [management] to a star in a pivot; and thusly [too] the Sun [and the lord of the Ascendant][310] in the day. But if the lord of the tenth [were] scorched in the cycle of the year, or there were an infortune returning to[311] the tenth, it leads to the end [of his rule]. And if the lord of [the house of] the king were eastern in the cycle of the year, it renews the duty of his kingdom and dignity; but being western taints it.

Moreover, in the cycle of the year, if the lord of the end[312] applies to the lord of the tenth, it makes the kingdom firm. But conversely if the lord of the tenth were applying to the lord of the fourth—and more so with the Sun being remote from the pivots and the Moon occupying the sixth[313] or the twelfth, while at the same time the year applied to an adverse place [by profection].

11ᵗʰ house

For the affairs of the eleventh, such as pursuing a hope, the same determinations which were laid out in the second [house] are prescribed.

12ᵗʰ house

But for [the affairs] of the twelfth, such as for avoiding punishment, the same things which were determined in the fifth [should be followed].

♌   ♋   ♌

After having carried out all of these things which were proposed, it [now] remains for the end of matters to be observed. But in finding the significator of the end, one must first take note of the Moon. If the Moon herself is the significator of the beginning of things, then the star to which the Moon

---

308 The "east of the year" is the calculated Ascendant at the time of the solar revolution: so, Sahl is speaking of the Midheaven of the solar revolution.
309 *Eorumque domini consentiat discutiendum.*
310 Adding with John's Sahl.
311 Again, John's Sahl reads, "retrograde."
312 That is, of the fourth.
313 Reading with John's Sahl for *septimum.*

applies obtains the signification of the end. Whenever the Moon does not regard the one to whom the lord of the Moon unites,[314] the beginning of things is empty. But whenever the Moon obtained the signification of the outcome of things, nor did she regard her own lord, it makes the beginning of the matter totter, and complicates the end.

But meanwhile, Bālīnūs distributes every question of the astrologers throughout the four pivots: he hands over the querent to the east, the quaesited matter to the seventh, the cause of the matter to the Midheaven, [and] the end to the pivot of the earth.

---

[314] *Communicat.* This could indicate either a connection by body or by ray. Namely, the one to which the lord of the Moon pushes its management.

BOOK III: VICTORS AND SIGNIFICATORS
OF CHARTS & TOPICS

Chapter III.1: The significator of the chart and of a topic[1]

Every matter to be judged entails at first a certain necessary discovery of a significator, so that when the significator over everything is observed, one may attain the purpose of the intention[2] rightly and absolutely. Because it has been looked at less diligently than the rest, we (following Māshā'allāh) are undertaking an investigation of it, more carefully so than the rest,[3] so that we may see this category [of significator] be more commonly embraced. We are correctly following the path which Māshā'allāh put in order [for] this work, in his book which is entitled *The Seven Keys*.[4]

Chapter III.1.1: General method for the significator of a chart[5]

He says: the stellar signification in the lower world is a wholly two-part path or method. One is of the nature of a star, the other of its accident. Of its nature is like that of the Sun and Saturn for the affairs of kings and fathers. Of its accident, like that of Jupiter for wives and Mars for enemies.[6] And the natural varies neither by the change of place nor contrary blending, nor some disposition[7] within any fortune:[8] whence, with respect to the daily successions of the accidents of the world it is less complicated (that is, [it is] simple), and it occasions nothing new nor different.

---

[1] Much of Book III seems to be an appropriation of, and inspired by, al-Kindī's *Forty Chapters* chs. 3.1-3.3 (see Appendix E). Like Hermann, al-Kindī outlines a victor for a chart (Ch. 3.2), for a topic (Ch. 3.1), and describes his method for finding the longevity releaser (Ch. 3.3). And just like Hermann, al-Kindī says that the longevity releaser can be used for questions as well as nativities (Ch. 3.4).
[2] That is, the "thought."
[3] I believe this refers to "other matters" rather than to "other astrologers." But this paragraph is rather tortured.
[4] I am not aware of a book with this title; it may be misattributed.
[5] An abbreviated version of this method (with only the points) appears above in Ch. I.3.4.
[6] That is, by house location or rulership or their various configurations and changes. See the next paragraph.
[7] *Affectu.*
[8] This seems to mean, "its disposition within any *fortunate or unfortunate* circumstances or planets."

But the accidental significations are three categories: [1] dignity, [2] strength,[9] [3] regard.[10]

[1] There are five dignities: domicile, sovereignty, bound, trigon, decan. Their relationship to the chiefs (which are that many in number) [is as follows]:[11] the Sun over a diurnal east ([but] the Moon over a nocturnal east), [the Ascendant],[12] the Lot of Fortune, [and] the assembly or opposition of the lights. If therefore one discerned which [planet] had more dignities in these places,[13] an order of this kind should be followed: with the beginning being taken up from the lord of the domicile, to whom 5 portions are given, they grant 4 to the lord of the sovereignty; 3 to the lord of the bound;[14] 2 to the first lord of the trigon; 1 to the decan. But the [points attributed to][15] the stars in these places is in this order, so that the one which obtains more portions in the places[16] of the chiefs is more worthy.[17]

Lords of the Chiefs	Points
Domicile	5
Exaltation	4
Bound	3
Primary triplicity lord	2
Decan	1

Figure 25: Ruler strengths for "Māshā'allāh's" significator

[9] That is, the types of strength found above in Ch. II.4.2, but also *ITA* IV.1-2.

[10] That is, in terms of what houses aspect the Ascendant (see below). Probably, the Persians saw this as a way to incorporate the various systems of "advantageous" or "busy" or "profitable" houses: see *ITA* III.4.

[11] This seems to be based on al-Kindī's victor over the whole chart (see his Ch. 3.2 in Appendix E below), although al-Kindī seems to use both luminaries no matter the sect of the chart (as Hermann does below). It seems to me that it might be worth using only the sect light, or at least preferring it.

[12] Adding based on al-Kindī, and because the text says there are five of them, and the Ascendant is obviously left out.

[13] Or rather, *over* these places, as I describe in my Introduction.

[14] Note that the bound receives 3 and the primary triplicity lord 2; in many medieval texts it is the other way around.

[15] Reading for "strength," which would mix up the categories being distinguished here.

[16] Reading *locibus* (ablative pl.) for *loci* (genitive sing.).

[17] That is, according to dignities (*dignior*, "worthy"; *dignitas*, "dignity").

[2] [But] the one which is in its own greater rulership, is stronger.[18]

[3] The regard of the degrees is an order of this kind: that which was in the east obtains 12 portions, the Midheaven 11, the domicile of hope 10, the western pivot 9, the fifth 8, the fourth 7, the ninth 6, the third 5. Among those which are in aversion [to the Ascendant] are: the eighth, 4; the second, 3; in the twelfth, 2; in the sixth, 1.[19]

But Dorotheus[20] put the tenth after the east, [and] the eleventh after the tenth; then the fifth, and thus the seventh and the fourth. Others prefer the pivots to the rest, in order.[21]

Therefore, once the significator has been chosen, one will have to compare all of the places of the stars through the circle, and first one must note the one [1] richer in dignities;[22] then the one [2] more powerful in strength; and finally the one [3] more blessed by regard. Therefore, that one among them which overflowed in number, that one plainly gets the signification.[23]

---

[18] Remember that being dignified in one's *own* position is not the only strength, as Ch. II.4.2 and *ITA* IV.1-2 show: below, Hermann includes being direct in motion as well as a favorable solar phase.

[19] The present version by "Māshā'allāh" favors the angles and the places of good spirit (11th) and good fortune (5th)—these are Hellenistic designations, and are the joys of the benefic planets—preferring those which are above the horizon and on the eastern side of the chart; then the cadent places which aspect the Ascendant (9th, 3rd), apparently favoring the 9th because it is above the horizon; then, of the places in aversion, he favors the 8th and 2nd (the 8th because it is above the horizon), then the 12th and 3rd (the 12th because it is above the horizon).

[20] See *Carmen* I.5. The version attributed to Māshā'allāh in Ch. I.3.4 above, is identical to this. The Dorotheus-based version follows his understanding of the advantageous or busy or good places (*ITA* III.4), all of which aspect the rising sign: he begins with the Ascendant and Midheaven, then the two succeedent places which aspect the Ascendant by sextile (11th) and trine (5th), apparently favoring the eleventh because it is above the horizon; then the other two angles (7th, 4th), then the cadent places which aspect from a trine (9th) and sextile (3rd), again favoring the ninth because it is above the horizon. Then he looks at the places in aversion to the rising sign, favoring first the succeedent ones (8th, 2nd), and the one which is succeedent to and supports the Ascendant (2nd); then the cadent places which are in aversion (12th, 6th), again favoring the one above the horizon.

[21] For example, Abraham ibn Ezra: see his victor of the chart in Appendix F.

[22] Again, by its types of rulership over the places of the five "chiefs."

[23] But remember that we are not supposed to add all of the points up indifferently (indeed, the types of strength do not have point values). Rather, as Hermann's example shows, we are to compare the planets across all of these categories.

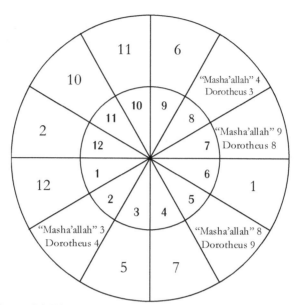

**Figure 26: House strengths: "Māshā'allāh" in Ch. III.1.1
vs. *Carmen* I.5**

Which if it were found, it must not be rejected on account of the disadvantageousness of the places: it can [indeed] be remote and averse, but in the number of portions [it must be] overflowing in both dignity and strength—in which case it obtains the high position of being the significator.[24] Because if it were not so, and the worthiness of the signification passed only to those which held onto a pivot or at least possessed accidents, there would not be different significations.[25] Since therefore one must pay attention to it in this craft, one will have to compare between the stars, signs, and the places of business,[26] and all natures, proper qualities and dispositions.[27] After looking at these things up and down from all sides, it will finally be clear which one is fit to hold down the fort with respect to the task of the high place of signification.[28]

---

[24] In other words, being an authoritative ruler over the chiefs or releasing places, and in terms of qualitative strength, is more important than house position.

[25] That is, in that case, the position by place alone would determine the significator, and there would be no need to take rulerships or planetary strength into account.

[26] *Negotia*. It is intriguing that Hermann chose this word, since it is one of the core meanings of the Greek term for the "advantageous/busy/profitable" places above in the diagram of house strengths (and described in *ITA* III.4).

[27] *Affectu*.

[28] *Quis aptus ducatus officio principatus arcem teneat.*

Chapter III.1.2: Example of a victor for a whole chart

An example:[29] the east was Gemini, in the bound of Mars, in the decan of the Sun. In Cancer: Jupiter 5°, in the decan of Mercury.[30] And in the same place, the Lot of Fortune. In Scorpio, the Head 28°. In Sagittarius, Saturn 22°. In Capricorn,[31] Mars. In Aquarius, the Sun 25°, the conjunction of the lights 24°. In Pisces, the Moon 10°; Mercury in the face of Mars;[32] also Venus 26°.

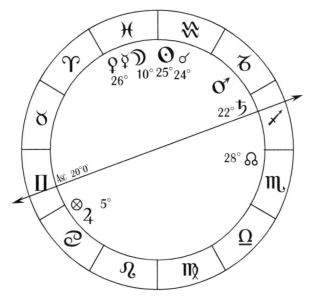

Figure 27: Hermann's example of a significator for a whole chart

---

[29] Below I propose the original chart, after the deaths of 'Umar and Māshā'allāh but during the careers of al-Kindī and Abū Ma'shar. Apart from the close positions of many of the planets, Hermann points out that Saturn rules the domicile and triplicity of the Sun: if the original position of the Sun were truly at 25°, he would rule the Sun's bound as well—which Hermann or the original Arabic author would surely have noted. But by modern calculations the Sun is in the bound of Mars, which explains the omission. Nevertheless, the positions of Mercury and Mars are far off, which would entail several serious errors in the manuscript transmission.

[30] But the decan of Mercury is between 10° and 20°.

[31] If my calculation is correct, this should be Gemini.

[32] If my calculation is correct, he should be in his own face, in Aquarius.

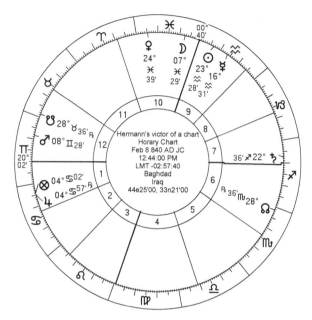

Figure 28: The likely chart for Hermann's example[33]

	☉	☽	Ascendant	♂	Fortune
Domicile (5)	♄ 5	♃ 5	♀ 5	♄ 5	☽ 5
Exaltation (4)		♀ 4			♃ 4
Bound (3)	♂ 3	♀ 3	♂ 3	♂ 3	♂ 3
Triplicity (2)	♄ 2	♀ 2	♄ 2	♄ 2	♀ 2
Face (1)	☽ 1	♃ 1	☉ 1	☽ 1	♀ 1

Figure 29: Worked-out dignity points for Hermann's example

After having made a comparison between the stars and signs by dignity, power and regard, among all of them Saturn is found to be more worthy over the places of the chiefs, and powerful in strength, and blessed in regard, surpassing the rest in number.[34]

[1] For he is the lord of the Sun, and confers 5 portions of dignity; as [the lord] of the conjunction, the same amount; as [primary] lord of the trigon of

---

[33] I have cast the chart using Alchabitius Semi-Arc houses.
[34] Note that the instructions said to use the Sun for a diurnal chart, and the Moon for a nocturnal one: here Hermann is using both. Until a source text is identified, we cannot know whether these results are Hermann's or the original author's.

the east, 2.[35] Therefore, [the chart] bestows 16 portions of dignity: that much is conceded to no other in this affair.[36]

[2] But [he has] portions of strength because he is direct, eastern, and the partner of the trigon of his place.[37]

[3] The western pivot bestows 8 portions of regard.[38]

But both Mercury and Mars are partners in this signification, because one is the lord of the sign of the east, the other [the lord of] its bound. And one is in the tenth, the other in his own sovereignty.[39] But the Moon [is] the lady of the Lot of Fortune. Of [these three], Mercury and the Moon confer years to Saturn,[40] [who is] in aversion to Mars, [so] Saturn is more powerful.

---

[35] Omitting a redundant sentence which repeats (in slightly different language) the points received for being the domicile lord of the Sun and the conjunction.

[36] I get 16 points in the following manner: as the domicile lord of the Sun (+5), the primary triplicity lord of the Sun (+2), the primary triplicity lord of the Ascendant (+2), the domicile lord of the pre-natal conjunction (+5), and the primary triplicity lord of the pre-natal conjunction (+2). This assumes that my calculation of the true chart is correct, so that the bound lord of the Sun is Mars, and not Saturn (which would have given Saturn 3 more points).

[37] Saturn is the partnering or third triplicity lord of all fiery signs.

[38] Venus and the Moon are in the tenth, which gives more points; but they do not have the same situation in dignities that Saturn enjoys.

[39] Again, if my calculation is correct, neither of these statements is true: Mercury is in the ninth sign, and Mars in Gemini in the rising sign. But in Hermann's chart, Mars is in his exaltation and Mercury is in the tenth.

[40] Probably because they are in an earlier degree, applying to a connection by aspect. But I see no basis for referring to longevity techniques here. Perhaps the manuscript originally read that they were conferring "rays" or "light," not "years."

Chapter III.1.3: The victor for a topic

Moreover, an example in choosing the more powerful one over parents, as above:[41]

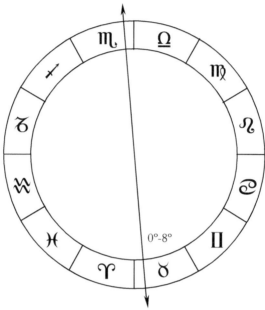

Figure 30: Incomplete figure for the victor over a topic[42]

So, to which planet do the above four places of parents[43] (that is, [the place] of the Sun, of Saturn, of the Lot of Parents, and [the place] of parents [itself]) concede the testimonies? I judge that Venus has got it, surpassing [the others] in the number of portions. That she is the lady of the pivot of the earth itself, bestows 5 portions; that of its bound, 3; that she possesses the trigon of the place of Saturn confers 2; by the decan of the solar place, 1. And these all come to be 11, which no other gets in this affair. And in this manner I investigate the things to be pursued in every affair.

---

[41] This section seems to continue Hermann's appropriation of al-Kindī (see *Forty Chapters* Ch. 3.1 in Appendix E), but note that Hermann does not include the lord of the hour in his reckoning below.

[42] This figure is based upon a handwritten figure in the manuscripts which included no planetary positions. The text only makes it certain that the degree of the IC is between 0°-8° Taurus (the bound of Venus). Since Venus is also the primary triplicity lord of Saturn, he must be in an earthy or watery sign.

[43] Reading *parentum* for *impotentum* ("the impotent").

Chapter III.2: The victor, releaser, and *kadukḫudhāh*

Next, we must appoint three assistants in every affair: the victor,[44] the releaser, and the *kadukḫudhāh*.[45] The victor has signification in the outcome of a matter; the releaser, the beginning; the *kadukḫudhāh*, the determination of the nature and disposition[46] of a star and place. Indeed the victor is the most powerful and elevated over the chiefs. The releaser, [the most] fit with regard to the five chiefs. The *kadukḫudhāh*, the partner of the place, [and is one] regarding the releaser itself.[47] But the judge of the end is the lord of the releaser, as [the releaser] is [the judge of] the beginning. This [is so] in every undertaking, both for a question and a nativity.[48]

Since therefore it was [already] discussed by what method the victor is to be chosen, we will investigate the releaser along with the *kadukḫudhāh*. In choosing the releaser from among the five chiefs, by day one must first consult the Sun; by night, first the Moon. But the places of a diurnal releaser are five; of a nocturnal one, eight. So, given a diurnal question or birth, one must first look at the Sun. Which if he occupied the east or the tenth or eleventh (whether [the sign] were masculine or feminine), he is fit to be the releaser. But in the seventh or ninth, let [the sign] be male. [Otherwise] he is unfit. But neither the Sun nor any other [would be] fit in any place unless in any place it had the regard of a partner: that is, unless there were a regard by the lord of its domicile or sovereignty, bound, trigon, or decan. Which if it were in aversion to [all of them], it will not be fit to be the releaser, nor [will any of its lords be] the *kadukḫudhāh*. But if the Sun is unfit [in a diurnal nativity], then one must consult the Moon. Which (as was said about the

---

[44] This is probably the victor over the chart as a whole, described in Ch. III.1.1-2 above.

[45] This planet is one of the lords (preferably the bound lord) of the longevity releaser, which must aspect the releaser at least by sign. The releaser is often called the *hīlāj* or *hyleg* in medieval Arabic and Latin texts.

[46] *Affectus.*

[47] That is, the victor is the most authoritative planet (by dignities) *over* the places of the candidate releasers or chiefs; the releaser itself is the most fit *among* them, and so must be one of them; the *kadukḫudhāh* was described in a footnote above. For the difference between victors among places and over them, see my Introduction, §3. For more on releasers and the *kadukḫudhāh*, see the references in Appendix F of *ITA*.

[48] See al-Kindī's statement at the end of *Forty Chapters* Ch. 3.4. Reading *nativitati* for *naturali*, since the releaser and *kadukḫudhāh* are natal positions used in longevity determinations, and both questions and nativities are paired immediately below.

Sun), if she is found in the other part of the circle,[49] in a place appropriate to her nature, she is fit.

But with a nocturnal question or birth, first the Moon must be examined: which if she is in a pivot or after a pivot, provided that she is in a female sign and regarded by a partner of the place, she will be fit to be the releaser, and the partner who regards [is fit] to be the *kadukhudhāh*. And it [also] happens that the Moon in the third is like the Sun in the ninth. Which if the Moon is unfit, the Sun will appear fit in the opposites of the upper places, [provided that he is in a place that is] appropriate [to himself].

Then, if neither of the lights were fit by day or night, and the birth or question is after a conjunction, the degree of the Ascendant will handle [the matter] before [turning to the] Lot of Fortune; [but] after the opposition, conversely. If the degree of the Ascendant is of either sex, [but] regarded by a lord of its dignity, it will be the releaser, and the regarding one is the *kadukhudhāh*. However, the Lot of Fortune will be the releaser [if] in a pivot or after a pivot [and] regarded by a lord of its dignity, and the regarding one is the *kadukhudhāh*.

Lastly, if all of these are unfit, let us embrace the conjunction or opposition [if it is] in a pivot or after a pivot, provided that it is regarded by the lord of one of its five dignities. Which if there were less than this, one will observe neither a releaser nor a *kadukhudhāh*.

Finally, [if] either of the lights were fit to be the releaser, [and] in its own domicile or sovereignty, it will equally be the releaser and the *kadukhudhāh*.

---

[49] That is, below the horizon. Hermann is trying to put the releaser in its own domain (see *ITA* III.2).

Chapter III.3: On discerning the path

After assigning the significators of judgments, one must then discern the path of judging. Generally, the method of judgments is three-fold: [1] by the place of the circle, [2] by the place from the Sun, and [3] by blending.[50]

[1] The place according to the circle is threefold: [1a] the pivot, [1b] the [place] advancing [to the pivot], and [1c] the remote [place].[51]

[1a] The pivot [makes something] certain, true, stable, present, completed, making the thing happen right before one's eyes.

[1b] The advancing [place]: arrival, going towards something which follows, it accelerates perfection, and confirms hope and grief.[52]

[1c] The remote [place]: transitory, idle, varying, lost and remote things, so that it speaks against the hope of good things just as it makes the grief of bad things fail.

And so that it might be briefly comprehended: the pivot, discovery; remote, loss; the advancing [place], in the middle. And so, a significator in a pivot or the Ascendant establishes perfection, with nothing absent from the unwavering matter; in remote [places], movable, doubtful, empty. And the place according to the circle is of this type.

[2] The place from the Sun is no less three-formed: [2a] eastern, [2b], western, [2c] under the Sun.[53]

[2a] Being eastern is akin to a pivot.

[2b] Being western, to an advancing [place].

[2c] Being under the Sun, to the remote [places].

---

[50] But see below, where Hermann inserts a fourth category related to solar phases: the direction of planetary motion.
[51] See *Forty Chapters* Ch. 1.2.3 and its §§106-07.
[52] That is, it confirms something even if it is bad.
[53] Cf. *Forty Chapters* §71 and §107.

Moreover, direct motion [is akin] to a pivot, the second station to an advancing [place], retrogradation along with the [first] station, to the remote [places].

[3] But blending is two-fold: [3a] application and [3b] conjunction, each one being ranked in two among each type of star.[54] [3b] Conjunction[55] is similar to a pivot, just as [3a] application is to an advancing [place], and being in aversion to the remote places, according to the disposition[56] of each kind of star.

But the east, the Sun, the Moon, and their lords, resemble the testimony and assistance of the above-stated significators.[57] The one of them which either appeared stronger or was exceptional in dignity, will be the victor itself.[58]

Then[59] one must examine the fortunate one among each, in terms of status and disposition, if it had power over all five releasers and the rest [of the planet], or at least the majority. A signification of this kind [must be examined according to] the places through the circle, the places from the Sun, the domiciles, sovereignties, and the entrance into their own bounds, the manner of its journey,[60] applications, separations, and the nature both of themselves and of the signs and degrees in which they were.

For, fortunate significators[61] in the pivots or advancing [places], conjoined [in the same sign] or bound [by degree from another sign] or even regarded [by sign alone], or in their own domiciles, establish the good without impediment. In the remote places, they shatter what is promised, divert what

---

[54] Hermann means that applying and completed connections mean different things for fortunes and infortunes. See a restatement of this below.

[55] That is, any connection actually completed by degree, not simply being assembled in the same sign.

[56] *Affectus.*

[57] That is, the victor, releaser, and *kadukḫudhāh.*

[58] *Quorum qui fortior extiterit vel ipse almubtez̧ erit vel dignitate eximius.* The sentence should be read more naturally as: "the one of them which appeared stronger, will be either the victor itself or one exceptional in dignity"—but this does not make much sense to me in this context.

[59] Very tentative translation of a very awkward sentence: *Deinde et caeteros ipsamque alhileg ut [aut?] 5 vel pro omnium si facultas fuerit, maioris saltem partis inter utrumque fortuna, statu et affectu pertractanda.*

[60] This must mean its speed and direct or retrograde motion, including the stations.

[61] This sounds like al-Kindī's approach in *Forty Chapters* Ch. 8.1, in which he analyzes the *separate* condition of each releaser, in order to yield a general appraisal of the chart, but without trying to select a victor from among them or over them.

is contracted, and frustrate the hope of good. But unfortunate ones[62] in the pivots or advancing [places], or their own domiciles, threaten the troubles of difficulty and harmful things. But in the remote [places], distresses, fears, and harmful terrors. Again, all of these [may be divided into] two parts: the good and bad, the advantageous and the troubled.

[There are also] three different orders or times: past, present future; the beginning, middle, end.

Therefore, this discovery of the Persians has been confirmed by the Chaldeans and Egyptians with an invincible abundance of evidence (as on the other hand the Indians' method of judging gathers together the numbers of stellar counsel and testimony between the equal and unequal).[63]

---

[62] Reading *infortunati* for *infortunia* ("the infortunes").
[63] I take this to be a criticism of Indian methods: it seems to say that the Persian method above distinguishes between planets which are important in separate categories (such as dignity, regard, and so on), which preserves the separate meaning of those categories; but the Indians are alleged to have mixed together all of these separate numbering and judging systems, therefore illegitimately combining unequal categories together.

APPENDIX A: AL-RIJĀL'S *THE BOOK OF THE SKILLED*

1. *Skilled* I.7: On the hour for taking the Ascendant

The ancients were discordant in this:

[1] Hermes said that the hour of taking the Ascendant over the question is at the meeting which is between the querent and the master, and the master should take the question then.[1]

[2] The Indians, and those from Persia, and those from Babylon, say that questions are put down upon the querent's will, and they say that the significations of questions are in disagreement according to the alternation of the querent's will in [those] hours.[2]

[3] Valens says[3] that the Ascendant of the question should be taken in the hour in which the questioner comes to the master.

But I say that[4] the hour of taking the Ascendant of the question should be [the Indian and Persian and Babylonian view]: when the querent says to the master that he should take it, and not when he comes to him; because if he would come and *not* state that he should take the Ascendant, there is not an Ascendant unless he said so.[5]

---

[1] This seems to mean that the astrologer decides if and when to cast a chart, and is close to our sense of a horary question.

[2] This sounds like statements by Māshā'allāh and 'Umar in *Judges* §§0.1 and 0.2 respectively, that the chart will reflect the clarity or confusion in the client's own mind.

[3] Cite unknown. It could belong to a pseudo-Valens in Arabic, or as part of a commentary on Valens which was mistaken for Valens's own view. It sounds like a straightforward casting of a consultation chart to determine thoughts.

[4] 1485 reads, "And I see well that…", which sounds like al-Rijāl's own personal experience.

[5] Al-Rijāl seems to mean that the casting of the Ascendant really requires the explicit decision and consent of the querent, after having explored the issue with the astrologer. In a way, this reflects the ultimate triumph of explicit horary questions, because the whole procedure of finding significators of thought is pointless if we prefer explicit discussions before casting the chart—in Hermann's words, we would only have questions "in speech," and not "in thought" (*Search* Ch. II.4.1)

2. *Skilled* I.5.2: On disagreements over significators of thoughts

They even disagree on learning the querent's thought, and how they can understand it, and what signification they[6] ought to have over him.

[1] Dorotheus[7] says: If you wished to know the querent's thought, look to the first lord of the triplicity of the Ascendant: which if it were in its own house or exaltation or triplicity or bound, judge through that place in which you found it. And if you found it in the second house, know that the question was about assets, or about what accrues to him; and judge about this according to the place in which it was, and in whatever house, and judge from the significations[8] of that house. On the other hand, if the planet found there were in the cadents or in its own fall, or in places in which it has no dignity, you will *not* judge through its place, but you will look to the planet which projects its own rays upon it, without the Sun or another planet cutting it off: and you will judge through *that* planet and *its* place.

[2] And this was [also] the opinion of Hermes and of the great fellowship of the ancients who followed him.

[3] Valens says:[9] If you wished to know the thought, look in this at the planet from which the Moon is being separated, or the one which is in her opposition or in her square, and you will know the thought from that. Which if you did not have such a planet, look at the planet to which the Moon applies herself first, and see if it has some dignity in the Ascendant or in the place in which she[10] is. And if it did not have dignity in the Ascendant nor in her place, look at the house of another planet which is regarding it,[11] and is in its own exaltation, and judge by that.

[4] And this[12] is [also] the opinion of the Persians, and the great fellowship of the Roman sages—nor do others operate with it.

---

[6] This is possibly an error in the Latin translation, accidentally reading *debent/debeant* (pl.) for *debet/debeat* (sing.).

[7] Cite unknown at this time, but the use of triplicity lords is certainly Dorothean.

[8] Reading with 1485 for "significators."

[9] Note that this is virtually identical to the opinion of "Māshā'allāh" on the victor of the whole chart, in *Skilled* I.5.2 (in excerpt 5), below.

[10] Here and in the next sentence, I am reading with the opinion of "Māshā'allāh" in excerpt 5 below, and assuming al-Rijāl is speaking about the Moon's sign.

[11] I believe this refers to the Ascendant: so it seems the last option is to take an exalted planet that can aspect the Ascendant.

[12] I believe al-Rijāl means that the last sentence about an exalted planet is the view of the Persians and Romans.

[5] Māshā'allāh said:[13] First, it is agreeable to divide matters into four parts, namely into animals, vegetables, minerals, and works. (And by works, understand things which men do, such as travels, marriages, visions, dreams, and other things which men engage in, all of which are comprehended in the twelve houses.) And when you wanted to know the thought of a querent, whether it is about the deed of some one of [these] works, or about one of the other three [categories], inspect any of the seven planets which is in some place (of the places of deeds), and consider whether another planet is elevated over it (but a planet is said to be "elevated" over another, when it is in the tenth sign from the sign in which the other planet is): and if you found this, judge that the question was about one of the deeds. But if you found no planet elevated over the other, judge that the question was about one of the other three things. And if it were so, and you wanted to know which of the other three it is, look to a planet which is elevated over another one of the seven planets (except for the Moon), and at the proper quality of that planet, and of the sign in which the one which is elevated over the other planet is, and judge from this. And lead your reason from that planet by looking [next] to the Moon: if she applies herself to that planet, or she would be joined to it before another, judge that the question was about vegetation. But if the Moon does not aspect that planet, nor is she being joined to it, and the Sun aspected it or he would be joined with it before another planet, judge that the question is about an animal. But if something of this with the Moon or Sun did not exist, judge that the question was about a mineral thing, or that it is not about some other of the things, and judge according to the proper quality of the planet and of the sign in which it is.

[6] ['Umar] al-Tabarī[14] says: If you wanted to know someone's thought, look at it from the planet which is in an angle or before it was[15] in an angle, and which would have some dignity in the Ascendant, and in [the place of] the luminary of the time (namely the Sun in the day, and the Moon in the

---

[13] Source unknown at this time. The logic of this passage seems to demand that we find an overcoming planet (see *ITA* IV.4.1 and its Glossary) in order to determine the thought. If a planet is in a place of action and has another overcoming it, then it is about an action. If not, then see if *any* planet has another overcoming it: if so, then if the Moon is applying to the overcoming planet, it is about vegetation; if not, but the Sun is applying to it, it is about an animal; if not, the question is about a mineral or something else.

[14] This seems to be an abbreviated version of the longer method below, corresponding to *Judges* §0.3 in Appendix D.

[15] *Ante fuerit.* Meaning unclear. Maybe this means that it is angular but still approaching the degree of the angle itself by the diurnal/primary motion of the heavens.

night), and judge according to the dignity of that planet, and its distribution[16] in the heaven. And if none of the planets were in an angle, but [one] was in the succeedents, and it was the lord of the Ascendant or its exaltation, and if it is the victor [of it], you should know that the signification is in the succeedent. And if you found two or three planets in this method, take the one which is stronger in its own place, and which has more dignities in the Ascendant or in the luminary of the time, and judge as before.

[7] In all the methods, it is appropriate for you to look at the significator, [to see] which of its own houses it aspects, and to judge the thought according to this.[17] But if all planets were cadent, take the one from the cadents which had greater dignity in the Ascendant, and take it as the significator, and see which one of its own houses it aspects, and judge according to this and according to its distribution [in the houses] and its dignity in heaven.

3. *Skilled* I.11: On the knowledge of the querent's thinking, and if there were many questions

[The querent's thought]

[1] Al-Kindī says:[18] if you wanted to know the querent's thought, count the degrees which are from the lord of the hour up to the degree of the Sun, and project what comes out from the beginning of Aries, and the thought will be in the place where the number is ended: and judge [the thought] according to the nature of the sign and its lord.

[2] Others[19] say that there are nine significators of thought in the Ascendant, and three outside the Ascendant. [Of] the ones which are in the Ascendant, they name the lord of the house, the lord of the exaltation, the lord of the triplicity, the lord of its bound, the lord of the face, the lord of its ninth-part, its victor, and the planet to which the degree of the Ascendant goes, and the planet which is found in the Ascendant. But the planets which

---

[16] *Partitionem.* That is, its place in the houses (not the predictive method of distributions).

[17] Reading this sentence with 1485, which is much clearer and reflects a method well used by al-Kindī (see my Introduction to *Forty Chapters*, §4 topic 5).

[18] This is probably not al-Kindī (it is certainly not in *Forty Chapters*). Moreover, I believe the calculation here is probably wrong: in Leopold's version (Appendix G, below), the distance is projected from the Ascendant, which makes more sense than Aries.

[19] Al-Rijāl must be referring to *Thought* and OHT §2, attributed to Māshā'allāh (see Appendix C, below).

are outside the Ascendant are: the Lot of Fortune and its lord, the lord of the hour, and the lord of the house of the Sun (in the day), [but] the lord of the house of the Moon (in the night). Therefore, of all of these, consider which has more and firmer dignities, and greater dominion in the figure: because that one will be the significator of the thought.

[3] Valens says: Multiply the degrees of the Ascendant by the number of the past hours of the day or night, and project what comes out from the place of the luminary of the time (namely, from the Sun if it were in the day, or from the Moon if it were in the night), and where the number is ended, the thought will be there—which you will judge according to nature of that sign and lord. And know that the applications of the first indicate a thought, and that of the second indicate a question.[20]

[4] Hermes says: First, know the ascending degree at the hour of the question, and after that seek the significator from the lords of the dignities of the ascending sign, and from the luminaries and the Lot of Fortune, and all of their virtues: because the most true and perfect signification of the significator exists among these when it has dominion in the nature of the thing.[21]

Nor[22] should you be deceived by a planet in which you saw many testimonies,[23] but look at the one which has dominion in its own greater motion,[24] or the one which has dominion in the Ascendant of the revolution of the luminaries,[25] or the one which has dominion over the revolution of the greater conjunction,[26] or the one which has dominion in the revolution of [year of] the world,[27] and the rest of the other significations, in the way it is said in the *Book of Conjunctions*.[28] Because the one which has some one of

---

[20] This sentence clearly distinguishes thoughts from questions, but I am not sure what parts of the instructions refer to each.
[21] This must mean, "if it is also the natural significator," such as if it is a question about wealth, and Jupiter is both the natural significator and the most authoritative lord of the places mentioned.
[22] Cf. a similar list in *OHT* §6 (in Appendix C below).
[23] This could mean "dignities," but might also refer to a planet which is being applied to by many planets.
[24] I am not sure what this means.
[25] This probably means, "at the moment of the conjunction or opposition which preceded the consultation."
[26] This probably means either "at the moment of the Saturn-Jupiter conjunction" or "at the Aries ingress for the year in which there was a Saturn-Jupiter conjunction."
[27] That is, in the chart of the Sun's most recent Aries ingress.
[28] Unknown to me at this time.

these rulerships is put first in signification, over and above one having many testimonies.

[When there are many questions]

[1] Dorotheus says:[29] If you have many questions, take the first one from the Ascendant, the second from the Midheaven, the third from the eleventh house, the fourth from the fifth [house], the fifth from the seventh [house], the sixth and seventh from the angle of the earth, and the eighth from the ninth house.

[2] Others say: You will take the first question from the Ascendant, the second one from the second house, and the third from the third, and thusly until you finally reach the twelfth house.

[3] Others say:[30] Take the first question from the first application which the Moon has, the second from the next one, and so on up to the end of the questions.

[4] Others claim that it works if you take the first question from the lord of the first hour, the second from the lord of the second hour, and the third from the lord of the third hour, and thusly up to the end of the questions ([whether they are] few or many).

But it is good that you should inquire and apply yourself if you wish to find it, with the guidance of God.[31]

---

[29] This virtually duplicates the Dorothean order of the houses which receive points according to Chs. I.3.4 and III.1.1 above. All of these places are the Ascendant or aspect the Ascendant; note that the places in aversion to the Ascendant are omitted, as is the third (which has an ambiguous position in such rankings of houses).

[30] Namely, Sahl in *On Quest.* §13.14.

[31] One might indeed need God's help, with such an array of contrasting opinions.

4. *Skilled* (*passim*): House-specific advice on interpreting thoughts

[2nd house]:[32] And if, in a question, a fiery sign and the thought of the querent were in this house (that is, if the significator of the thought were in it), judge that the question is about assets. But if it were earthen, you should say that it is about entering into a city; if airy, about attendants;[33] if watery, about livelihood[34] and profit.

[5th house]:[35] And if, in questions of this house, the significator of thoughts happened [to be in it], and a fiery sign would be in it, it signifies a legation. But if an earthy sign were in it, it signifies the seeds of vegetation, and the returns of fields; and if it were airy, it signifies children; and if it were watery, it signifies gifts and drinks.

[6th house]:[36] Moreover, if the sign of this house in a question were fiery, and the significator of the question were in it, the question is about fear; but if earthy, the question is about a thing which has escaped; if airy, it is about a slave or captive; if watery, it is about a sick person.

[7th house]:[37] Moreover, if the question were about some thing demanded, and the thought of the querent fell in this house, you should know that this house—by its own nature and proper quality—signifies women, adversaries, and the place which someone absent goes to, and the place of a robber, and theft. Moreover, if in a question of this house you found a fiery sign, and the significator of the question and thought were in it, say that the question is about adversaries, enemies, or people speaking against him; and if you found an earthy sign in it, say that it is a question about a theft; and if you found an airy sign there, say that it is about a woman; and if you found a watery sign there, say that the question is about an absent man.

[8th house]:[38] Moreover, if a fiery sign were in this house in questions, and the thought of the querent were in it, the question is about inheritances; if earthy, the question is about a dead person; if airy, the question is about the Devil, or about a tough and bold evildoer and giant; if watery, the question is

---

32 *Skilled* I.24.
33 *Satellitibus*. 1485 reads: "those who serve" (*sargentibus*), the root of the English "sergeant."
34 Or, "one's means of subsistence" (*victu*).
35 *Skilled* I.40.
36 *Skilled* II.1.
37 *Skilled* II.13.
38 *Skilled* III.1.

about a man's assets—because the Ascendant always belongs to the querent, and the seventh to him about whom it is asked.[39]

[9th house]:[40] Therefore, when a question from these things has been presented to you, and you wanted to know the querent's thought, and you found the significator of thought in this house, and it were a fiery sign, say that the question is legal or sacred, and about prayers; if earthy, it is about travel or [something] of this sort; if airy, it is about the sciences and wisdom; if watery, it is about a rulership far from his status, or to which something has happened. And if you found Jupiter to be the significator of the querent's question, [and] in this house, judge that the question is about having a dream. And if you wanted to know what it is, look to see from what planet Jupiter is separating, or the one which is being separated from him, and judge the vision according to the nature and proper quality of that planet.

[10th house]:[41] So if the thought of the querent about some matter were in this house, and a fiery sign [was] in it, judge that the question was about the king; if earthy, about the commerce of a man and his profession; if airy, about slaves; if watery, about his enemies.

[11th house]:[42] If, in questions, you found the significator of thought in his house, and it were a fiery sign, say that the question is about a matter in which he has trust, and about a thing which he fears he will not have. But if it were a watery sign, say that the question is about fortune; just as if [it were] airy, about friends; and if earthy, about ancestors.[43]

[12th house]:[44] And if it happened in questions that the significator of the question is in this house, and it is a fiery sign, the question was about misery and pain; and if earthy, about prison or a captive; and if watery, about beasts; and if airy, about enemies.

---

[39] Al-Rijāl is pointing out that the eighth is the second (assets) from the seventh (another person).
[40] *Skilled* III.3.
[41] *Skilled* III.19.
[42] *Skilled* III.27.
[43] *Antecessoribus.* This signification does not really make sense to me.
[44] *Skilled* III.33.

5. *Skilled* I.5.2: On disagreements over significators of the chart

Likewise, they disagree in understanding the significator.

[1] Because Ptolemy[45] says that the significator (which is called the "victor")[46] is the planet having greater power in the degree of the Ascendant, and in the two luminaries, and in the conjunction and opposition. And if it did not have this, the significator will be a diurnal planet appearing in the day above the earth, and in the night below the earth (or a nocturnal planet appearing in the night above the earth, and in the day below the earth).[47] And if it did not have this, the significator will be the planet nearer the Sun.

[2] Dorotheus[48] says that the significator is the planetary ruler over the degree of the Ascendant, and over the luminaries, and [over] the Lot of Fortune. And if it did not have this, the significator will be the planet nearer the Moon (before and after [her]), because that is the planet to which the Moon goes first, or from whom she separates.[49]

[3] And in this opinion, Hermes agrees with Dorotheus.[50]

[4] Valens[51] said that the significator is the planet which was eastern from the lord of the Ascendant,[52] and western from the lord of the seventh, and that every such planet is a significator. But if such a one was not found there, we should look to the angles: and the planet found there, having some dignity in the Ascendant, is the significator. Which if none of this kind were found there, one should look to the planet which will first go to the degree of the Ascendant by the motion of the firmament, and not by the advancement of the planets through the signs,[53] and that one will be the significator.

---

[45] I believe this is a pseudo-Ptolemy (for the releasers, probably based on longevity material in *Tet.* III.11), perhaps combined with some thoughts about sect and solar phase from *Tet.* III.3 (see Appendix H below).

[46] Lat. *almutez*.

[47] A planet in this condition is said to be in its *ḥalb* (see *ITA* III.2).

[48] Probably a pseudo-Dorotheus.

[49] This is evidently referring to statements such as *Carmen* V.5.24 and V.5.28. The idea is that the most recent separation or next application will reveal the circumstances of the question, just as Hermann says about the significator in Ch. I.6.3.

[50] See also below, where Hermes and Dorotheus are said to agree. According to Pingree (*Carmen* p. *vii*), this is a confusion arising from the fact that Dorotheus was addressing a student whom he named Hermes (following a mystical tradition). It would be easy to confuse such an addressee with the legendary Hermes Trismegistus.

[51] Source unknown at this time.

[52] This sentence is very close to *Carmen* III.1.12.

[53] That is, not by transit but by primary or diurnal motion. This will be the one which rises on the horizon next, or in other words to whose body the Ascendant is directed first.

[5] The philosopher[54] who made the book of examples says that the significator is taken from three schemes, each one after the other (and they are the angles, succeedents, and cadents from the angles). And you should focus your mind and look at the status of him for whom you are looking: which if he were a king, you would look for him from a shining planet which has dignity in the angles, and especially rulership in the Midheaven, and in the day over the Sun and in the night over the Moon: and that planet will be the significator. Which if the man for whom you are looking were of the middle [classes], you should look for him from a planet which has dignity and rulership in the succeedents, and especially the one which has dignity in the eleventh house, and over the Sun in the day and over the Moon in the night: and that one will be the significator. And if the man for whom you are looking were of the lower [classes], look for him from the planet which has dignity and rulership in the cadents, and especially if it has dignity in the twelfth house, and over the Sun in the day and the Moon in the night: and that will be the significator.

[6] Māshā'allāh[55] says that we should look to the significator and understand it from the two squares of the Moon and her opposition: because if you found a planet with the Moon, or in her square or opposition, which would have dignity in the Ascendant or in the sign in which the Moon is, that will be the significator. And if you did not find a planet in this manner, consider the Moon: if she is aspecting some one of the planets having dignity in the Ascendant, that planet will be the significator. Which if the Moon aspected no planet which has dignity in the Ascendant, the Moon herself will be the significatrix.

[7] ['Umar] al-Tabarī[56] says that the significator is the planetary ruler over the degree of the Ascendant and the one which has greater dignities in that degree; and if none were this, the planetary significator will be the one which will first go out of the sign in which it is, into another sign.

---

[54] Unknown at this time. Note that this approach reflects the notion (in Sahl's *On Elect.* and elsewhere) that the value of questions and elections depends on the status and nativity of the client. If the client is successful or has an eminent nativity, then his or her choices and questions will be accordingly powerful and are signified through planets ruling the most important places of the chart; the opposite would be true for people who are low-class or have weak nativities.

[55] This closely resembles *Carmen* III.1.10-14, and may be based on Māshā'allāh's own translation of *Carmen.* But note that this section of *Carmen* is on longevity (and favors bound lords), and so is another example of adopting natal material for use in questions.

[56] Source unknown at this time.

6. *Skilled* I.10: On the knowledge of the victor of the conjunction and opposition

The conjunction of the Sun and Moon was in 15° 10' Virgo, around the tenth hour of the night,[57] and I looked at the significators of Virgo, and I found Mercury to be the lord of the house and the lord of the exaltation, and the Moon to be the lady of the triplicity (for the conjunction was at night), and Venus the lady of the bound. And Mercury was the victor over Virgo and that degree, because he was the lord of the house and the lord of the exaltation. Therefore, because the Moon was the lady of the triplicity there, Mercury was the victor over her, because she was in his house; likewise, Mercury was the victor over Venus (who is the lord of the bound), because Venus was in the house of Mercury. Likewise, Mercury was the victor over the two luminaries, because both were in his house. Seek the victor over the Ascendant and over the other houses in this way.

And I hold that if the lord of the hour were in one of the angles, and the Moon cadent from an angle, and likewise the lord of the Ascendant, it will be the significator through itself, and the one to which it applies, and the one which approaches the house in which it is. For I speak thusly: when the significator of a question gives its own virtue to another planet, the one which receives the management will be the victor; and if that receiver gives its own virtue to another, that other one (namely, the receiver of the receiver) will be the victor. And if in this matter there were three or more, the last receiver will be the victor—except that if a giver were strong and the receiver weak, then [the last planet] does not receive its power but returns it.[58] And understand thusly in all questions.

---

[57] This would probably have made Leo rising.
[58] This is the "returning" of light. See *ITA* III.19, which lays out specific conditions for returning.

7. *Skilled* I.9.1: The significator of the question and the querent according to ʿUmar al-Tabarī[59]

[Primary significators]

You should know that the querent's victor with respect to himself, or for the thing which he seeks, or for a matter which is between him and another, is the lord of the Ascendant—if it aspected the Ascendant. But if it were cadent from the Ascendant,[60] look at the Moon: which if she aspected the Ascendant, take her as the significator of the querent. And take the lord of the seventh house as the significator of that about which it is asked, if it aspects the seventh house: which if it does not aspect the seventh house, take the lord of the house of the Moon as the significator.

Which if the Moon did not aspect the Ascendant either, but she was departing from one planet [and going] toward another, take the planet from which she is departing as the significator of the querent, and the planet toward which the Moon advances will be the significator of the one about which it is asked.

But if the lord of the Ascendant were cadent from the Ascendant, and did not aspect it, and the Moon did not do so either, and the Moon is not departing from some planet, nor is she being conjoined to another, take the Moon herself as the significatrix of the querent, and the lord of her house as the significator of the one about whom it is asked. And if the Moon—in this situation—were in her own dignity, take her as the significatrix of the querent, and the lord of the triplicity in which she is as the significator of the one about whom it is asked.

But if there were a planet bearing[61] the light of the lord of the Ascendant to the lord of the seventh, or one who collects it between the Moon and any of the other planets, take that planet as the significator of the one about whom it is asked, and the Moon as the significator of the querent.

---

[59] This is al-Rijāl's version of ʿUmar's view, as also found in *Judges* §0.4 (see Appendix D below). It is on choosing the significators for an explicit horary question, and is very close to Māshā'allāh's view in his *On Reception* (in *WSM*).
[60] That is, in aversion to it.
[61] That is, "transferring." See *ITA* III.11.

[Secondary significators]

And help yourself in the significator of the querent, from the planets which were peregrine [and] in the Ascendant (that is, which did not have some dignity in the Ascendant) and from the lord of the Ascendant, even if it does not aspect the Ascendant. And likewise reinforce yourself with respect to the significator of the one about whom it is asked, from peregrine planets in the seventh house, and [from] its lord, even if it does not aspect it.

8. *Skilled* I.9.2: The victor according to others

[1] [Al-Kindī says]:[62] The planet over the querent and that about which it is sought, and the quaesited matter, is the one having more dignities in that house; and [also], the planet which is of the nature of the question, and the Lot which signifies the question, and the lord of the hour.

[2] [Al-Kindī says]:[63] And the significator of the querent is the planet having more dignities in the five releasers: which are the Sun and Moon, the Ascendant, the Lot of Fortune, and the place of the conjunction or opposition preceding the question. The dignities are had in this way: the lord of the house has 5 dignities, the lord of the exaltation 4, the lord of the bound 3, the lord of the triplicity 2, the lord of the face 1.

[3] ['Umar] al-Tabarī says[64] that the victor is the significator—namely, the planet which rules in the nature of the question, and the planet having more dignities there (as, the lord of the house and the lord of the exaltation, and the lord of the bound, triplicity, and face). Some of [the older authorities] give one dignity to the lord of the hour, just as to the lord of the face.

When you wanted to learn this, first you will look to the lord of the Ascendant, and you will give him privilege and strength, and if perhaps in addition to its rulership in the Ascendant it had the exaltation or bound, or triplicity or face,[65] you will take it as the significator, and you will call it the

---

[62] This is the victor over the topic from *Forty Chapters* Ch. 3.1.

[63] This is the weighted victor over the querent (taken from all releasing places), from *Forty Chapters* Ch. 3.2. Note that the points assigned to the lords of the bound and triplicity are 3 and 2 respectively, whereas in later authors like al-Qabīsī and ibn Ezra they are 2 and 3 respectively.

[64] Cf. *Judges* §0.3 (in Appendix D) for this entire opinion of 'Umar's.

[65] For example, if the degree of the Ascendant were not only in Scorpio (ruled by Mars), but also in Mars's bound.

victor, and no other significator will have sharing nor partnership with it. But if you found the lord of the Ascendant in one of the four angles (and especially in the Midheaven), even if it has no dominion in [its place] besides [having] the domicile of the Ascendant,[66] still it will be the significator, and none will participate with it in the signification, unless perhaps there were another planet which has the exaltation, bound, and triplicity in the Ascendant, and it were likewise in an angle: then *that* planet will have a signification with the lord of the Ascendant in [its] signification. And this will be [so], if the lord of the Ascendant were *not* remote from the degree of the angle, up to 3°. For if the lord of the Ascendant were remote by more than 3°, and the other planet with three dignities were in that very degree of the angle, the one which occupies the degrees of the angle will be stronger, and it will have its own separate signification.

In addition, if the lord of the Ascendant had no dignity [where it was], nor were it in an angle, then that lord of three dignities will be stronger, if it is appearing at the beginning of [its] sign. But if it were at the end of the sign, a lord of two dignities will be stronger than it, if it appeared as the lord of the bound [or][67] exaltation [or] triplicity: for the lord of the face is weak in this, unless it [also] has rulership in the domicile in which the Sun is (by day) or the Moon (in the night), or unless it was the lord of the hour.

And you should know that the angles are the roots of significations, and their lords are strengthened through them, and they are weakened by being cadent.[68]

If the lord of the house of the Sun (in the day) and the lord of the house of the Moon (in the night), or the lord of the hour, were equal in strength, the significator will be the lord of the house of the Sun in the day, and the lord of the house of the Moon in the night, or the lord of the hour at that hour.

And judge [the chart] by coming to know the significator and its motion, until you know the signification—if it pertains to one planet, or two, or more than two. And if you had two planets equal in strength, and partners in the signification, and you doubted whose signification it was, consider whether the Moon would incline herself to one of them, with her appearing in the Ascendant [and] in her own domicile; or whether the planet is the lord of the

---

[66] Reading this phrase more with *Judges* §0.3.
[67] Reading *aut* ("or") for *et* ("and"), with the logic of the sentence.
[68] Lit., falling (*casus*).

bound of the Sun (in the day) or of the Moon (in the night), or whether it is the lord of the Lot of Fortune: for such [a planet] has greater strength than the other, and it will be the victor, especially if it were in its own domain.[69]

An even greater power is if the Moon applied to it from the Ascendant: afterwards, the dominion will belong to whichever of the two planets was firmer,[70] especially if the Moon applied to it just as we said before.

Even the Lot of Fortune has power in the signification or the question, in nocturnal questions.

Then,[71] look to see to whom the significator would be adjoining itself in the sign in which it is, or which one of the others inclines itself to it: because the applications are according to the quantity of the lights of the planets (which are their rays). The lights of the infortunes even disturb and harm questions, in the way the lights of the fortunes make them active and hasten them. But the lights of the planets are those which we have already said before.[72]

[4] Al-Khayyāt[73] said that the victor is taken from the lord of the Ascendant and from the planet giving its power[74] to it, and from its place in the figure.

[5] Antiochus,[75] Dorotheus, and Valens said that the victor is taken from the Lot of Fortune and its lord, and from the place in which it is.

[6] [Al-Rijāl:] But I say that if a planet would put itself in the house of another planet, the lord of that house will be the victor in the nature of that house. For example, if the Ascendant were Aries, and its lord Mars in Capricorn, then Saturn is the victor over Mars. And if each of them were in the house of its associate, and they were equal in dignities, the firmer of them

---

[69] See *ITA* III.2.
[70] That is, "angular." But I do not see how this differs from the previous paragraph, in which the Moon already applies to one of them from the Ascendant.
[71] This paragraph is interpretive, telling us what to do once we have found the significator. It resembles *Forty Chapters* Ch. 2.1.1, and *Search* Chs. I.3 and I.6.2-6.3.
[72] Al-Rijāl is referring to *Skilled* I.6, in which he gives different opinions about planetary orbs (but since this view comes from 'Umar, it must refer to a similar passage in his work). Al-Rijāl prefers the unequal medieval orbs endorsed by Sahl (in his *Introduct.* §5.3), in which the Sun gets 15° on each side, the Moon 12°, Saturn and Jupiter 9°, Mars 8°, and Venus and Mercury 7°.
[73] Source unknown at this time, but surely part of al-Khayyāt's book on questions (much of which is contained in *Judges*).
[74] This sounds like "pushing power" (see *ITA* III.16).
[75] This is from *OHT* §2, and is on finding the significator of thought. But in *OHT*, the place of the Lot itself (not its lord) shows the topic of the thought.

in the house is the victor.[76] And likewise, that one of them which is closer to the degree of an angle, is the victor. And if they were equal in the number of degrees [from] the angle, the one which was closer to the degree of the east is the victor. And if they were equal in the eastern situation, the one which was closer to the degree of the Sun is the victor. And if they were equal in the degree neighboring the Sun, that one of them which was in the angle[77] is the victor. And if they were equal in the angle, that one of them which had more dignities is the victor. And a lord of two dignities conquers a lord of one: for example, let two victors be in the angle, and let the angle be the house or exaltation or triplicity [of them]: the lord of the house conquers the lord of the exaltation, and the lord of the exaltation conquers the lord of the triplicity.

When a luminary puts itself in some sign, it strengthens the lord of that sign: if the luminaries are in the house of some planet, the strength goes to the lord of the house. [But] if a planet is in the house of some luminary, the strength goes to the luminary. (A planet is even weakened when equalizing itself[78] with the luminaries.) For example, [if] the Ascendant is Leo, and both the luminaries are already in Taurus, the signification belongs to Venus, because she is the lady of the house of the lord of the Ascendant, and the lady of the house of the Moon.

---

[76] This does not really make sense, since if Mars were in Capricorn but Saturn in Aries, then Saturn would be in fall and less desirable under any circumstances (unless al-Rijāl is suggesting we adopt his triplicity rulership in fiery signs, or in his bound, as substitutes). The point is that if two planets are equal in dignities, then the more angular one (the "firmer" one) will be dominant.

[77] But according to the previous sentences, each is already equally in an angle, or is equally angular.

[78] I think this means that when a luminary and a planet are roughly equal in their claims to be the significator, the luminary wins.

APPENDIX B: SAHL BIN BISHR'S *ON QUESTIONS*

1. *On Questions* §1.9: A chapter on the corruption[1]
of the Ascendant (*excerpt*)[2]

And it is not good that this should be missing from it in nativities (and likewise questions). And indeed it corrupts questions, and corrupts the life of the native. Indeed Māshā'allāh, cutting off hidden things from this…[3] And it is that you should look at [1] the star leading[4] or conquering in nativities and questions, and at [2] the star with which the lord of the Ascendant or the lord of the matter is joined,[5] or [3] the one to whom the Moon is joined, when[6] the Moon is the partner of the lord of the Ascendant—or it is [4] the one leading or conquering over the Ascendant and its lord and the lord of[7] the matter in a question.

2. *On Questions* §13.18: On the significations
of the hours of the planets in questions[8]

These are the three partitions of the hours:

The first is divided into three parts: he who comes in the first part (belonging to the hour of the Sun) asks for the king or for [his] master or a man or a great evil whence he has great fear; in the middle [part], either on account of a great fear or an infirm person; in the end [part], about his livelihood or merchant business, and acquiring.

---

[1] Reading *corruptione* for *coniunctione*.

[2] This section does not appear in the *BN* manuscript.

[3] This sentence fragment has no clear operative verb, and I am not sure of its function besides saying that Māshā'allāh has something to do with this doctrine.

[4] Reading *ducentem* for *lucentem*. In Arabic, the verb "to indicate" or "to signify" also means to "lead one's attention to." Hence, translators such as Hugo frequently refer to significators as "leaders."

[5] Reading *iunctus* for *iunctas*.

[6] *Quando.* One might expect *cum*, "since," since the Moon is generally one of the significators of the querent as well.

[7] Or perhaps, "house of the matter," which sounds more correct.

[8] This section does not appear in the *BN* manuscript, and the Latin style has changed. It is probably an addition by a later author.

In the first part of the hour of Venus, he asks you about the taking of a wife or about the cares of women; in the middle [part], about the vestments of women or their decoration; in the end [or third part], for a reason which is being born or a friendship which cannot come to pass.

In the first part of the hour of Mercury, for a legal case[9] or personal fortune,[10] or something engraved;[11] in the middle [part], for a fit vestment or for the soul of the one asking; in the end [or third part], because of loss.

In the first part of the hour of the Moon, for moving from place to place, or for an infirm person, or for something which has a blemish on it;[12] in the middle [part], for a reason which went out of his hand and is not returning, or for a man who comes from the road, or a beast, or for a man who is dying; in the end [or third part], for something going to be completed or because of something which is born of the earth.

In the first part of the hour of Saturn, because of a fleeing slave (if you are worried about him, [whether] he will return);[13] in the middle, for a strong man or an association which he wants to make, or he wants to walk from place to place, or some petition; at the end, for a bad cause whence he has already escaped.

In the first part of the hour of Jupiter, he comes to ask you with a particular name[14] or something public;[15] in the middle, for a vestment to be fitted, or for an infirm person to be healed;[16] at the end, for a man who made money and is now losing from his personal fortune.

In the first part of the hour of Mars,[17] stolen property [that is] red or gold or copper, or a vestment; in the middle, for an infirm person, especially one injured (perhaps by heat);[18] at the end, because of some deception or a purpose that is worked in fire.

---

9 *Causata.* My phrase "legal case" is somewhat speculative.
10 Reading *avere* or *avero* for *avo.*
11 *Causa sculpta.*
12 Perhaps because the Moon's craters appear as blemishes or smears to the naked eye?
13 *Si fatigas pro eo [utrum] revertitur.*
14 *Proprio nomine.* This could also mean he comes on behalf of an important person.
15 *Aliquod forum.* Perhaps, "market goods."
16 Reading *sanari* for *sanati.*
17 Omitting a word that appears to be *primo.*
18 *Afflicto vel calore.*

APPENDIX C: MATERIAL ATTRIBUTED
TO MĀSHĀʾALLĀH

1. *On the Interpretation of Thought*[1] (excerpt)

Māshāʾallāh instructs that you should establish the Ascendant by its degree and minute, and the houses, most precisely. And he said that questions come to be[2] in three ways:[3]

First, for what reason the questioner has come, so that you might know [it] and about what he is asking.

Second, that you should know what was the cause of the question.

Third, that you should know whether it might be perfected or not, and what end it will have.[4]

Therefore, if you wished to know this, first know the significator according to what I will tell you—the knowledge of which is that you should look at:[5] [1] the Ascendant and [2] its lord, and at [3] the Moon, and [4] the lord of her house, [5] (the Sun, too, and the lord of his house),[6] and [6] the lord

---

[1] In my 2008 *WSM*, I called this "The Interpretation of Cognition." It is probably the work in eight books (!) which is attributed to Hermes in the Prologue to Māshāʾallāh's *Book of Aristotle* (in *PN I*), which is described as being about "what new thing the mind deliberated on inwardly, and what endings that deliberation would have; and, if a matter is really going to be, how it would come to be; but if not, how and for what reason it would be prevented from being in the future." Indeed, both Hermann and Leopold recognize that this material and the chart accompanying it (see Ch. I.7 above, and Appendix G) properly belongs to Hermes, though it was used by many later astrologers.
[2] Reading *fiunt* for *sint*.
[3] The "reason" is shown by the condition and the nature of the significator; the "cause" is shown by the planet the significator separates from; the "end" is shown by the planet to which it is being joined. See the last paragraph of this section: it is just like the "two circumstances" of the question in *Search* Ch. I.6.3.
[4] Heller reads these differently, but is not much more helpful in making sense of the different causes: "First, that you should know the cause, concerning which he is asking; second, what cause impelled him; third, that you should know whether the matter would be perfected or not, and what end it is going to have."
[5] Note that Māshāʾallāh gives two slightly different lists, here and a few paragraphs below.
[6] Below, Māshāʾallāh clarifies that this is in diurnal charts.

of the hour, and [7] the Lot of Fortune. And operate through the one which had more authorities[7] and was in a better place. Which if you did not find something of those which I told you, look at the lord of the Ascendant or the lord of its exaltation, also the lord of the bound and the triplicity and the face—and know which one of these is stronger in the Ascendant by the multitude of its dignities.

And you would look, and you would establish this one as the significator, if it were in a good place. (And the goodness of a place is that it is in one of its own dignities, or in a good place from the Sun, or in the angles, free from the bad ones). Therefore, operate through the one which is stronger and had more dignities and was in a better place.

And know that the lord of the Ascendant, if it were in the Ascendant, is more worthy,[8] more so than the rest. Which[9] if it were [not][10] in the Ascendant, and the lord of the exaltation of the Ascendant were in it, that one will be the sole significator. But if both were in the Ascendant, they will both be partners. If however one of them had, in addition, another dignity, and it were stronger by place, it will be the significator and be more worthy. If some planet which had a dignity in the Ascendant would be joined to one of them, or the Moon were in the house of one of them and she were joined to it[11]—if it were so, that one will be the significator on account of the multitude of dignities. Which [if] it were not in the Ascendant, [seek][12] the significator or the Moon or a planet which was in the Ascendant or in the rest of the angles, and was stronger than the rest in the figure.[13]

And know that each sign has a lord, and ascends within two hours, and many things can be asked in them. And if the lord of the Ascendant had been the significator of all things, [then] all things asked under the same sign would be all good or all bad according to the signification of the lord of the

---

[7] See *OHT* §6, below.

[8] Omitting *ascendente illo*.

[9] Heller's text reads rather differently for the rest of this paragraph: "Which if it were not in the Ascendant, and the lord of the exaltation of the Ascendant were in it, it will be the sole significator and be more worthy; and you would look thus at the one which was stronger in the circle by the multitude of dignities, even if it were not in the Ascendant or in the rest of the angles, and it was stronger than the rest in the sign."

[10] Adding *non* with Heller, else these sentences would not make sense.

[11] This would be a case of pushing nature or what I call "classical reception" (see *ITA* III.15 and III.25).

[12] Reading *quaere*.

[13] Note the similarity to 'Umar's view in *Judges* §0.3 (in Appendix D below) and *Skilled* I.9.2 (in Appendix A above).

Ascendant—but it is not so. Likewise, the Moon is being joined to some planet throughout the whole day, and throughout the greatest part of the day, but the significations[14] of matters are diverse in that same day: because certain ones of them are effected, but certain ones not. Wherefore, it is necessary for us always to seek the significator.[15]

Therefore, know which one is the significator, and I will tell you out of which ones you should choose—namely, out of: [1] the lord of the Ascendant, and [2] the Moon, and [3] the lord of her house, [4] (and from the Sun, too, in the day, and from the lord of his house), and from [5] the house of the Lot of Fortune, and from [6] a planet which was in the angles (and especially in the Ascendant or in the Midheaven), the one which was stronger in the figure.

And know that a more truthful intention is one which the questioner has had in his heart for one day and night,[16] or more.

Therefore, if you found the significator, and you wished to know the cause of the question—that is, whence the question has arisen—look to see from whom the planetary significator of the intention is being separated. And know that the cause of the intention would be according to the nature of the planet from whom the significator is separated. And if you wished to know the end of the intention, know to whom the significator is being joined. And know how the end of the intention will be through the signification of the planet to whom it is being joined.

2. *On Hidden Things* §2: On discovering the significator

A chapter on the knowledge of the significators of an intention, from the diverse sayings of the ancients.

Know[17] that the intention will be more accessible if his thought retained it in his heart for one day and night (or more). But[18] if he did not know how to

---

[14] Omitting *significatorem*.
[15] This also helps to explain various instructions on how to handle multiple questions: see *Search* Ch. I.10 above, and al-Rijāl's list in his Ch. I.11 (in Appendix A above).
[16] That is, for 24 hours. See the second paragraph of *OHT* §2 below.
[17] This sentence is also reflected in *Thought*, above. Note that in *Thought*, the querent's thought is more "truthful" after waiting, whereas here it is more "accessible."
[18] This is similar to statements in *Judges* §0.1, in which Māshā'allāh suggests that people who are insincere or want to trick the astrologer will have difficulty even forming a

ask about his intention, you[19] would not be able to find the significator of the question, because the circle will be according to the intention of the one asking, and according to the thought of his heart. Therefore, [if] he who asked you [did so] well, you will not go astray—but not every man knows how to ask.

And now I will tell you something about the intention, inasmuch as[20] if the questioner asked well, you will not go astray, if God wills. This is what I have found to be stronger, concerning the significations:

[1] Now you should establish [1a] the lord of the Ascendant as the first significator, and [1b] the planet which receives its management, because the intention will be according to the lord of the Ascendant's place in the circle, or according to the place of the reception of management (from out of the circle)—that is, the signification of the intention is taken from these places.[21] The intention is also found from that same ascending degree: that is, that you should look to see [1c] to what planet the degree of the Ascendant is being joined, because the intention will be according to that planet's place in the circle. Nor should you overlook [1d] a planet which is in the Ascendant, if it were not remote from the degree of the Ascendant: because the intention or thought will be according to the nature[22] of that same planet. Therefore, look to see of what house of the circle [that] planet[23] is lord of, because the intention will be according to that house [of its own] which it aspected.[24]

[2] Also, the second significator is according to Dorotheus[25] and Antiochus and Ptolemy and Valens: this is that you should look at the sign in which the Lot of Fortune is, because the intention will be according to the nature[26] of that same house from the Ascendant. That is, if it were in the Ascendant, the question will be about himself; and if it were in the second, it

---

question. Likewise, both there and in *Judges* §0.2 (by 'Umar), it is suggested that the chart itself will display evidence of confusion and insincerity in the client's mind.

[19] Reading *potueris* for *potuerit*.

[20] Reading *quatenus* for *quatinus*.

[21] In other words, the house in which the lord of the Ascendant is, or the one in which the other planet is, will indicate the thought.

[22] *Substantiam.*

[23] I.e., the one near the degree of the Ascendant.

[24] That is, see which of its domiciles it aspects, by a whole-sign aspect. The shortcoming of this approach in whole signs is that it does not allow a planet in the Ascendant to indicate 12th, 2nd, 8th, or 6th house matters, since by definition those houses are in aversion to the rising sign.

[25] See Hermann's independent citation of this view (attributed to Dorotheus), in Ch. I.9.1 above, and al-Rijāl's variation in *Skilled* I.9.2 (Appendix A above).

[26] *Substantiam.*

will be about assets; and if it were in the third, it will be [about] his brother; and thus concerning the remaining twelve signs.[27]

[3] The third significator is according to the Indians, who said if you were asked about some matter which he was concealing from you, look at the lord of the dignity of the degree of the Ascendant, and at the lord of its bound or face (that is, the one which is stronger), and see to whom it is being joined. Because what he was concealing from you will be according to[28] that.

[4] And[29] what is stronger than all of these is that you should look at the twelve-degrees[30] of the degree of the Ascendant—upon which sign they fell. Which if the lord of that same sign were there, or another planet were there, the intention will be according to the place of that house in the circle. If however you did not find a planet in that place, look to see where the lord of that house is: because the intention will be according to the twelfth-[part] of the Ascendant from the Ascendant, and according to its lord. An example of which is this: that the Ascendant was the twelfth degree of Aries, which, when I had projected two-and-a-half degrees for each sign, beginning from Aries (which was the Ascendant), the number was ended in Leo, which, from the Ascendant, is the domicile of children—in which neither the Sun nor another planet was journeying.[31] Therefore I looked at the Sun, whom I found in the seventh from the Ascendant. And I said that the question was about a child who sought a woman, wanting to take her as his wife. And if the Sun had been in the sixth, I would have said that he was seeking concerning an infirm child; and so on with the rest of the twelve signs.

---

[27] *Search* Ch. I.9.1 also includes material on the type of sign (such as being four-footed) and the bound of the Lot.

[28] *Apud.* That is, it will pertain to or belong to matters associated with that planet.

[29] According to Hermann in *Search* Ch. I.9.3., this is the second of the methods among the Indians.

[30] That is, the twelfth-part. See *ITA* IV.6, and Hermann's use of this example in *Search* Ch. I.9.3.

[31] *Peregrinus.*

3. *On Hidden Things* §6: According to "Ptolemy"

Ptolemy said[32] if the significator[33] aspected the Ascendant, the kind of the hidden thing will be of the nature of the Ascendant; and if it did not aspect it, it will be of the nature of the significator's place. And the lord of the hour signifies its color. And the place of the Moon signifies its time: which if she were above the earth, it will be newly buried; and if she were under the earth, it will be old. And from the lord of the Lot of Fortune is signified the length or shortness of the thing—that is, the length and shortness of the matter whence it was taken.[34] And from the lord of the bound of the degree of the fourth,[35] and from the lord of the Midheaven— that is, from the one of them which was in an angle—and from the lord of the bound of the Moon, is known its nature. (He wants the bound of Ptolemy to be understood here.)[36]

The significator of which Ptolemy speaks is not the lord of the Ascendant, nor [the lord of] the Moon,[37] nor one which was more worthy in the Ascendant—but rather the one to which are joined many strengths, namely, one who was more worthy in the Ascendant *and* in the places of the luminaries. And were it joined to no one,[38] that is, it did not commit its own management to another, and it were strong in its own place (or perhaps it were joined to another, and that other were joined to no one, and it were strong in its own place), such a one will be the significator of the intention and the thought. And the place in which it was, will signify the intention or thought:[39] and if it were in the tenth sign, the question will be about the king; and if it were in the house of foreign travel [it will be about foreign travel], and so on with the rest.

---

[32] Source unknown, but definitely a pseudo-Ptolemy. Cf. a similar list in *Search* II.3.2.
[33] See the next paragraph for the definition of the significator in this instance.
[34] I am not sure what distinction or clarification is being made here.
[35] That is, the degree of the IC itself.
[36] Lit., "the bound of Ptolemy wants to be understood here." This may be a comment by the Latin translator, or by the original compiler/author. At any rate, we are apparently supposed to use Ptolemy's bound rulerships when using Ptolemy's method.
[37] *Lunae.* But it could be a scribal error for *luna*, meaning simply "the Moon."
[38] Reading *nulli* for *ulli.*
[39] This description is reminiscent of Māshā'allāh's accounts in *On Reception* of which planet in a horary will have final disposition over the nature and outcome of a question. But compare this method with Māshā'allāh's other ways of determining the significator of the intention, as described in *Thought* and in *OHT* §2 above.

Also, for the increase of the strength of this significator, other authorities[40] for seeking this are namely that it should have dignity in the degree of the conjunction or the prevention which was before the question, and in the Ascendant of that same conjunction or prevention,[41] because then it will be stronger. Also, one must seek out whether it would have a power or dignity in the Ascendant of the revolution of that same year, and in the Ascendant of the lesser[42] conjunction (that is, in the present conjunction of Saturn and Jupiter), and in the sign to which the profection of that same year is coming.[43] Such a one, if it were strong in the figure (that is, if it were direct and free from every impediment, and it were in an angle, and had some dignity in that same place, and likewise in the Ascendant, and it were in the rest of its own praiseworthy conditions), it will be made fortunate, stronger than all of the planets, or more worthy than the others in signification.

Which [if] you were not able to have all of these (because such a one is rarely found), at least it should have a portion of them—that is, it should have a role in the Ascendant of the question, and in the places of the luminaries, and in the Ascendant or degree of the conjunction or the prevention just finished, and let it be strong in its own place in the figure (that is, let it be direct and strong, just as it is said concerning the strength of the planets), and let it lack every weakness, and let it be in an angle, and let it have [something] of those authorities[44] which we stated—that is, let it have a role in the Ascendant and in the places of the luminaries, or in the Ascendant of the revolution of the year, and in the Ascendant of the present conjunction of Saturn and Jupiter, or let it be the lord of the conjunction of the prevention just finished. (The lord of the conjunction or prevention is said to be the one which has dignity in the degree of the conjunction or the prevention, and in the sign which is ascending at the hour of the conjunction or the prevention—for this one, as the philosophers say, had authority in all

---

[40] The author does not mean astrological authorities, but planetary conditions that will give the *planet* more authority (see below).

[41] That is, the Ascendant of the chart cast for the moment of the conjunction or prevention itself.

[42] Reading *minoris*, but the text might also be read as *maioris* ("greater"), especially considering the following clause about the current Saturn-Jupiter conjunction (which is considered to be lesser than the conjunction signaling a change in triplicities).

[43] That is, the profection of the most recent Saturn-Jupiter conjunction. It would be amazing if a planet had to have so many testimonies—asking the astrologer about your missing watch does not seem like it should have import in relation to Saturn-Jupiter conjunctions.

[44] Reading *auctoritatibus* for *auctoribus*.

things which come to be in that same conjunction or prevention, and it must participate with the lord of the Ascendant in all questions which come to be [asked?][45] in that conjunction or prevention). And certain experts of the astrologers, if they found this one strong in an angle, they used to give it some[46] partnership. But they used to *judge* by it alone (and they used to declare their judgments true).[47] Such a one, therefore, to whom two or more of the aforesaid authorities were joined, and was in a good condition (as we said above) in the hour of the question, will be the significator of the philosophers. And there will be no doubt in all judgments that they are judged by it. And know that it is of the secrets of astronomy, and the ancient sages among the astrologers used to conceal this from the rest who were less learned in this Art.

---

[45] The *BN* manuscript has an unclear abbreviated word here.
[46] *Ullum.*
[47] Or perhaps, "and they used to profess true judgments of [these things]," in both cases treating *fitebant* as a version of *fateor.*

APPENDIX D: 'UMAR AL-TABARĪ ON VICTORS AND SIGNIFICATORS

1. *Judges* §0.3: On choosing the significator of the querent and the question[1]

Therefore, with these things having been managed by such a method, we should deal with the appropriate choosing of the useful and very necessary "leader" (or rather, "significator").

And so, the star specially embracing the signification of the quaesited matter is deservedly allotted the name of "leader" and "minister." And it is the one which obtains the most dignity in the place of the question, or whom the most testimonies support, from wherever.[2]

We enjoin [you] to pursue the establishment of this matter in such a way: namely that once the beginning is taken up from the lord of the house, 5 points are devoted to it: being stronger and more worthy, [and] engaged in the manifold gift of dignity, it is put before all the rest. From that one, the minister of the high command or sovereignty[3] holds second place, with 4 being taken. But the lord of the bound exceeds by 3. But the one who is in charge of the triplicity possesses twin dignities. On the other hand, the [planet] which is influential over the decan or face deserves to be enriched by only 1, because the signification of its leadership is weaker than of the others. Some astrologers even, wanting to ascribe a certain portion of dignity to the lord of the hour, seem to have strayed far from the opinion of certain others.[4]

Then, once this consideration is had, take note especially of the eastern lord (because this one signifies the querent), [since] a certain excellence and strength is ascribed to it. If it obtained the principal position of sovereignty or bound, triplicity or even decan (apart from its own proper dignity which it collects from the Ascendant), it will merit being enriched with the more excellent benefit of leadership, wholly denying the partnerships of the rest.

---

[1] See al-Rijāl's rendering of 'Umar in *Skilled* I.9.2 (Appendix A above).
[2] This seems to mean, "no matter what house the supporting aspects come out of."
[3] *Principatus vel regni*: namely, the exaltation.
[4] For example, ibn Ezra's method for determining the victor of the entire chart, uses both the lord of the day and the lord of the hour (Appendix F below). But al-Kindī does this too in his Ch. 3.1 (Appendix E).

However, if this same [lord of the Ascendant] is traversing in a pivot (especially in the tenth), without, I say, any dignity, that partner[5] will be single in the leadership of the east, [and] fully claims the signification of the whole question (to the extent that it pertains to the querent), without the fellowship of [another] partner—unless (I say) any star is blessed with the rulership of the kingdom and bound (but even of the triplicity) [in the Ascendant],[6] likewise appearing in a pivot. Which if [that] sometimes happens, [such a star] seems not to be foreign from a partnership with the eastern lord, provided that the lord of the east possesses the beginning of the sign up to 15°.[7] For if the significator of the triple power is in the tenth, and placed in that same degree, [then] it takes possession of the signification, as the one individually stronger.

On the other hand, with the lord of the east being deprived of every dignity, and being cadent,[8] the minister of the three-fold power merits a stronger signification [if it is] at the beginning of [its] sign. Which if it held onto the end, reckon a stronger one to be one which is blessed by a twin dignity,[9] if it were fully in control of the bound and the sovereignty or, at least, the triplicity. For the one which is in charge of the decan is weaker than all the rest, unless it manages the power and ownership of the house which the Sun is holding onto by day (and the Moon by night), or at least that of the hour.

Moreover, the pivots strengthen their own lords in the power of signification; but [if the lords are] cadent, a not-moderate humbleness is noted.

Moreover, [if] the lords of the Solar house in a diurnal question (even the Lunar one in a nocturnal [question]), but even of its hour, are co-equal in power of this kind, they bequeath this gift of superiority to the one which is in control of the Solar rulership by day (of the Lunar one by night), or rather[10] that of the hour.

Therefore, one must use discernment about this leader and significator, until you discover [whether it is] the power of one star or two, or even many.

---

[5] That is, the lord of the Ascendant.
[6] That is, if it has all of these three dignities; it will continue to be compared to the domicile lord below.
[7] The Latin al-Rijāl reads as though the lord of the Ascendant cannot be more than 3° beyond the angle of the axis, not that it must be in the first half of its sign.
[8] The Latin al-Rijāl has the lord simply non-angular, which would still allow it to be succeedent.
[9] That is, if it rules two dignities in the Ascendant.
[10] The Latin al-Rijāl simply says "or," which does not help distinguish between them.

Which if the strength of two partners were equal, you will note to which of them the Moon will be applying, or at least [if] the Moon would possess her own house in the east,[11] or preferably if it[12] would be the minister of the Solar dignity[13] by day or the Lunar one by night (for I advise that the stronger signification of this belongs especially to the one which obtains the shift);[14] I say the stronger one will be the one to which the Moon applies from the east.

And so that I might tie all of this up briefly: any star blessed with the support of many witnesses [and] the Lunar application (and after observing these things which were said), is preferable in the principal rulership.

Even the Lot of Fortune always exhibits a stronger signification in the night for nocturnal affairs.

2. *Judges* §0.4: Another chapter on the same thing

[Primary significators]

Now that things have been attended to in an order of this kind, in every affair we must next investigate the nature of that significator which is called the "victor" among the Arabs, and the one which is in charge of the question.

And so, the lord of the east principally claims this dignity, if it itself regarded the east. But with it being cadent [from the Ascendant],[15] the Moon principally acquires the signification of the querent if she blesses the east with *her* own regard. (One must even note whether it[16] is applying or

---

[11] I take this to mean that even if the Moon rules the Ascendant (and even if she rules it and is in it), we should still look at the planet to which she is applying.

[12] I take this to be one of the candidate planets just mentioned.

[13] The Latin al-Rijāl has "the bound of" the Sun and Moon.

[14] That is, the sect light. Arabic writers use "shift" (*nawbah*) to describe the alternating command over charts taken by the luminaries, as the charts are diurnal or nocturnal. The Latin al-Rijāl adds that it would be good if it were also the lord of the Lot of Fortune.

[15] That is, in aversion to it.

[16] This probably refers to both the lord of the Ascendant and the Moon, but especially whichever one is taken as the significator of the querent.

receding. For although it may be deprived of the gift of the proper quality of each, in no way will it lose the signification which it holds onto.)[17]

And the lord of the seventh, [if it is] regarding [the seventh], will be in charge of the question; or [if it does not regard it, take] rather the lord of the lunar lodging-place.

Which if the Moon would be[18] regarding the east (as was just stated), provided that she has an application and withdrawal, the star from which she is being separated belongs to the querent; but the one to which she applies merits the signification of the question.

On the other hand, once the eastern lord is discovered to be cadent [from the Ascendant], [and] the Moon cadent from the east, while she neither applies to nor withdraws from [a planet], it will be permitted to establish her as belonging to the querent and the lord of her lodging-place[19] as the significator of the question. Moreover, the Moon lingering in her own sovereignty (and being foreign to any application and recession), will still belong to the querent, and the lord of her triplicity will have to be put over the question.

Which if some star would be transferring light, or would be collecting it, between the lords of the east and the seventh (or at least between the Moon and another star), that star will belong to the question, but the Moon will be allotted the command of the querent.

[Secondary significators]

But generally, if a star were in the east (and the seventh), even if it is [not][20] the lord of the east and the seventh, they present testimonies to the querent and the question, even if they are deprived of a mutual aspect.[21] But

---

[17] This parenthetical statement is not in the Latin al-Rijāl, and I am not sure exactly what it means.

[18] The Latin al-Rijāl has the Moon *not* aspecting the rising sign. I am unsure which is correct, since the Moon is always supposed to indicate things according to her applications and separations. Below, 'Umar covers situations in which the Moon has no application or separation.

[19] That is, of her sign.

[20] Adding with the Latin al-Rijāl, which specifically addresses peregrine planets in the first and seventh houses.

[21] That is, a planet in the Ascendant (or the seventh) will be an important significator, even if the lord of the Ascendant does not aspect the Ascendant (based on the Latin al-Rijāl).

the victor of the affair is said to be the star that is stronger in the place of the matter, even one established in that same place.[22]

It seems that everywhere, the Moon must be brought to bear upon all of these.

---

[22] I feel rather confident about this somewhat awkward sentence in Hugo, which is not mirrored in the Latin al-Rijāl. 'Umar is referring to the victor of the topic by dignities, as described in §0.3 above.

APPENDIX E: AL-KINDĪ'S *FORTY CHAPTERS*

Chapter 2.4: The planet in charge[1]

§130. No less too, does the minister which the Arabs call the "the one in charge"[2] mean the highest fortune, if it crossed the Sun and would appear eastern, so that it would be separated from the Sun by 12° or a little more, and would appear in the east in the morning. Which if it would be arising distant from the Sun by double the number of degrees of the first [distance], it is a sign of middling luckiness. But if it is remote from him by the tripled prior distance, it introduces lesser fortune.

§131. Also, with that same [distance] being quadrupled and it being foreign to[3] the Sun, it signifies a lesser punishment. But fivefold, it designates middling anguish. After that, it harms with greater misfortune until it undergoes scorching.

Chapter 3.1: Victor for a topic[4]

§136b.[5] But whichever one had more powers in the domicile of the matter, and its Lot, and its significating star[6] and the lord of its hour, will be considered to be the manager and administrator of that matter.

---

[1] This subchapter seems to give criteria for judging the favorability of the victors to be determined immediately below—it does not identify a wholly separate victor or ruler. If so, then it should be considered *in addition to* the determinations of strength by dignity, just as Ptolemy (*Tet.* III.3 and III.5, in Appendix H), and Dorotheus (*Carmen* III.1.1-6) and ibn Ezra (in Appendix F) stress the importance of solar phase in their versions of victors and chief significators. See especially *ITA* II.10.

[2] Or, "ruler, administrator": Ar. *al-mustawli* (Lat. *almuzeth, almustaul*), from *waliya* (forms I and V), "to be in charge, manage, assume responsibility for." Thanks to Charles Burnett for pointing this out.

[3] I believe this means that it is in a trine from the Sun by sign, so it is "cadent" from the whole-sign angles of the Sun. This would place the planet near the beginning of its retrogradation. But it might also mean that it is in aversion to the Sun (i.e., in the eighth sign from the Sun).

[4] Cf. al-Qabīsī's version of victors for topics in *ITA* I.18.

[5] This part of §136 is only in Robert of Ketton's translation.

[6] I take this to be the natural significator (such as Jupiter for wealth, Venus for love, and so on).

Chapter 3.2: Weighted victor for the querent,
taken from all releasing places[7]

§137. Moreover, the significator of the querent is distinguished according to the majority of the stars participating in the five places of releasing. For [the releasers] are the Sun, Moon, Ascendant, Lot of Fortune,[8] [and] the degree of the assembly or opposition which preceded the matter. However, the lord of the house obtains 5 portions or dignities, the lord of the sovereignty 4, the lord of the bound 3,[9] the lord of the triplicity 2, but only 1 is bequeathed to the lord of the face.

Chapter 3.3: The releaser & *kadukḫudhāh*[10]

§138. If one were eager to find the releaser (that is, the significator of life), one will consult the Sun in a diurnal nativity; which if one found him being received in a sign or quarter of the masculine sex, and viewed by[11] a [planet] ruling with any power over his place, it would establish him as the releaser, and the viewing one as the *kadukḫudhāh* (that is, the giver of the years of life). But if the Sun did not bear himself thusly, then the Moon should be considered: and if she were received in a sign or quarter of the female sex, and regarded by a lord with any power in that place, she should be taken as the releaser, and the one regarding her as the *kadukḫudhāh*. But if the Sun and Moon were forsaken of such a condition, [then] if he is born after an assembly [of the luminaries], the degree of the east—being regarded by any of its lords—should be taken as the releaser, and the aspecting one as the *kadukḫudhāh*. Moreover, if one has allotted the stated condition to none of these three, then if the Lot of Fortune bore itself thusly, let it be assigned as the releaser, and the one looking at it as the *kadukḫudhāh*.

---

[7] Cf. al-Qabīsī's victor for the chart in *ITA* VIII.1.4.

[8] The Lot of Fortune is taken in the day from the Sun to the Moon, and projected from the Ascendant; by night, from the Moon to the Sun and projected from the Ascendant.

[9] Note that al-Kindī follows the earlier practice found in *Search*, which assigns 3 points to the bound and 2 to the primary triplicity lord, rather than the other way around. Already in al-Qabīsī they are reversed.

[10] This chapter is only in Robert. For more on releasers, see *ITA* VIII.1.3 and the list of *PN* sources in its Appendix F.

[11] That is, "aspected" by. I believe this requires only an aspect by sign, not necessarily by degree.

§139. But with the aforesaid four lacking the manner [of bearing] indicated above, finally the degree of the assembly should be judged as the releaser [if it is] allotting that condition, and the one aspecting as the *kadukḫudhāh*. But if none of the aforesaid five bore themselves thusly, the native will lack a releaser and *kadukḫudhāh*. But in a nocturnal nativity, the Moon should be considered in the aforesaid way;[12] and, being found thus, she is appointed as the releaser and the one seeing her as the *kadukḫudhāh*. But if not, after [her] the Sun; and with these [conditions] being lacking, if he were born after the opposition, [look at] the Lot of Fortune (if it were fit); but if not, the degree of the east is allotted the aforesaid dignity; [but] if not, finally the degree of the opposition[13] should be taken as the releaser, and the one regarding it as the *kadukḫudhāh*. [But if none of the five bore themselves thusly, the nativity will lack releaser and *kadukḫudhāh*.][14] And so, with these things being found, the force and power of the *kadukḫudhāh* should be noted: for, being strong grants the greatest gifts, being weak the least. But its strength is that it would be advancing,[15] eastern, direct, and in its own *ḥalb*, and in one of its own dignities.[16]

§140. Moreover, the releaser should be directed to the rays and bodies of the fortunes and the bad ones with the greatest accuracy. For whenever and wherever it applied itself to a good one, it bestows good fortune from out of its manner and nature; and conjoined to a bad one, it shows misfortune according to its quality—but especially if it were the conjunction, tetragon, or opposite.

Chapter 3.4: The use of Lots & natural significators (excerpt)

§141 (in part). This chapter must especially be noted as being appropriate to a native, but by it a similar judgment can also come to be with respect to the rest of matters and their beginnings.[17]

---

[12] In feminine places, however.
[13] Reading for "assembly."
[14] Adding with the logic of the method, as above.
[15] That is, in an angle or a succeedent.
[16] For more on strength, see *ITA* IV.1-2, and *Search* II.4.2 above.
[17] Or perhaps, "and initiating them" (*initiis*), which in al-Kindī's mind probably includes both horary questions and elections proper.

APPENDIX F: IBN EZRA ON THE VICTOR OF THE CHART

What follows are two versions of Abraham ibn Ezra's victor method for the whole nativity. The first is according to his *Book of Nativities and Revolutions*, which was recently translated from the Hebrew by Meira Epstein; I have translated it from Peter Abano's Latin version from the late 13th or early 14th Century, and printed in 1507. The second is according to Latin editions of his work entitled *On Nativities* (1485 and 1537).

The difference between these two methods is this: the first version lacks the lords of the day and the hour, while the second version lacks the solar phase relationships.

1. Ibn Ezra on the victor over the native (1507)

Also, Ptolemy and Dorotheus say one should always seek the planet principally ruling over the native, which we will find thusly. We know firmly that the places of life are five, of which two are the places of the luminaries in the day and night; and the third is the place of the conjunction of the luminaries (or the place of the opposition) preceding the nativity; the fourth is the degree of the Ascendant; the fifth is the place of the Lot of Fortune, just as I have laid out in the *Book of Reasons for the Beginning of Wisdom*.[1]

And it is reckoned that the lord of the house [of each] has five strengths, the lord of the honor[2] four, of the triplicity three,[3] of the bound two, but of the face, one. And one must do thusly for all of those [planets] having power in all the five places.

[Likewise, if one of the superior planets is rising before the Sun, then if it is between the Sun's rays and a sextile to the Sun, it receives 3 strengths; if between the sextile and the square, 2 strengths; if between the square and its first station, 1 point.][4]

---

[1] This is actually two books, both of which have been translated from Hebrew by Meira Epstein.
[2] That is, of the exaltation.
[3] This would include only the primary triplicity lord, not all of them.
[4] I have added this consideration based on the Hebrew, as it is lacking in Latin. Ibn Ezra is referring to statements he makes in other books, which are similar to the view of the

In the same way, one must look into the houses: because the native has 12 strengths in the first house, 11 in the tenth, 10 in the seventh, 9 in the fourth, 8 in the eleventh, 7 in the fifth, 6 in the second, 5 in the eighth, 4 in the ninth, 3 in the third, 2 in the twelfth, 1 in the sixth.[5]

And the nature of the native is according to the nature of the principal ruler. Which if the principal ruler were in the belt of the firmament,[6] the native will be thin. But if it had latitude, he will be plump, and you will judge according to its latitude. Which if the latitude were southern, he will be light in motion; but if northern, he will be heavy.

	Saturn	Jupiter	Mars	Sun	Venus	Mercury	Moon
☉:							
☽:							
Asc:							
⊗:							
♂/☍:							
Houses							
Superiors							
Totals							

Figure 31: Table for ibn Ezra's victor (1st version)

---

superior planets' solar phases in *ITA* II.10 (see especially the diagram of the synodic cycle according to Abū Ma'shar).

[5] Note that these values differ from both the Māshā'allāh and Dorotheus attributions (see Ch. III.1.1 above).

[6] That is, right on the ecliptic, with no latitude.

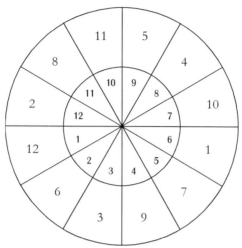

Figure 32: House points for ibn Ezra's victor

2. Ibn Ezra on the victor over the native (1485, 1537)

But the most powerful of all testimonies is that we consider the status of the planet having power over the whole circle, which the Saracens call the "victor": for its testimony, in terms of the quality of its status, is equal in power to all the others taken together. But you will find it thusly: therefore, one must know that the principal places are five: one, the Sun; the next, the Moon; the third is the place of the uniting or opposition (whichever of these preceded the nativity). But the sages disagreed in this, because they doubted whether the place of the Sun or the place of the Moon [in the case of an opposition] should be taken as the third. Ptolemy always affirms that the place of the one which held onto the upper hemisphere in the opposition, should be put third. But Hermes and Dorotheus claim that the place of the one holding onto the upper hemisphere in the *nativity* should be put third. But the Indians and Māshā'allāh say that the place of the Moon in the hour of the opposition, should be put third—with whom the sages of the Saracens and I agree. Fourth, the rising degree. Fifth, the Lot of Fortune, which according to Ptolemy is always to be taken by day and night from the Sun to the Moon.

Calculate how many virtues each of the planets would have in these five places, and in the place in which it is, and in the day of the nativity and the hour. Give 5 virtues to the lord of the house, but 4 to the lord of the honor,

3 to the lord of the triplicity (whichever one of these it was),[7] 2 to the lord of the bound, 1 to the lord of the face.

If one were in the first house, give it 12 virtues; appearing in the tenth, 11; in the seventh, 10; in the fourth, 9; in the eleventh, 8; in the fifth, 7; in the second, 6; in the ninth, 5; in the eighth, 4; in the third, 3; in the twelfth, 2; in the sixth, 1.

Attribute 7 virtues to the lord of the day, 6 to the lord of the hour.

And therefore, the planet which had more virtues, will be the victor. And its virtue will appear in the one being born, according to how the number of the virtues of any of the rest approached the number of its virtues.

	Saturn	Jupiter	Mars	Sun	Venus	Mercury	Moon
☉:							
☽:							
ASC:							
⊗:							
♂/☍:							
Lord day							
Lord hour							
Houses							
Totals							

Figure 33: Table for ibn Ezra's victor (2nd version)

---

[7] In other words, use the primary triplicity lord.

APPENDIX G: LEOPOLD OF AUSTRIA'S *COMPILATIO*[1]

Comment by Dykes. This little treatise at the end of Leopold of Austria's *Compilatio* (pp. 215-17) deals with interpreting thoughts, but note that Leopold seems to suppose that the client already has an explicit horary question, and simply does not want to tell the astrologer what it is.

The Tenth Treatise: On Intentions

[Leopold's method, from ibn Ezra][2]

You will know the intention[3] of someone wanting to pose a question to you, if he came to you for this [purpose] (with him being silent),[4] through:

[1] The lord of the Ascendant and its place, once the figure of heaven is arranged and the planets put into their places, in the hour at which he intended to ask. For if the lord of the Ascendant is in the first house, he wanted to ask about himself; if in the second, about assets; and thusly through all the houses, just as they signify.

[2] If the lord of the Ascendant is retrograde or burned up, do not judge through it but [rather] as before by means of the Moon—unless she is burned up by the Sun or in the burnt path.

[3] And[5] then judge by means of the lord of the hour, thusly: multiply the degrees which he has finished in the sign in which he is, by 12, and distribute the sum from the Ascendant in [increments of] 30: and where it is ended, judge the intention according to that part of the sign,[6] since it signifies it.

---

[1] From Leopold's *Compilatio*, pp. 215-17.
[2] These first four methods are directly from ibn Ezra's *Particular Treatises* (see Appendix J).
[3] Reading *intentionem* for *intentionum*.
[4] *Interposito sibi silentio.*
[5] That is, if the Moon is burned up or in the burnt path.
[6] See ibn Ezra's way of dividing the houses into subtopics, in Appendix J.

[4] And if this one—namely the lord of the hour—is impeded, take up the degrees which have already ascended in the rising sign (those above the earth), [and] divide them by 2 ½, and distribute this from the beginning of the rising sign, giving 2 ½° to each sign: where it is ended, there is the intention.

	0°-2.5°	2.5°-5°	5°-7.5°	7.5°-10°	10°-12.5°	12.5°-15°	15°-17.5°	17.5°-20°	20°-22.5°	22.5°-25°	25°-27.5°	27.5°-30°
♈	♈	♉	♊	♋	♌	♍	♎	♏	♐	♑	♒	♓
♉	♉	♊	♋	♌	♍	♎	♏	♐	♑	♒	♓	♈
♊	♊	♋	♌	♍	♎	♏	♐	♑	♒	♓	♈	♉
♋	♋	♌	♍	♎	♏	♐	♑	♒	♓	♈	♉	♊
♌	♌	♍	♎	♏	♐	♑	♒	♓	♈	♉	♊	♋
♍	♍	♎	♏	♐	♑	♒	♓	♈	♉	♊	♋	♌
♎	♎	♏	♐	♑	♒	♓	♈	♉	♊	♋	♌	♍
♏	♏	♐	♑	♒	♓	♈	♉	♊	♋	♌	♍	♎
♐	♐	♑	♒	♓	♈	♉	♊	♋	♌	♍	♎	♏
♑	♑	♒	♓	♈	♉	♊	♋	♌	♍	♎	♏	♐
♒	♒	♓	♈	♉	♊	♋	♌	♍	♎	♏	♐	♑
♓	♓	♈	♉	♊	♋	♌	♍	♎	♏	♐	♑	♒

Figure 34: Table of twelfth-parts

For example,[7] the Ascendant was 12° Aries. I distributed by 2 ½, beginning from Aries, and the distribution was ended in the fifth [house], which is Leo, the house of children.[8] Therefore I know that he wanted to ask about a child. And because the lord of that place (namely Leo), the Sun, was in the seventh, I know that he wanted to ask about the wife of [his] child. Which if he had been in the sixth, he would have intended to ask about the illness of the child—and speak thusly about the others.

---

[7] See also *Search* Ch. I.9.3, and *OHT* §2 (in Appendix C above).
[8] That is, he divided 12 by 2.5 (yielding 4.8), and gave the first 4 to the signs in order, starting with Aries (because it is the rising sign); the remainder (.8) fell into Leo. One can also simply use the above table of twelfth-parts.

[According to "Ptolemy"]

Ptolemy[9] used to judge the intention by means of the stronger signifier in the circle: so that if it is in the tenth, [it is] about an honor; if in the first, about life, and so on.

[According to Māshā'allāh]

And [according to Māshā'allāh],[10] in every case, consider [1] the Ascendant and [2] its lord, [3] the Sun and [4] his lord, [5] the Lot of Fortune and [6] its lord, and [7] the lord of the degree of the twelfth-part of the Ascendant: and judge the intention according to the one among them which appeared stronger.

But he[11] teaches that one is the degree of the significator[12] which is taken from the lord of the hour to the lord of the Ascendant, and [on top of that] are added the degrees which the lord of the hour has made in the sign in which it is, and it is projected from the degree[13] of the lord of the hour: and the significator will be the planet in whose sign the projection was ended (but I believe that it ought to be projected from the beginning of the sign of the lord of the hour).[14] And if the victor is in the first face of a sign, it signifies a

---

[9] See *OHT* §6, paragraph 2 (in Appendix C above) for a fuller statement of "Ptolemy's" significator of thought.

[10] This is perhaps a misunderstanding of *Thought* §2, as also found in Ch. I.9.4 above. This list is taken from a combination of the many views Māshā'allāh mentions.

[11] Source unknown. The simpler way to put the calculation is: measure from the lord of the hour to the lord of the Ascendant, and project that distance from the position of the lord of the hour. This is similar to two other versions of Lot-like projections involving the lord of the hour. In *Search* Ch. I.3.2, Dorotheus is credited with a significator of thought which is measured from the lord of the hour to the lord of the Ascendant, and that distance is projected from either the Sun or the Midheaven (but see my note there: I believe the Midheaven might be a mistake for a different Lot-like projection in Ch. I.11.1). And in *Search* Ch. I.11.2 there is a Lot-like projection to determine whether the outcome will be useful: it is measured from the lord of the Ascendant to the lord of the hour, and projected from the Sun.

[12] *Pars ducis*, "leader." Leopold's use of *dux* in this section leads me to believe he was relying on Hermann or another colleague such as Hugo of Santalla for this material. Likewise, some of his phrases and vocabulary later on match *Search* exactly.

[13] As Leopold will note just below, this is an error in his source manuscript: the instructions should read "sign" or "beginning of the sign."

[14] Leopold is right: in many traditional texts, the degrees of the rising sign or another planet are added so that one can easily project in increments of 30° from the beginning of that sign. See my own example of this in *ITA* VI.1.1.

matter indicated by the first lord of the triplicity of that sign; and speak likewise with respect to the second and third [faces].

Also,[15] a projection of the intention happens from the lord of the hour to the degree of the Sun;[16] the equal degrees are taken and extended from the Ascendant, and the intention is in that house where the extending is ended. Whence if the Sun [himself] is the lord of the hour, the lord of the hour[17] is in the Ascendant.

[An example from Hermes]

Also, a figure which is said to belong to Hermes:[18] I have calculated it fully for the latitude of the completed third clime.[19] The Ascendant was 9° 55' Taurus.[20] The Midheaven, 26° 29' Capricorn. The eleventh, 29° 20' Aquarius (in the right circle, 61° 30').[21] The twelfth, 4° 50' Aries (in the right circle, 94° 30'). The first, 9° 55' (in the right circle, 127° 30'). The second, 6° 25' Gemini (in the right circle, 154° 30'). The third, 1° 34' Cancer (in the right circle, 181° 30'). Venus was in 15° Cancer, in her own triplicity. The Moon in the tenth degree of Libra, in no dignity of her own. The Sun was in Cancer. The Lot of Fortune in Sagittarius. Saturn in Leo, in no dignity of his own.

Therefore, Venus was the significator of the question: but because the Moon was separated from Saturn (having been bound [to him from] the sixth), Hermes judged that the question was about the mother (for the Moon is in charge of mothers), and about an infirmity [because the Moon is in the sixth]; and because the Moon was being separated from Saturn, he said that the infirmity was cold and dry; and because Leo is the stomach in the human body, he says the cause [of the infirmity] is in the stomach; and because Saturn was in the first degree of Leo, he says the infirmity is in the mouth of the stomach.

---

[15] This is very similar to the Lot-like projection in *Skilled* I.11, in which al-Rijāl projects the distance from Aries instead of the Ascendant (see Appendix A above). Leopold's version seems more likely.

[16] But probably the Moon in a nocturnal chart.

[17] This should probably read, "then the intention is in the Ascendant."

[18] See Hermann's treatment in Ch. I.7 above (including my own proposed original chart), and the version in the complete *Thought* (in *WSM*).

[19] The chart is calculated for 30° N latitude, and Leopold is using Alchabitius Semi-Arc houses.

[20] Leopold's text omits the number, so I have supplied it from the diagram in his book.

[21] This is the right ascension (RA) of the cusp: in older tables, RA was measured from 0° Capricorn instead of 0° Aries.

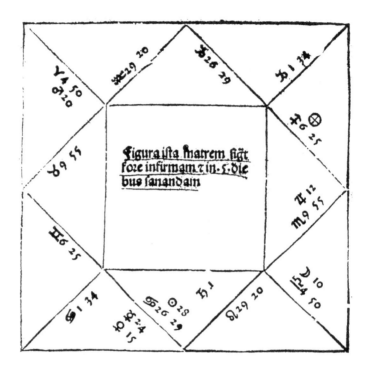

Figure 35: Hermes's thought of sick mother (Leopold)

From there, since the Moon applies to Venus [who is] receiving [her], he said she would be cured. And because there were 5° between the Moon and Venus, for that reason he said she would be cured within 5 days (because the sign was convertible).[22] And if the Moon had been in a firm sign, she would have signified 5 years; if in a double-bodied one, 5 months. And if the Moon had applied to Saturn in such a way, he would have said the sick woman was going to die within so many days.

Conversely, if it[23] had been Venus instead of the Moon, the question would have been about some woman of his own people; if Saturn, about his father; if Mercury, about a child; if the Sun, about the king. If Venus [had been the significator and were] in the seventh, about betrothals. The Sun is

---

[22] That is, a movable sign (often called "cardinal" signs).
[23] That is, the significator. There seem to be two reasons for the Moon to be the significator. According to al-Rāzī here, the Moon is the lord of the lord of the Ascendant, and so shows the *cause* of the situation. But note step #2 in Leopold's own method above: if the lord of the Ascendant is burned up, we defer to the Moon.

male in the day and female in the night; the contrary for the Moon. Likewise, if Jupiter had been [the significator and] in the ninth, the question would have been about a dream; if Mars in the seventh, about a controversy.

And also al-Rāzī, looking at this figure, said: since I saw that the east was feminine and its lord feminine, and in a feminine [sign], it was plain that the question as going to be about a woman. And since the lord of the lord of the east (namely, the Moon) was in the sixth, applying to Venus in the house of brothers, [and the Moon was] separated from Saturn (who was in the fourth, which belongs to parents), I know [it was] about the mother, because mothers belong to the Moon; and because she was applying to the lord of the sixth from the sixth [itself], I knew she was infirm; and because she was being separated from Saturn (to whom the harm belongs) and is applying to Venus, it establishes that she is going to be cured. And because there were five degrees within the transfer, and the transfer was happening from a movable sign, I knew that what was signaled should have happened in five days.

APPENDIX H: HELLENISTIC ANTECEDENTS

In these passages we can clearly see some of the Hellenistic natal inspirations for the use of victors (1-3). Ptolemy seeks the victors over topics by examining the rulers of a place and their solar phase, treating each relationship as being one point or count. Porphyry (4) describes a victor for the entire chart (according to several views), as well as the releaser and domicile-master (the Persian *kadukḫudhāh*). Finally, (5) Hephaistio describes four types of thought-interpretation.

1. Ptolemy: Chief rulership over the degree of the syzygy before birth, used for rectification (from *Tet.* III.3):[1]

Comment by Dykes. In this passage, we are to find a planet which has more of the five relationships listed below, counting each relationship equally. For example, I take it that if a planet were both the domicile and primary triplicity lord of the pre-natal lunation, and also coming out of the rays, then it would have three of the five relationships. But so would a planet which was the exalted and bound lord, and also coming out of the rays. The planet with the most relationships has the *oikodespotia* or "house rulership."

After we discover the approximate degree of the Ascendant in the path of ascensions (by means of the hour which is given to us),[2] it is good that we should find the degree of the conjunction or prevention which was before the nativity [and] closer to it, and we should learn it truly. Which if there were a conjunction in the one we found, we will take the degree of each luminary; but if it were a prevention, we will observe the degree of the luminary appearing above the earth.[3]

After this, we will inquire as to which of the planets at the hour of the nativity has the management of this degree. But generally, the path by which the management agrees with a planet, is explained in these five things, which

---

[1] I use the chapter divisions of Robert Schmidt, but my translation is from Plato of Tivoli's translation of *Tet.* III.2.

[2] In other words, one should first determine the approximate hour of birth based on the best information possible (in this case, by determining the Ascendant by rough ascensional times).

[3] That is, the one above the horizon at the time of the opposition itself.

are: [1] triplicity, [2] house, [3] exaltation, [4] bound, and [5] [its] appearance (or relationship with the Sun) in the figure. And the management of the place will belong to the planet which has more than one (or all) of these strengths in it.

But if we find that all of these (or many) belong to one planet, we will observe its truly-found degree in the sign in which it had been at the hour of the nativity. And we will say that the degree of the sign which was taken approximately by ascensions, which is [then] made equal to [the planet's degree] in number, is the degree of the Ascendant.

But if we found two or more planets being associated with each other,[4] we will look at the number [of the degree] which each [of them] walked through at the hour of the nativity, and whichever number was closer to the [approximate] degree of the Ascendant which appeared to us by ascensions, that one will be the Ascendant of the hour of the nativity.

Should we find the number of the degrees of two or many of the planets to be near the number of the degree of the Ascendant which came out for us by ascensions, in this we will imitate the one which had more authorities in the angles, and whose sect[5] it was.

But if the distance of the degree of the manager[6] from the degree of the Ascendant (which is found without a fine observation)[7] were greater than the distance of its [degree] from the [number of the] degree of the [approximate] Midheaven,[8] we will establish that number as the degree of the Midheaven, through which we will [then] calculate the other angles.

2. Ptolemy: The victor over a topic (from *Tet.* III.4):

First it is right that we should look in the place of the circle of signs which agrees with the thing which we seek, from those we wish to judge: just as, for example, of those things which the native gets involved with, the place of the

---

[4] That is, sharing in these rulerships or the "five things."
[5] Lat. *haiz*, a transliteration of the Ar. *ḥayyiz*. Here, Ptolemy at least means a planet of the sect of the birth (a diurnal planet in a diurnal birth, or nocturnal planet in a nocturnal one). But we might also give extra emphasis to a planet of the sect which is also in its own proper domain (see *ITA* III.2).
[6] Lat. *almudebit*, ultimately from either the Ar. *ḍābiṭ* (governor) or *dabara* (to manage, organize, *etc.*).
[7] That is, the approximate Ascendant.
[8] Omitting *ipsa eadem via exquisitio*.

Midheaven agrees with masteries and works; or, just as the place of the Sun agrees with the things pertaining to fathers.

And afterwards, we will inspect which planets have the right to manage that place, by means of the ways which we said before.[9] And if one planet would rule over that place in all of these ways, we will attribute the management of the matter to it.

But if two or three would rule over it, we will give the management to the one which had the strength of more numbers.

3. Ptolemy: The victor over a topic (from Tet. III.5):

Comment by Dykes. In this passage, Ptolemy recognizes that planetary significators might be hard to reconcile if they indicate different qualities or times. [1] For the quality of the topic and its timing, Ptolemy recommends taking the one with the most authorities (see the excerpt from Tet. III.3 above, on the five types of authority). But [2] if more than one star had the same number and was in the same solar phase, we must mix their natures together. [3] If they were otherwise equal but in different solar phases, they will indicate distinct things at *different times*. [4] Only planets with this type of natal connection to the topic will govern the general nature of the topic—all other influences are more temporary and occasional. [5] Finally, Ptolemy reminds us that being authoritative is not the same as indicating a time: only solar phase and placement in the eastern or western quarters indicate times.

[1] But of the types of occasion for the mutual combination [of planets],[10] it is appropriate for us to hold this in our memory, here and everywhere: that we should consider that if the planets which rule over the places we are looking into, were not of one kind but of different kinds, or [they were] of planets producing a contrary,[11] we will take the one[12] which had greater authorities—of those whose powers over [the place] are of greater author-

---

[9] That is, the "five things" from *Tet.* III.3 above.

[10] *Modorum autem coadunationis occasionum adinvicem.*

[11] This must mean if the relevant planets seem to indicate conflicting and incompatible things, such as Venus and Saturn often do.

[12] Here and later in the sentence, the Greek text suggests that we are looking for more than one planet with many authorities; but I follow Plato of Tivoli and Schmidt in treating this as singular, since Ptolemy deals with multiple planets a few sentences later.

ity—so that it agrees with the future matter: and the natures of these things would turn out according to it.

[2] Which if their authorities were equal, and [other] stars were elevated along with them,[13] we will arrive easily to the knowledge of the combined matter from the commingling of these different natures.

[3] But if they were separate,[14] we will attribute what is likened to them (in terms of accidents) according to the particular hours[15] belonging to each of them. But at first we will attribute [events] to those which were morning [stars], but lastly to those which appeared as evening [stars].

[4] But it is necessary that [a star] be likened to [the place] from the beginning: for if they did not bear themselves thusly, it would be able to do nothing of the future [event], since they retained no partnership in the beginning.[16]

[5] But [a planet's] primary management is not [itself] the occasion of the future time, but [rather] the quality of the star which was the lord of the management at the time of the nativity, by the regard of the Sun and of the angle of the world.[17]

4. Porphyry/Antiochus on victors in the nativity[18]

In material attributed to Antiochus, and in summaries of it by Porphyry, several types of victors are described:

[1] The longevity releaser and domicile-master.[19] The procedures for determining these are very similar to those in the medieval period, including the material from *Forty Chapters* Ch. 3 (see Appendix E above).

---

[13] Ptolemy seems to mean that at least two planets have the same number of relationships (including solar phases), as described above in the excerpt from *Tet.* III.3.

[14] This seems to mean that the relevant stars are equal in the number of relationships, but they have *different* solar phases: in Ptolemy's astrology, planets eastern of the Sun (and/or in eastern quarters) indicate earlier times, while those western of the Sun (and/or in western quarters) indicate later times. Therefore, equally authoritative planets in different solar phases can be distinguished according to *when* their indications are relevant.

[15] That is, the times of life.

[16] Here Ptolemy is saying that only such stars with these authorities and relationships to the place of the topic in the nativity can have a general signification for the topic as a whole; any other planet will have only occasional and temporary indications for the topic.

[17] This simply means that the victor alone does not give us the *time* of the events: instead, we must rely on a planet's solar phase and its relationship to the angles and quarters.

[18] See Schmidt 2009, pp. 315-37.

[2] The "lord" (*kurios*) of the nativity, which seems to be the victor of the whole chart. Porphyry describes several competing views:

The first concerns the Midheaven, preferring first the lord of the Midheaven, if it is angular; if not, a planet in or right on the Midheaven; if not, a planet ascending after the Midheaven.

But another view concerns some other places: the lord of the Ascendant, or a planet transiting the rising sign and the bound of the degree of the Ascendant; or, the lord of[20] the Moon; or, the lord of the Lot of Fortune; or, a planet entering or exiting the Sun's rays, within seven days. To the strongest of these, this second view adds the bound lord of the pre-natal conjunction or opposition (using the Moon's degree in an opposition). Whichever one is chosen, it should also be situated the best in terms of houses and planets, *etc.*

5. Hephaistio on thought-interpretation (*Apotel.* III.4)

The *Apotelesmatics* of Hephaistio of Thebes (early 5th Century) reports several methods of thought-interpretation and predicting their outcomes.

[1] First,[21] Hephaistio says that one must make a general appraisal of the chart in a way similar to nativities. He specifically instructs us to examine the triad of angular signs around the Midheaven (and planets in them), to study the past (ninth), current (tenth), and future (eleventh) characteristics of the client's actions or activities.

[2] Next,[22] he advises us to examine the axial degrees and other characteristics of the signs (such as their quadruplicity, triplicity, being dry signs, *etc.*). The Ascendant signifies the nature of the inquiry, the Midheaven the activity itself, the Descendant the result, and the IC hidden things. Likewise, the Moon's connections and separations indicate results according to the nature of the stars involved.

---

[19] In the Persian and later medieval tradition, this is known as the *kadukhudhāh*, preferably the bound lord of the longevity releaser.

[20] That is how I read Schmidt's text, both here and in the next clause about the Lot of Fortune.

[21] *Apotel.* III.4.1-4.

[22] *Ibid.,* III.4.7-11.

[3] Third,[23] foretelling the thought and results can be examined by the Lot of Fortune and its lord, including houses derived from the Lot. For example, Hephaistio says that if the Lot falls on the third (close friends) but the lord of that sign is in an opposition to it (i.e., in the seventh sign from that), then the inquiry is about an enmity (derived seventh) with friends (the third). He also suggests chart examples that would show an action to be helpful or "pointless."

[4] Finally,[24] Hephaistio endorses his own version of the method attributed to the Indians (*Search* I.9.3) or unknown persons (*OHT* §2): namely, the twelfth-part on the Ascendant indicates the thought. After reminding the reader how to compute the twelfth-parts,[25] Hephaistio provides 144 separate interpretations, one for each twelfth-part. Since his material is basically in the form of a prose table, I have put the interpretations in a table below.

The number of the twelfth-part indicates the whole-sign house at the basis of the thought, and I have added the name of the sign for easy reference: by comparing the various meanings across signs and houses, one can see that the content of the thought is generally a combination of (1) the qualities of the sign itself, (2) its whole-sign house position, (3) the nature of its domicile or exalted lord, and (4) its original house position relative to Aries. For example, if the Ascendant at the consultation falls between 7.5°-10° of Capricorn, it falls on the 4th twelfth-part: by definition this means the 4th house from Capricorn, which is Aries. Of the three thoughts listed in the table, "flock-animals" must be due to the fact that Aries is a four-footed sign, plus the agricultural meaning of the 4th house;[26] according to Valens, "clothing" is an attribution of Mars (the domicile lord), "because of Aries."[27]

---

[23] *Ibid.*, III.4.14-18. Note that this method is attributed to people such as Antiochus and Valens elsewhere: see the table in the Introduction.
[24] *Ibid.*, III.19ff.
[25] See the table in *Search* I.9.3 above.
[26] Some medieval texts also say that Mars (the domicile lord of Aries) signifies the tending of animals.
[27] *Anthology* I.1.

Twelfth-parts of Aries		
	Sign	Thoughts
1st (0°-2.5°)	♈	Freedom or rulership
2nd (2.5°-5°)	♉	Livelihood or household goods[28] or living things or land or a woman or elegant persons or the like
3rd (5°-7.5°)	♊	Ambushes or theft or a runaway
4th (7.5°-10°)	♋	A theft of silver,[29] or plunder
5th (10°-12.5°)	♌	One's property[30] or rulership, and the like
6th (12.5°-15°)	♍	Household management, feminine adornment
7th (15°-17.5°)	♎	Enemies and a fight, or demanding [something] back, or a court of judgment[31]
8th (17.5°-20°)	♏	A secret and obscure matter
9th (20°-22.5°)	♐	Travel by land, or change, or a voyage
10th (22.5°-25°)	♑	Hope or union or a covenant[32]
11th (25°-27.5°)	♒	Loss or theft or some such indication
12th (27.5°-30°)	♓	A woman or especially female matters, or flourishing things[33]

Twelfth-parts of Taurus		
	Sign	Thoughts
1st (0°-2.5°)	♉	Being occupied with the means of living and eating
2nd (2.5°-5°)	♊	Shameful affairs or sensual pleasure or the like
3rd (5°-7.5°)	♋	Theft or some work or household management
4th (7.5°-10°)	♌	Enmity and plunder
5th (10°-12.5°)	♍	Harmony and being carefree, friendship and goodness
6th (12.5°-15°)	♎	The matter under consideration has fallen into uncertainty and doubt
7th (15°-17.5°)	♏	Trouble and anxiety and warfare
8th (17.5°-20°)	♐	Travel by land and a voyage and suchlike
9th (20°-22.5°)	♑	Interchanges[34] with respect to women, and the like
10th (22.5°-25°)	♒	Complete liquidation[35] and loss and toil
11th (25°-27.5°)	♓	Sensual pleasures
12th (27.5°-30°)	♈	Foreign women or living abroad or agriculture

[28] *Oikou.*
[29] Or, "money" (*arguriou*).
[30] *Ousias.*
[31] *Kritēriou*, which can also refer to a standard or a test (just as a court is supposed to test and assess competing claims).
[32] *Harmonias.*
[33] *Tethēlummenōn.*
[34] Or, "reconciliations" (*sunallagēs*).
[35] *Diapraseōs.*

Twelfth-parts of Gemini		
	Sign	**Thoughts**
1st (0°-2.5°)	♊	Fellowship and civil affairs and ambiguity[36]
2nd (2.5°-5°)	♋	Loss of gold or silver
3rd (5°-7.5°)	♌	Loss and bad luck
4th (7.5°-10°)	♍	Loans and loss and damage penalties[37]
5th (10°-12.5°)	♎	A deed and a business transaction
6th (12.5°-15°)	♏	A theft from a fire that has occurred
7th (15°-17.5°)	♐	A chased runaway, or travel by land, or suchlike
8th (17.5°-20°)	♑	A profitable craft and some cheerful affair
9th (20°-22.5°)	♒	Words and deeds
10th (22.5°-25°)	♓	A fight and enmity and similar significations
11th (25°-27.5°)	♈	Some loss or fear or repentance or death[38]
12th (27.5°-30°)	♉	Agriculture or living abroad, and what is like that

Twelfth-parts of Cancer		
	Sign	**Thoughts**
1st (0°-2.5°)	♋	Rulership or the chief priesthood or worship
2nd (2.5°-5°)	♌	The greatest deed, and rank, and priesthood
3rd (5°-7.5°)	♍	Fear on account of something done regarding a woman
4th (7.5°-10°)	♎	Trusts[39] or loss or things demanded back
5th (10°-12.5°)	♏	A secret stash or treasure or something deposited
6th (12.5°-15°)	♐	Travel by land or a voyage or foreign[40] persons
7th (15°-17.5°)	♑	A fight because of feminine persons and jealousy
8th (17.5°-20°)	♒	Loss or theft or fines or denials
9th (20°-22.5°)	♓	A marriage agreement and good matters
10th (22.5°-25°)	♈	Rulership and rank and a priesthood and what is like that
11th (25°-27.5°)	♉	Theft or escape or the damage of something deposited
12th (27.5°-30°)	♊	Fellowship and harmony in affairs and what has been joined together

[36] Lit., "having the same name" (*homōnumias*).
[37] Or, "fines" (*zēmias*).
[38] Or, "releasing, dissolution" (*analuseōs*).
[39] *Pisteōs*, which might also mean "confidences, things in which we have trust." But along with the 4th-house theme, I take this to mean property which is being taken care of by or entrusted to someone.
[40] *Xenōn prosōpōn*, which could possibly refer to one's guests.

Twelfth-parts of Leo		
	Sign	**Thoughts**
1st (0°-2.5°)	♌	Rank and desire for others' [things], or greed
2nd (2.5°-5°)	♍	Great deeds and damages and injustice
3rd (5°-7.5°)	♎	A fight and greed and uncertainty
4th (7.5°-10°)	♏	Accomplishing a great deed
5th (10°-12.5°)	♐	No small thing, but rather a nobleman, or founding [something][41]
6th (12.5°-15°)	♑	Some toil or foreign labors, or returns[42]
7th (15°-17.5°)	♒	Enemies and the like
8th (17.5°-20°)	♓	The things of another, or anxiety [about] another
9th (20°-22.5°)	♈	Fear and uncertainty
10th (22.5°-25°)	♉	A lounging-place or country life or living abroad
11th (25°-27.5°)	♊	A fight and unexpected things
12th (27.5°-30°)	♋	Sacred things or some such thing

Twelfth-parts of Virgo		
	Sign	**Thoughts**
1st (0°-2.5°)	♍	Feminine adornment and reaping the fruits of kindness[43]
2nd (2.5°-5°)	♎	Revenues or costly adornment or clothing
3rd (5°-7.5°)	♏	A secret, contrived matter[44]
4th (7.5°-10°)	♐	An occasion for an exchange, or sharing in a kindness[45]
5th (10°-12.5°)	♑	Agriculture and building, or some suchlike
6th (12.5°-15°)	♒	A person or hope and actions[46] and toil
7th (15°-17.5°)	♓	Enmity with women, skirmishing with friends
8th (17.5°-20°)	♈	Crafts, or holy works or business[47]
9th (20°-22.5°)	♉	Merchandise for sale or a burdensome time abroad
10th (22.5°-25°)	♊	Some open insult or a foreigner or a rustic
11th (25°-27.5°)	♋	Theft or a secret matter or treasure
12th (27.5°-30°)	♌	Wounds or sickliness or the like

---

41 *Ktiseōs*, which can also mean "creating."
42 In the sense of returns or yields from labor, crops, *etc.* (*prosodou*).
43 *Karpou charin.*
44 *Pragmatos lathraiou belouleumenou.*
45 *Aphormōn allagēs ē koinou tinos charin.*
46 This can also mean "revenge" (*praxeōn*).
47 Or, "a divine warning" or a response from an article (*chrematismōn*).

Twelfth-parts of Libra		
	Sign	**Thoughts**
1st (0°-2.5°)	♎	Revenues or a court or gifts, or things received
2nd (2.5°-5°)	♏	Theft or absence
3rd (5°-7.5°)	♐	Commerce or agriculture in a foreign land
4th (7.5°-10°)	♑	Secret or crooked actions
5th (10°-12.5°)	♒	One's business, or failure, or the anticipation of hopes
6th (12.5°-15°)	♓	Another's matter, or the command of a woman
7th (15°-17.5°)	♈	Ill-timed unpleasantness and passion and a fight, or some peacefulness
8th (17.5°-20°)	♉	Sickliness or wounds or royal anxiety
9th (20°-22.5°)	♊	Fellowship or words or contracts
10th (22.5°-25°)	♋	Revenues or rank or an assessment or good times
11th (25°-27.5°)	♌	Ignorance or sudden hubris[48]
12th (27.5°-30°)	♍	Bodies[49] or public goods

Twelfth-parts of Scorpio		
	Sign	**Thoughts**
1st (0°-2.5°)	♏	Warfare or a foreign matter, or sudden affair that has occurred
2nd (2.5°-5°)	♐	A voyage or changes and the like
3rd (5°-7.5°)	♑	The crowd or a fight, and a dangerous unpleasantness
4th (7.5°-10°)	♒	Deliverance from bad actions
5th (10°-12.5°)	♓	Likemindedness or a voyage or joint matters
6th (12.5°-15°)	♈	An injunction and might and unexpected strength
7th (15°-17.5°)	♉	Something that has occurred in another land or on account of a foreign person
8th (17.5°-20°)	♊	Provisions for a journey
9th (20°-22.5°)	♋	Thefts or authority or quarrels with powerful people
10th (22.5°-25°)	♌	Living abroad or some craft or rank
11th (25°-27.5°)	♍	Theft because of a woman
12th (27.5°-30°)	♎	Revenues or danger or unsatisfied thief[50]

---

[48] I.e., an attack, insult, gross arrogance.
[49] *Sōmatōn*, which can mean sensual pleasures but has the special meaning of "slaves," i.e., humans considered merely as bodies or objects: this latter is probably what Hephaistio means.
[50] *Kerdous aplēstou.*

Twelfth-parts of Sagittarius		
	Sign	Thoughts
1st (0°-2.5°)	♐	Merchandising in a foreign land
2nd (2.5°-5°)	♑	Warfare or living abroad or encampments[51]
3rd (5°-7.5°)	♒	Maritime[52] matters and transactions
4th (7.5°-10°)	♓	A voyage and the like
5th (10°-12.5°)	♈	Merchandise
6th (12.5°-15°)	♉	Four-footed animals
7th (15°-17.5°)	♊	Unpleasantness or a runaway
8th (17.5°-20°)	♋	Theft or loss
9th (20°-22.5°)	♌	Travel or ambushes
10th (22.5°-25°)	♍	Love or the like
11th (25°-27.5°)	♎	Revenues on account of female or male foreigners
12th (27.5°-30°)	♏	Theft

Twelfth-parts of Capricorn		
	Sign	Thoughts
1st (0°-2.5°)	♑	Not-clean matters, or an insult
2nd (2.5°-5°)	♒	A runaway or loss
3rd (5°-7.5°)	♓	Love or a voyage
4th (7.5°-10°)	♈	Flock-animals, buildings or clothing
5th (10°-12.5°)	♉	Agriculture or household management
6th (12.5°-15°)	♊	Matters of disagreement with others
7th (15°-17.5°)	♋	Theft or unpleasantness
8th (17.5°-20°)	♌	Fear or warfare
9th (20°-22.5°)	♍	A craft or feminine adornment
10th (22.5°-25°)	♎	Revenues or unpleasantness
11th (25°-27.5°)	♏	A secret matter that has arisen
12th (27.5°-30°)	♐	A matter that has arisen, or a voyage

---

[51] Or, "a fleet" (*stratopedou*).
[52] *Kathurgōn.* This can also indicate matters involving much moisture.

Twelfth-parts of Aquarius		
	Sign	**Thoughts**
1st (0°-2.5°)	♒	Favor regarding bodies
2nd (2.5°-5°)	♓	Maritime[53] matters or merchandise
3rd (5°-7.5°)	♈	Some gossip
4th (7.5°-10°)	♉	One's own toils
5th (10°-12.5°)	♊	Fellowship or maritime matters
6th (12.5°-15°)	♋	Theft or sudden unpleasantness
7th (15°-17.5°)	♌	A craft or fellowship
8th (17.5°-20°)	♍	Public loafers
9th (20°-22.5°)	♎	Revenues or adornment and some just matter or being in a foreign land
10th (22.5°-25°)	♏	Theft and treasure
11th (25°-27.5°)	♐	A voyage or maritime matters
12th (27.5°-30°)	♑	Others' matters or feminine faithfulness

Twelfth-parts of Pisces		
	Sign	**Thoughts**
1st (0°-2.5°)	♓	Revealing damaged maritime goods
2nd (2.5°-5°)	♈	Adornment or a wedding union
3rd (5°-7.5°)	♉	Those who are trying to accomplish something secretly, or a feminine matter
4th (7.5°-10°)	♊	Toil or a partnership or a foreign matter
5th (10°-12.5°)	♋	Merchandise or marriage
6th (12.5°-15°)	♌	Others' merchandise
7th (15°-17.5°)	♍	A feminine craft or like things, those relating to a woman
8th (17.5°-20°)	♎	Others' matters
9th (20°-22.5°)	♏	Revenues and a fine deed
10th (22.5°-25°)	♐	A voyage or a good time abroad
11th (25°-27.5°)	♑	A feminine matter or a disagreement with a woman
12th (27.5°-30°)	♒	Loss or a runaway, and the like

---

[53] See footnote about *kathurgōn* above.

APPENDIX I: THE *LETTER OF ARGAFALAU TO ALEXANDER*

What follows is a partial translation of the anonymous *Letter* of "Argafalau"[1] to Alexander the Great, which is part of a Latin collection from the mid- to late-10th Century.[2] The *Letter* describes four main topics: how to predict or interpret the thoughts of a client beforehand, as well as what objects the client holds in his hand (§§1-2), the outcomes of those thoughts (§3), answers to explicit questions (§§4-7), and advice for elections based on the planetary hours (§8, not included here).

Three sections (§§2-3, 6) suggest that the purpose of thought-interpretation or identifying objects in the hand, is to impress doubters. For one thing, §2 speaks of the client specifically asking what is in his hand; for another, §3 speaks of when the client "persists in inquiring" about something, after the thought is interpreted; and in §6, surely only a doubter or tester would care to ask an astrologer which way his door or bed points. Since Argafalau leaves it open as to whether or not the client will persist in inquiring after the thought is interpreted, it seems he views thought-interpretation as distinct from, but sometimes a preliminary to, answering specific questions.

The numbering system in the paragraphs below follows Juste's edition. The italicized section titles are my own, and I use ellipses (…) to indicate that a particular section continues with further planetary hours (or signs or houses) after the portion I have translated.

---

[1] According to Juste (personal communication), Argafalau (or Ergafalau or Ergaphalau, *etc.*) is a pseudonym drawn from the Arabic name for the 26th mansion of the Moon, *al-Fargh al-Awwal* (which Bos and Burnett 2000 translate as "the first spout").

[2] See Juste 2007 and Burnett 1987, p. 140. I have used Juste's edition for my partial translation.

[§1: Introduction]

[1.2-3]: You say that in a certain work of Plato the philosopher, you have read that a summary of the whole work is inscribed, [and] that that philosopher was accustomed to responding to the silent thought of men, and that you were shaken with great admiration over this—namely how a man can identify hidden and hitherto unshared[3] thoughts…[and]…this is the greatest usefulness of this art: to know hidden things beforehand, and to predict future things…

[§2: Interpreting thoughts and objects by one-thirds of the planetary hour]

[2.2] And therefore, if someone came to you to ask something of this kind which he has not yet asked about (as you say, this is very wondrous), you will respond to the silent human thought, [and] you could say what it is—on top of that, even if he conceals something unseen in his hand—according to the planet of the hour in which he has come.

[2.3] Therefore, if he came to you in the first part of the hour over which the Sun is in charge, for the sake of seeking something or inquiring as to what it is he conceals in his closed hand,[4] you should respond that he wants something or to engage with you about himself or his associate, according to the nature of that planet; but what he holds in his hand is something of earth.

[2.4] But if in the second part of that same hour, [he comes for the sake] of proposing counsel, namely [about] war, a siege, fortifications, or a position of power which he believes he is going to get, or he [wants] to engage with you about panic over some enmities; in his hand he holds silver or copper[5] or earth.

[2.5] If he came at the end of that hour, he is angry [and] seeks counsel as to by what art he can avoid the threats which some powerful judge has made [against him]; [and he] has white wool in his hand, or a little white piece [of something], or a white woolen string…

---

[3] *Latentes et adhuc inexpertas.*
[4] This sounds like a client who is challenging the skills of the astrologer.
[5] Reading *aes* for *os.*

[§3: The outcomes of thoughts]

[3.1-2] With these things happening according to your reason, if you are foretelling these things to him, if he persists in seeking counsel from you over an affair of this kind (on account of which he has come), consider in what sign any of the planets presiding over this or that hour, would be lingering, and [see] if, in that part of this hour, the sign in which the planet is then staying, would be arising.[6] Because the power of the signs is signified by the course of the planets, let your response be tempered according to their proper qualities and their managements.[7]

[3.3] If in fact anyone came to you in the hour of the Sun, [and] if the sign in which [the Sun] is, is then raising itself, he will fall into difficulties: namely he will be whipped by a powerful person and his things will be snatched away…

[§4: Answering questions from the Ascendant]

[4.1] Moreover, respond in a simple way to anyone questioning you about some matter, once you have considered the sign which raises itself from the east while he has come to ask.

[4.2] If Aries is lifting itself up, what he seeks will be profitable, but [only] through great energy and his labor.

[4.3] If Taurus, one seeking medicine will get well from any infirmity…

[§5: Answering questions from the Moon]

[5.1-2] If someone came to you for the sake of asking about the fate of his journey, once his constellation[8] has been considered according to the rule which we stated above, you should know that while the Moon is in his life-giving constellation,[9] he is not going to undertake a journey successfully because [*omitted*].[10]

---

[6] Argafalau does not tell us what to do if this sign, is *not* arising.
[7] *Administrationes.* This probably refers to rulerships, but generally anything signified by them.
[8] *Astro.* This is not an endorsement of a sidereal zodiac, but simply a reference to the rising sign from the previous section. *Astrum* can also simply mean "star."
[9] Namely, the first house. This passage suggests whole-sign houses.
[10] The Latin reads, *de vita componit*, which literally means, "he is putting [it together] from [his] life." I believe that either the original Latin writer misunderstood his Arabic sources, or there is something wrong with the text.

[5.3] If [she is] in the constellation of gain, he will lose his things.

[5.4] If she went forth in [the constellation] of siblings and friends, he will prosper....

[§6: Answering questions from triplicities]

[6.1-2] Above, we stated that the twelve signs are allotted the proper qualities of the four elements and the four climes, so that just as three of them (namely Aries, Leo and Sagittarius) were fiery and eastern, so three (Taurus, Virgo and Capricorn) [are] earthen and southerly; and again three (Gemini, Libra, Aquarius) [are] airy and western; but the last three (namely Cancer, Scorpio and Pisces) [are] watery and northern. And so...[11] If someone would inquire of you in what direction the line of his doorway[12] is turned or the head of his bed is placed, or [if] at that time he would ask what had happened or would happen with respect to what is his, or himself (or brothers, friends, parents, his wife, or infants, or travel, or [his] standing, or any matter), you should respond thusly:

[6.3] If his life-giving constellation is an eastern [sign], the line of his doorway is turned toward the east; if southern, toward the south; if western, toward the west; if northern, toward the north.

[6.4] But if you want to know the place of his bed, consider to what region the seventh constellation from his life-giving constellation ([namely], that which belongs to his wife) is ascribed, as I have stated, and you would know to what region it is ascribed: the head of the bed or the whole bed is turned toward that [region].

[6.5] If however someone would ask of you what had happened to him or would happen to what is his, you should respond according to this procedure: consider diligently the course of the seven planets through the twelve signs, and, according to what we have described above, with them entering this or that [sign], you will pronounce what has either happened then or is going to happen then: adverse things from adverse [planets], gentle things from gentle ones, now for his own life, now for brothers and friends, and thus in order.

---

[11] Omitting a remark about using Hebrew letters to make notations on the chart.

[12] *Cardo ostii.*

[§7: More on answering questions from the triplicities]

[7.1] If excessive worry would consume someone, namely so that he craves to know whether his wife would survive him or if there would be a future, prosperous union [for him] in nuptials not yet brought to pass, you should inquire according to this rule: in the regular way (as we have taught above), consider the constellation of each,[13] and thus contemplate the truth.

[7.2] If the constellation of each is found to be in a sign of the fiery nature (or airy or watery or earthy), the union will be prosperous and the one who outlives [the other] will follow the preceding one [in death, after] a not-long interval.

[7.3] But if one is found to be in a fiery one, [and] the other in an airy one, since air arouses fire, the union will be happy but the one in the airy [sign] will be the survivor.

[7.4] But if one is in a fiery one [and] the other in a watery one, the union will be contrary, and, because water extinguishes fire, the one in the watery one will be the survivor.

[7.5] But if one is in a fiery one, the other in an earthy one, they will live together in quarrels and tribulations and, because fire dries up earth, the one in the fiery one will remain standing.

[7.6] But if [one] is in an airy one, [but] the other put the constellation in a watery one, the union presents neither evil nor good, [but] the one in the airy one will prevail.

[7.7] But if one is in an airy one, the other in an earthy one, they will come together poorly, [and] the one in the earthy one will endure.

[7.8] But if one is in a watery one, the other in an earthy one, the union [is] happy but the one in the watery one will be the survivor.

---

[13] I believe the text is instructing us to look at the natal charts of the male querent and his current wife. If we were looking only at one chart (namely, at the first and seventh houses), the instructions below would not make sense: since no sign on the Ascendant can be of the same triplicity as that on the seventh, the first possibility—that the "constellation of each" would be fiery (or airy, *etc.*), would be impossible.

APPENDIX J: IBN EZRA'S *PARTICULAR TREATISES*

What follows is a translation of the introduction and first chapter of the first Treatise of ibn Ezra's *Particular Treatises* (Latin edition, 1507). I have numbered each of the separate methods, many of which are recycled from other texts.

The second chapter, on the querent's thought and what he holds in his hand, leads with material virtually identical to Argafalau §2 (see my partial translation in Appendix I), and is followed by a small amount of additional material I have translated below.

[Introduction to first Treatise]

This book contains four chapters. The first, on a man's notion,[1] and his question. The second, what it is that he hides in his hand. Third, on a concealed thing and its place. Fourth, on the place of a fugitive.

First chapter: [Eleven ways to discover a man's notion and his question]

[1] Also, you should look at the lord of the Ascendant, to see in which of the twelve houses it is, so that it is not burned nor retrograde nor in a sliding[2] house (for if it were in one of these places, no response should be given through it). Therefore, let it be put that the lord of the Ascendant is of a good condition:

If it were in the Ascendant, he is asking about himself.

And if it were in the second, about assets.

But the third house is divided into two: if the lord of the Ascendant were in the first part of the third house, he wants to go from place to place. In the second one, from brothers to sisters.[3]

The fourth is divided into three. And if the lord of the Ascendant were in the first part, he is thinking about his father who produced him. In the

---

[1] *Cognitione.* That is, his thought.
[2] That is, cadent (lit., "falling").
[3] Or rather, he wants to ask about brothers and sisters.

second, a ship or building or something underground. In the third, he is thinking about himself.

The fifth is divided into four. The first, children or those who are learning, or slaves; the second, joy; the third, vestments; the fourth, the news of messengers or of letters.

The sixth is divided into two parts. The first, diseases; the second, male and female slaves and small animals.

The seventh is [divided] into three. The first, women; the second, associates; the third, enemies, robbers, or litigators, or what is contrary to him.

The eighth is divided into three. The first, death or fear, and he fears lest something touch him; the second, his own houses and fields, and his lands, and everything acquired by him; the third, something owed.

The ninth is divided into four. The first, that of faith and truth; the second, travel; the third, honor and a name with respect to knowledge; the first is that of dreams.

The tenth is divided into three. The first, the king or a powerful person; the second, knowledge, character, and mastery; the third, mothers.

The eleventh is divided into three. The first, merchandising; the second, what is rich, or opulence; the third, a male or female friend.

The twelfth is divided into three. The first, his enemy; the second, captivity and infirmities and prison; the third, beasts.

[2] If the lord of the Ascendant *were* burned, retrograde, or cadent, or [it is masculine and][4] in a feminine sign, you should leave it behind and respond through the Moon. And see in what house she is, and you should respond according to the place of the house in which she is, following the partitions [of the houses] which I have laid out for you.

[3] But if the Moon were in a masculine sign or cadent or burned, you should not respond through her, but you must do it thusly through the lord of the hour.[5] See how many degrees the lord of the hour[6] was in, in its own sign, multiply them by 12 and divide by 30, and project from the Ascendant: you will give 30 to the Ascendant and likewise to the second and third, and in the same way until the degrees arising from the multiplication are ended. And

---

[4] Reading for "and it is in the Ascendant," to match similar statements below.
[5] The following method is used by Leopold in Appendix G.
[6] Reading with Leopold for "sign."

where they are ended, there is his thought, according to the partitioning already stated.

[4] But if the lord of the hour were burned or retrograde or cadent, or [it is] masculine and is in a feminine sign, look at how many [degrees] of the ascending sign have ascended:[7] and you should give 2 1/2° to the Ascendant, and likewise to the second, and again to the third, and where this number will be ended, there will be his thought, according to the division of the houses stated above.

Also, Abraham said that the sages of interrogations said one man can know what is in the heart of the querent, and [they] labored much in this:

[5] For[8] there are some saying that we always look at the ninth-part of the degree of the Ascendant, to see in what house it appears.

[6] And others say one must always look to the Moon and to the Lot of Fortune.

[7] Some say[9] one must look to the planet having strength in the five places of dignity, and to the lord of the hour or the lord of the day.

[8] And it is closer to the truth if one knew the nature of every degree of the zodiac, just as it is written in the *Book of Tamedas*.[10] And one should adjoin [that nature] to the lord of the degree of the Ascendant, if it is regarding [it], or if some planet would appear in the Ascendant. And you should always conjoin [that] with a planet appearing in the Ascendant (whichever one it is that is in it), and know what its nature is, and from what house it aspects, or in which one it has dignity.[11] And it is right that a man should not put himself into perplexity nor respond with respect to a thought, unless he knows what any [particular] degree signifies. And this is a noble book.

---

[7] For other approaches to using the twelfth-part of the Ascendant, see below and *Search* Ch. I.9.3, *OHT* §2 (in Appendix C), and Appendix G.

[8] See for example the Indians (method #3) in *Search* Ch. I.9.3.

[9] I take this to mean the weighted victor over the Ascendant. Note the resemblance to ibn Ezra's own version of the victor over the chart, in Appendix F.

[10] Perhaps a *Book of Degrees*, from the Hebrew *middah* ("degree"). See another reference in the second chapter below.

[11] This really should read, "and which one of its houses (in which it has dignity) it aspects." Al-Kindī in particular emphasizes that a planet will indicate the topic of that one of its domiciles which it aspects better and more strongly (see my Introduction to *Forty Chapters*).

And Māshā'allāh says[12] the significators of thoughts are three:

[9] One,[13] the lord of the Ascendant, and the receiver of [its] strength (or the significator which receives the lord of the orb), and the one to which the lord of the Ascendant is being conjoined.[14] And you should not dismiss planets[15] on account of being in the Ascendant, because the querent's thought will be according to this. And attend to the sign belonging to [the planet in] the Ascendant, [namely which it aspects], and judge in the thought according to this.

[10] Second, that you should look at the significator of the sign,[16] to see in which of the houses it is: if in the Ascendant, it signifies him himself; in the second, assets, and thus with the other houses.

[11] Third,[17] according to what the sages of the Indians said, if it were about a hidden thing: regard the victor of the lord of the bound and face of the Ascendant, and regard the one to which the stronger of them is being conjoined. For the hidden thing will be according to the nature of that.[18]

[4] The stronger of them is the strength of the twelfth-part [of the Ascendant].[19] For example, the Ascendant was 12° Aries. When we have given one house to every 2 1/2° (and you will begin from the Ascendant of Aries), the number will leave off in Leo, which is the lord of the children, following the Ascendant. And there is no planet there. Then, regard the Sun: and I found him in the seventh house. And I said that the interrogation was about the querent's woman and his child: also, that he does not care about her. And if the Sun had been in the sixth, he would have been asking about an infirm child.

---

[12] See OHT §2 (in Appendix C).
[13] For a more accurate version, see OHT §2 (in Appendix C), the first significator of thought according to Māshā'allāh. This Latin version (or ibn Ezra's own account) is rather garbled, and I have done the best I can with it.
[14] Ibn Ezra's version omits planets aspecting the degree of the Ascendant.
[15] Reading planetas for parva.
[16] If we go by this Latin text, ibn Ezra must mean whichever of the planets in the previous paragraph is identified as the main significator. But this paragraph is exactly parallel to the view in OHT §2 (in Appendix C), which refers to the house in which the Lot of Fortune is.
[17] See Search Ch. I.9.3 and OHT §2 (in Appendix C).
[18] Reading for the puzzling "for the nature of the thing [fem.] will be according to the nature of that [masc.] which was hidden."
[19] For other versions of this same method and example, see Search Ch. I.9.3 and OHT §2 (in Appendix C), and Appendix G.

Second chapter: [Interpreting thoughts and identifying objects held in the hand]

[Omitting material virtually identical to Argafalau's Letter §2]

[12] Abraham [ibn Ezra] says: We have stated that the sages [consulted] the *Book of Tametas* already stated,[20] so that they would know what the questioner has in his hand, according to the nature of the ascending sign and its lord. Wherefore, Aries, Leo, Sagittarius, signify life; Taurus, Virgo, Capricorn, vestments; Gemini, Libra, Aquarius, colors;[21] Cancer, Scorpio, Pisces, pierced things. And [also judge] according to the planet appearing in the Ascendant.

[13] Also, the lord of the hour signifies a color: Saturn, gray; Jupiter, green; Mars, red; the Sun, shining white; Venus, a resplendent, beautiful [color]; Mercury, varied color; the Moon, whiteness so that it shines well.

[14] Also, they said that the lord of the bound signifies if the hidden thing is old or new, according to its relationship with the Sun.[22]

[15] But some say one must always look to the place of the Moon.

---

[20] See the reference to the *Book of Tamedas* above.
[21] *Colores.* Perhaps this means either paints or pigments, or things which are painted or colored.
[22] See for example Ch. II.3.4 above.

APPENDIX K: DIRECTIONS USING ASCENSIONAL TIMES

The following passage appeared just before Book I of *Search*, following a version of Hermann's 1140 translation of Abū Ma'shar's treatment of Lots in *Gr. Intr.* (Readers interested in the Lots should consult *ITA* VI, which is based on John of Spain's translation.) Below I offer some comments and explanations.

"In distributing[1] the ascensions of the stars' rays according to the opinions of the Persians, it is good first that equal degrees be calculated diligently from the beginning of Aries up to the place of a star, and the whole number should be found among the ascensions of the right circle, and how many equal [degrees] it denoted: the whole number is the right tetragon of the star.

"For example, with a star in the twentieth degree of Gemini, we are going to find the tetragon. We take 80°, which denote 19 equal degrees of Pisces in the right circle. However, the 79° 54' of the ascensions of the right circle are barely more than 5' over. And so, we say the right tetragon of the star falls in 19° 54' Pisces,[2] the opposite of which [is] the right tetragon in Virgo.

"Then, to find the hexagon, we take it from the degree of the star up to its left tetragon, and however many equal degrees there were between two-thirds of the number [of the tetragon] being added to the place of the star, establishes the left hexagon of the star, the opposite of which is its right trigon.

"For its left trigon, whenever it had to be taken up, we take it from the left tetragon of the star up to the opposite of the star, and one-third of the number [of the tetragon] being added to the left tetragon establishes the left trigon of the star, the opposite of which is its right hexagon."

---

[1] *Disponendis.*
[2] Reading *54* for *04*. The numeral 5 in Arabic looks just like our 0.

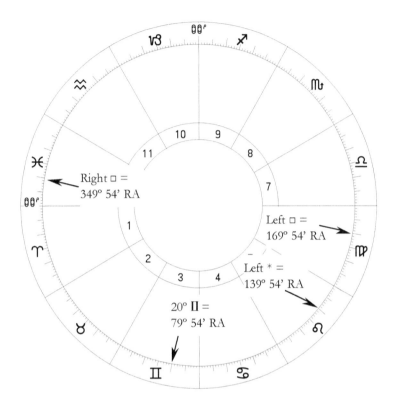

Comment by Dykes. The instructions above are rather opaque. Hermann is describing the use of ascensional times in primary directions. Ascensional times are used in the predictive method of "distribution" or directing through the bounds, but the instructions here pertain more to what I sometimes call "ascensional directions" (as opposed to Ptolemy's proportional semi-arc directions).[3] Readers may find a table of ascensional times with instructions on my own site (www.bendykes.com), and a discussion of proportional semi-arc directions in *ITA* Appendix E. Here, let me discuss what I believe Hermann is trying to do.

---

[3] Actually there is more than one way to perform ascensional directions. First, one may apply ascensional times to the signs themselves, so that every degree in a sign gets the same number of ascensions: this is probably the older method. Or, one may use tables to convert any single degree (even with its minutes) directly into positions of right ascension: this is probably a later method because it takes more sophisticated mathematics. Hermann seems to be using this latter method, but using tables I am not familiar with.

Zodiacal longitude is to the zodiac as right ascension (RA) is to the celestial equator, each measuring distance around these respective circles. Now, since all primary directions are measured using the celestial equator, we need to convert zodiacal positions to equatorial ones.[4] But since the ecliptic (where the zodiac is) is askew from the celestial equator by approximately 23° 25',[5] the positions on one circle do not match neatly those on the other. For example, 0° Aries corresponds to 0° RA, because the two circles intersect at that point. But a point on 15° Taurus, which is 45° in zodiacal longitude from the beginning of Aries, does not correspond to 45° in RA: it is rather closer to 42° 30' RA. So if we want to perform a primary direction, we need to convert zodiacal positions to equatorial ones, and determine the aspects that way.

Hermann is either using tables with a different obliquity value, or which calculate ascensions slightly differently (i.e., not using modern trigonometry), or else he is leaving out some steps. At any rate, he imagines a point at 20° Gemini, and we want to know where its aspects are on the equator for purposes of directing. Now, 20° Gemini is equivalent to 80° in zodiacal longitude, which we want to convert into RA. Using an unknown table, he says that this 80° corresponds to a position 79° 54' "from the beginning of Aries"—in other words, at 79° 54' RA. This means that the right square or tetragon of that position is 90° RA to its right, or at 349° 54' RA, which he equates to 19° 54' Pisces. This is not really the *zodiacal* position, but it is close to it: Hermann might be confused between the two kinds of position, or might have misunderstood whatever text he was reading. Anyway, the left square or tetragon is opposite this position on the equator, which we can also get by adding 90° RA to the left: 169° 54' RA, which again Hermann would have called 19° 54' Virgo.

The rest of the instructions use proportions instead of straightforward degrees in order to find the positions of the other aspects. So, instead of saying that the left hexagon is 60° in RA to the left, he says it is 2/3 of a square away (2/3 x 90° = 60°), and that its opposite position is the right trine or trigon. Likewise with the other hexagon and trigon.

In a fuller treatment, one would then use an RA table (or a calculator) to convert the equatorial position in RA back into zodiacal positions, or

---

[4] Good instructions for these may be found in Gansten 2009, Appendix I; see also Peter Duffett-Smith, *Practical Astronomy with Your Calculator*, 3ʳᵈ Edition (Cambridge: Cambridge University Press, 1988), p. 40.

[5] This rather constant value is called the "obliquity of the ecliptic" (OE).

compare the RA positions of two points. For example, suppose that Mars were at 20° Gemini, and we found his square lying at 169° 54' RA as Hermann suggests. Now suppose that there were some planet late in Virgo, whose position converted into 172° RA. The difference in RA (2° 06') is converted to years, so that roughly two years after birth there will be a direction of that planet to the square of Mars—even though the *zodiacal* distance between them may be more or less than 2° 06' on the ecliptic. This is an example of an ascensional direction.

APPENDIX L: TABLES OF BOUNDS, DECANS, & TRIPLICITIES

♈	♃ 0°-5°59'	♀ 6°-11°59'	☿ 12°-19°59'	♂ 20°-24°59'	♄ 25°-29°59'
♉	♀ 0°-7°59'	☿ 8°-13°59'	♃ 14°-21°59'	♄ 22°-26°59'	♂ 27°-29°59'
♊	☿ 0°-5°59'	♃ 6°-11°59'	♀ 12°-16°59'	♂ 17°-23°59'	♄ 24°-29°59'
♋	♂ 0°-6°59'	♀ 7°-12°59'	☿ 13°-18°59'	♃ 19°-25°59'	♄ 26°-29°59'
♌	♃ 0°-5°59'	♀ 6°-10°59'	♄ 11°-17°59'	☿ 18°-23°59'	♂ 24°-29°59'
♍	☿ 0°-6°59'	♀ 7°-16°59'	♃ 17°-20°59'	♂ 21°-27°59'	♄ 28°-29°59'
♎	♄ 0°-5°59'	☿ 6°-13°59'	♃ 14°-20°59'	♀ 21°-27°59'	♂ 28°-29°59'
♏	♂ 0°-6°59'	♀ 7°-10°59'	☿ 11°-18°59'	♃ 19°-23°59'	♄ 24°-29°59'
♐	♃ 0°-11°59'	♀ 12°-16°59'	☿ 17°-20°59'	♄ 21°-25°59'	♂ 26°-29°59'
♑	☿ 0°-6°59'	♃ 7°-13°59'	♀ 14°-21°59'	♄ 22°-25°59'	♂ 26°-29°59'
♒	☿ 0°-6°59'	♀ 7°-12°59'	♃ 13°-19°59'	♂ 20°-24°59'	♄ 25°-29°59'
♓	♀ 0°-11°59'	♃ 12°-15°59'	☿ 16°-18°59'	♂ 19°-27°59'	♄ 28°-29°59'

Figure 36: Table of Egyptian bounds

♈	♂ 0°-9°59'	☉ 10°-19°59'	♀ 20°-29°59'
♉	☿ 0°-9°59'	☽ 10°-19°59'	♄ 20°-29°59'
♊	♃ 0°-9°59'	♂ 10°-19°59'	☉ 20°-29°59'
♋	♀ 0°-9°59'	☿ 10°-19°59'	☽ 20°-29°59'
♌	♄ 0°-9°59'	♃ 10°-19°59'	♂ 20°-29°59'
♍	☉ 0°-9°59'	♀ 10°-19°59'	☿ 20°-29°59'
♎	☽ 0°-9°59'	♄ 10°-19°59'	♃ 20°-29°59'
♏	♂ 0°-9°59'	☉ 10°-19°59'	♀ 20°-29°59'
♐	☿ 0°-9°59'	☽ 10°-19°59'	♄ 20°-29°59'
♑	♃ 0°-9°59'	♂ 10°-19°59'	☉ 20°-29°59'
♒	♀ 0°-9°59'	☿ 10°-19°59'	☽ 20°-29°59'
♓	♄ 0°-9°59'	♃ 10°-19°59'	♂ 20°-29°59'

Figure 37: Table of "Chaldean" decans/faces

	Primary by day	Primary by night	Partnering
Fire	☉	♃	♄
Air	♄	☿	♃
Water	♀	♂	☽
Earth	♀	☽	♂

Figure 38: Table of "Dorothean" triplicity lords

APPENDIX M: THE *ESSENTIAL MEDIEVAL ASTROLOGY* CYCLE

The *Essential Medieval Astrology* cycle is a projected series of books which will redefine the contours of traditional astrology. Comprised mainly of translations of works by Persian and Arabic-speaking medieval astrologers, it will cover all major areas of astrology, including philosophical treatments and magic. The cycle will be accompanied by compilations of introductory works and readings on the one hand, and independent monographs and encyclopedic works on the other (including late medieval and Renaissance works of the Latin West).

I. Introductions
- *Introductions to Astrology: Abū Ma'shar & al-Qabīsī* (2010)
- Abū Ma'shar, *Great Introduction to the Knowledge of the Judgments of the Stars* (2011-12)
- *Basic Readings in Traditional Astrology* (2012-13)

II. Nativities
- *Persian Nativities I*: Māshā'allāh's *The Book of Aristotle*, Abū 'Alī al-Khayyāt's *On the Judgments of Nativities* (2009)
- *Persian Nativities II*: 'Umar al-Tabarī's *Three Books on Nativities*, Abū Bakr's *On Nativities* (2010)
- *Persian Nativities III: On Solar Revolutions* (2010)

III. Questions (Horary)
- Hermann of Carinthia, *The Search of the Heart* (2011)
- Al-Kindī, *The Forty Chapters* (2011)
- Various, *The Book of the Nine Judges* (2011)

IV. Elections
- *Traditional Electional Astrology: al-'Imrānī, Abū Ma'shar, and others* (2011-12)

V. Mundane Astrology
- *Astrology of the World*: Abū Ma'shar's *On the Revolutions of the Years of the World, Book of Religions and Dynasties*, and *Flowers*, Sahl bin Bishr's *Prophetic Sayings*; lesser works on prices and weather (2012-13)

VI. Other Works

- Bonatti, Guido, *The Book of Astronomy* (2007)
- *Works of Sahl & Māshā'allāh* (2008)
- *A Course in Traditional Astrology* (TBA)
- Al-Rijāl, *On the Judgments of the Stars* (TBA)
- *Astrological Magic* (TBA)
- *The Latin Hermes* (TBA)
- Firmicus Maternus, *Mathesis* (TBA)

BIBLIOGRAPHY

Adamson, Peter and Richard C. Taylor eds., *The Cambridge Companion to Arabic Philosophy* (Cambridge: Cambridge University Press, 2005)

Al-Rijāl, 'Ali, *In Iudiciis Astrorum* (Venice: Erhard Ratdolt, 1485)

Al-Rijāl, 'Ali, *Libri de Iudiciis Astrorum* (Basel: Henrichus Petrus, 1551)

Aristotle, *The Complete Works of Aristotle*, Jonathan Barnes ed. (Princeton: Princeton University Press, 1995)

Bos, Gerrit and Charles Burnett, *Scientific Weather Forecasting in the Middle Ages: The Writings of al-Kindi* (London and New York: Kegan Paul International, 2000)

Burnett, Charles ed., *Adelard of Bath: An English Scientist and Arabist of the Early Twelfth Century* (London: Warburg Institute Surveys and Texts 14, 1987).

Burnett, Charles, "Hermann of Carinthia," in Peter Dronke ed., *A History of Twelfth-Century Philosophy* (Cambridge: Cambridge University Press, 1988), pp. 386-404.

Burnett, Charles, "Al-Kindī on Judicial Astrology: 'The Forty Chapters'," in *Arabic Sciences and Philosophy*, v. 3 (1993), pp. 77-117.

Burnett, Charles, "Al-Kindī on finding buried treasure," *Arabic Sciences and Philosophy* v.7, 1997, pp. 57-90.

Burnett, Charles, "A Hermetic Programme of Astrology and Divination in mid-Twelfth-Century Aragon: The Hidden Preface in the *Liber novem iudicum*," in Charles Burnett and W.F. Ryan, eds., *Magic and the Classical Tradition* (London: The Warburg Institute, 2006), pp. 99-105.

Dorotheus of Sidon, *Carmen Astrologicum*, trans. David Pingree (Abingdon, MD: The Astrology Center of America, 2005)

Dykes, Benjamin trans. and ed., *Works of Sahl & Māshā'allāh* (Golden Valley, MN: The Cazimi Press, 2008)

Dykes, Benjamin trans. and ed., *Persian Nativities* vols. I-III (Minneapolis, MN: The Cazimi Press, 2009-10)

Dykes, Benjamin trans. and ed., *Introductions to Traditional Astrology: Abū Ma'shar & al-Qabisi* (Minneapolis, MN: The Cazimi Press, 2010)

Dykes, Benjamin trans. and ed., *The Forty Chapters of al-Kindī* (Minneapolis, MN: The Cazimi Press, 2011)

Dykes, Benjamin, trans. and ed., *The Book of the Nine Judges* (Minneapolis, MN: The Cazimi Press, 2011)

Gansten, Martin, *Primary Directions: Astrology's Old Master Technique* (England: The Wessex Astrologer, 2009)

Hermann of Carinthia, trans. Charles Burnett, *De Essentiis* [On Essences] (Leiden: E.J. Brill, 1982)

Ibn Ezra, Abraham, *Abrahe Avenaris Judei astrologi peritissimi in re iudiciali Opera* (Venice: Peter Liechtenstein, 1507)

Ibn Ezra, Abraham, *De Nativitatibus* (Marburg: Joannes Dryander, 1537)

Ibn Ezra, Abraham, *Liber de Nativitatibus* (Venice: Erhard Ratdolt, 1485)

Ibn Ezra, Abraham, *The Book of Nativities and Revolutions*, trans. and ed. Meira B. Epstein and Robert Hand (ARHAT Publications, 2008)

Juste, David, *Les Alchandreana Primitifs: Étude sur les plus anciens traités astrologiques Latins d'origine Arabe (Xe siècle)* (Leiden: Brill, 2007)

Lemay, Richard, *Abū Ma'shar and Latin Aristotelianism in the Twelfth Century* (Beirut: American University of Beirut, 1962)

Leopold of Austria, *Compilatio Leupoldi ducatus Austriae filii de astrorum scientia decem continens tractatus* (Augsburg: Erhard Ratdolt, 1489)

Lilly, William, *Christian Astrology*, vols. I-II, ed. David R. Roell (Abingdon, MD: Astrology Center of America, 2004)

Low-Beer, Sheila M., *Hermann of Carinthia: The "Liber Imbrium," the "Fatidica," and the "De Indagatione Cordis"* (New York: City University of New York, 1979)

Māshā'allāh, *On Reception*, ed. and trans. Robert Hand (ARHAT Publications, 1998)

Pingree, David, trans. and ed., *The Yavanajātaka of Sphujidhvaja* vols. I-II (Cambridge, MA and London: Harvard University Press, 1978)

Pingree, David, *From Astral Omens to Astrology: From Babylon to Bīkīner* (Rome: Istituto italiano per L'Africa e L'Oriente, 1997)

Ptolemy, Claudius, *Quadripartitum* [Tetrabiblos], trans. Plato of Tivoli (1138) (Basel: Johannes Hervagius, 1533)

Ptolemy, Claudius, *Tetrabiblos* vols. 1, 2, 4, trans. Robert Schmidt, ed. Robert Hand (Berkeley Springs, WV: The Golden Hind Press, 1994-98)

Schmidt, Robert H., trans. and ed. *Definitions and Foundations* (Cumberland, MD: The Golden Hind Press, 2009)

Schmidt, Robert trans., Robert Hand ed., *The Astrological Record of the Early Sages in Greek* (Berkeley Springs, WV: The Golden Hind Press, 1995)

Sezgin, Fuat, *Geschichte des Arabischen Schrifttums* vol. 7 (Leiden: E.J. Brill, 1979)

Valens, Vettius, *The Anthology*, vols. I-VII, ed. Robert Hand, trans. Robert Schmidt (Berkeley Springs, WV: The Golden Hind Press, 1993-2001)

INDEX

CPSIA information can be obtained
at www.ICGtesting.com
Printed in the USA
BVHW040222270321
603431BV00008B/581

9 781934 586181

Essential Medieval Astrology: Horary Series Vol. I

"Every question of astronomy...
is either in thought or in speech."

In the 1140s AD, Hermann of Carinthia assembled instructions from medieval Arabic-speaking authorities on interpreting the unstated thoughts of clients (now called "consultation charts"), often using a "victor" or *mubtazz* or *almuten* for topics or the chart. Hermann also offered his own reflections on the proper balancing of dignities, house rank, and planetary strength.

The Search of the Heart is now available for the first time. To Hermann's book, Dr. Benjamin Dykes has added similar instructions and source texts from such notable astrologers as al-Rijal (Haly Abenragel), Sahl bin Bishr, Masha'allah, 'Umar al-Tabari, al-Kindi, Abraham ibn Ezra, Leopold of Austria, Ptolemy, Hephaistio of Thebes, "Argafalau," and others.

In his lengthy Introduction, Dykes suggests that thought-interpretation and its victors in horary were supposed to identify what a client's interest is or should be as a preliminary to crafting a horary question.

With its huge number of approaches and never-before translated texts, *The Search of the Heart* is essential for traditional astrologers.

DR. BENJAMIN DYKES is a leading medieval astrologer and translator who earned his PhD in philosophy from the University of Illinois. He has taught college-level philosophy in Illinois and Minnesota. In 2010 he published *Introductions to Traditional Astrology: Abu Ma'shar & al-Qabisi*. In 2007-10 he published Bonatti's *The Book of Astronomy*, as well as numerous works of Sahl & Masha'allah, and *Persian Nativities I-III*, on natal astrology. He offers philosophy courses on MP3 for astrologers. For more, see www.bendykes.com.

ISBN 978-1934586-18-1

90000

9 781934 586181